the TEN COMMANDMENTS ACCORDING to JESUS

ELMER L. TOWNS

© Copyright 2021–Elmer L. Towns

All rights reserved. This book is protected by the copyright laws of the United States of America. This book may not be copied or reprinted for commercial gain or profit. The use of short quotations or occasional page copying for personal or group study is permitted and encouraged. Permission will be granted upon request. Unless otherwise identified, Scripture quotations are taken from the New King James Version. Copyright © 1982 by Thomas Nelson, Inc. Used by permission. All rights reserved. Scripture quotations marked NLT are taken from the Holy Bible, New Living Translation, copyright 1996, 2004, 2015. Used by permission of Tyndale House Publishers, Wheaton, Illinois 60189. All rights reserved. reserved. Scripture quotations marked BBJ are from the Bible By Jesus®. Copyright © 2018 by Destiny Image and 21st Century Press. All rights reserved. Scripture quotations marked ELT are the author's paraphrases; Elmer L. Towns. Scripture quotations marked KJV are taken from the King James Version. Scripture quotations marked LB are taken from The Living Bible; Tyndale House, 1997, © 1971 by Tyndale House Publishers, Inc. Used by permission.

All emphasis within Scripture quotations is the author's own. Please note that Destiny Image's publishing style capitalizes certain pronouns in Scripture that refer to the Father, Son, and Holy Spirit, and may differ from some publishers' styles.

DESTINY IMAGE® PUBLISHERS, INC.
P.O. Box 310, Shippensburg, PA 17257-0310
"Promoting Inspired Lives."

This book and all other Destiny Image and Destiny Image Fiction books are available at Christian bookstores and distributors worldwide.

For more information on foreign distributors, call 717-532-3040.

Reach us on the Internet: www.destinyimage.com.

ISBN 13 TP: 978-0-7684-7602-6

ISBN 13 eBook: 978-0-7684-7603-3

For Worldwide Distribution.

1 2 3 4 5 6 7 8 / 28 27 26 25 24 23

TABLE OF CONTENTS

Preface 9

Introduction 11

Part One

Chapter One   You Shall Put God First in Your Life 17

        The command, "Thou shalt have no other gods before me" is a choice about God's rulership in your life.

Chapter Two   You Shall Not Allow Anything Between You and God 25

        The command, "Thou shalt not make any carved images" means worship only the Lord.

Chapter Three   You Shall Reverence God 33

        Because God's name stands for His presence, "Thou shalt not take the name of the Lord in vain."

Chapter Four   You Shall Worship on the Lord's Day 43

        The command, "Remember the Sabbath Day to keep it holy" is not about quitting work but is about worshipping God.

Chapter Five   Honor Your Parents 51

        When you "Honor thy father and thy mother," you learn to live under the authority of God which He gave for parents to teach us obedience.

Chapter Six   You Shall Preserve the Life of Your Neighbor 59

        Jesus taught us to control our anger that will keep us from breaking the commandment, "Thou shalt not kill."

Chapter Seven   Your Body Shall Be My Sanctuary 67

        Because the Lord lives in our bodies, we should keep the commandment, "Thou shalt not commit adultery."

Chapter Eight	Respect the "Stuff" of Others	77

When we respect the rights and property of others, we will keep the commandment, "Thou shall not steal."

Chapter Nine	Live by the Standard of Truth	85

When truth is your criteria in all things, you will keep the commandment, "Thou shalt not bear false witness against thy neighbor."

Chapter Ten	Be Satisfied with the "Stuff" You Have	91

When you are contented with what God gives you, you will keep the commandment, "Thou shalt not covet…"

Epilogue	99
Appendix A	101
Appendix B	103
Appendix C	105

Part Two

Day 1	What Is Important about Law?	110
Day 2	Life Is Choice	112
Day 3	His Holiness	114
Day 4	Other Gods	116
Day 5	What Does "Have" Mean?	118
Day 6	What Is in God's Face?	120
Day 7	Lordship Is a Choice	122
Day 8	An Idol Is Not Like God Your Father	124
Day 9	Worship Is Relationship	126
Day 10	Worship God Your Father	128
Day 11	Why Put God First?	130
Day 12	God Doesn't Have a Body	132
Day 13	Graven Image	134
Day 14	Make for Yourselves	136
Day 15	No Vain Words	138
Day 16	Do Not Trivialize God's Name	140

Day 17	Be Careful What You Say	142
Day 18	Guiltless	144
Day 19	Words Are Powerful	146
Day 20	Speak Your Heart	148
Day 21	Truthful Words	150
Day 22	A Positive Command to Rest	152
Day 23	Remember	154
Day 24	The Seventh Day	156
Day 25	Jesus' View of the Sabbath	158
Day 26	Sabbath a Shadow of Christ	160
Day 27	Finish Your Work	162
Day 28	To Honor Is to Obey	164
Day 29	Obedience Brings Long Life	166
Day 30	Example of Jesus	168
Day 31	Family	170
Day 32	Promise of Long Life	172
Day 33	Why Honor?	174
Day 34	Obey Your Parents	176
Day 35	Murder	178
Day 36	A Sin to Murder	180
Day 37	You Must Not Murder	182
Day 38	Seeking Worship	184
Day 39	Murder in God's Sight	186
Day 40	Love Your Neighbor	188
Day 41	Killing and Murder, Is There a Difference?	190
Day 42	Transforming Murders	192
Day 43	Your Body Shall Be God's Sanctuary	194
Day 44	Avoid Adultery	196
Day 45	Wider View of Adultery	198

Day 46	Beautiful	200
Day 47	Clean in Mind and Body	202
Day 48	Remedy Now (Part 1)	204
Day 49	Remedy Now (Part 2)	206
Day 50	Reasons Not to Steal	208
Day 51	Work Not Steal	210
Day 52	What Have They Stolen?	212
Day 53	Stealing from God	214
Day 54	Stealing Many Ways	216
Day 55	Good Stewards of Money	218
Day 56	Who Controls Your Money?	220
Day 57	Bearing False Witness	222
Day 58	Many Ways to Lie	224
Day 59	Truth Tellers	226
Day 60	Lying	228
Day 61	How to Be a Truthful Person	230
Day 62	Four Steps to Lying	232
Day 63	Live and Speak Truth	234
Day 64	The Last Is the Worst	236
Day 65	What Coveting Does to You	238
Day 66	Spiritual Eyes Needed	240
Day 67	Controlling Covetousness	242
Day 68	Controlling Covetousness (Part 2)	244
Day 69	Controlling Covetousness (Part 3)	246
Day 70	Keeping All of Them	248

Part Three

Lesson Introduction: (**A Key**) The Ten Comandments by Jesus 252

Lesson Introduction: (**Q**) The Ten Comandments by Jesus......255

Lesson 1:	**(A Key)** The First Commandments	258
Lesson 1:	**(Q)** The First Commandments	262
Lesson 2:	**(A Key)** The Second Commandment	266
Lesson 2:	**(Q)** The Second Commandment	269
Lesson 3:	**(A Key)** The Third Commandment	272
Lesson 3:	**(Q)** The Third Commandment	275
Lesson 4:	**(A Key)** The Fourth Commandment	278
Lesson 4:	**(Q)** The Fourth Commandment	282
Lesson 5:	**(A Key)** The Fifth Commandment	286
Lesson 5:	**(Q)** The Fifth Commandment	289
Lesson 6:	**(A Key)** The Sixth Commandment	292
Lesson 6:	**(Q)** The Sixth Commandment	295
Lesson 7:	**(A Key)** The Seventh Commandment	298
Lesson 7:	**(Q)** The Seventh Commandment	301
Lesson 8:	**(A Key)** The Eighth Commandment	304
Lesson 8:	**(Q)** The Eighth Commandment	307
Lesson 9:	**(A Key)** The Ninth Commandment	310
Lesson 9:	**(Q)** The Ninth Commandment	314
Lesson 10:	**(A Key)** The Tenth Commandment	318
Lesson 10:	**(Q)** The Tenth Commandment	322

Part Four

Additional Resources....327

PREFACE

THE manuscript gives the positive side of the *negative* Ten Commandments, and their application to faith-based living as emphasized by Jesus Christ.

Elmer Towns taught this book as a series in his Sunday school class, May - July 2002, and had a very strong response from individual members:

- "I didn't know there was so much depth to the Ten Commandments."
- "I expected you to 'beat' me over the head, telling me what not to do, but this was great. I looked forward to each lesson."
- "I have never heard a series on the Ten Commandments, and I looked forward to each lesson."

Refraining from presenting the NEGATIVES of the Ten Commandments in his series, Towns chose rather to look at the POSITIVE "reasons" why God gave each of the commandments. That purpose was reflected in several original titles for this book:

- The Ten (-derly) Commandments
- The Positive Side of the Ten Negative Commandments
- The Soft Side of the Ten Commandments
- Why God Gave Us Ten Commandments?

Towns decided to add "Jesus" to the book title; because in His earthly ministry, Jesus not only emphasized keeping the Ten Commandments, He explained the positive, inner motivations for keeping them. For example, a positive, healthy view of sex within the context of marriage served as a motive for not committing adultery. The bottom line for not committing adultery is that the body is the temple of God.

The end of the Law is worship of God. So, each chapter concludes by focusing on worship. The worship factor is evident throughout the Ten Commandments. And since everything a Christian does should praise God, worship is continually reinforced in living by the Ten Commandments.

INTRODUCTION

I struggled with two things as I began teaching a series on the Ten Commandments to the Pastor's Bible Class in Lynchburg, Virginia (average approximately 1000 in attendance). First, I knew Christians were not under Law, but grace. We don't celebrate Saturdays, but the Lord's Day. So, how could I teach the Ten Commandments to people that were not under Law?

There was a second problem, I wanted people in America to live by the Ten Commandments, even though I knew keeping them wouldn't save anyone. America has had a *god-consciousness* in the past and a consciousness of the Ten commandments. But America has lost its consciousness of God, and its awareness of the Ten Commandments. What do I mean? There's more cursing in the media and in public than ever before. Sexual permissiveness is rampant. The murder rate is up, and there doesn't seem to be much respect for parents today, at least not as in the past. Then there is a "stealing" by corporate CEOs and the average worker. When elections come around, both candidates accuse the other of lying. If all of that was not enough, what about a society that's driven by greed? Can we live by the commandment, "You shall not covet…"

I know keeping the Ten Commandments can't save my soul but if America kept them, we'd have a better society. So how could I meaningfully teach these lessons? Then I looked at Jesus. If I interpreted the Ten Commandments the way Jesus did, then my class members could live by these principles and apply their meaning to their lives. The key to the Ten Commandments is Jesus. So, this book presents two new levels. First, the Ten Commandments are presented in the Old Testament context, so as you read the text you will understand each commandment. Second, the interpretations of Jesus are given to explain the meaning of each commandment. You find Jesus' view of each commandment in the boxes. So let's begin our study with the question:

WHY TEN COMMANDMENTS?

Some people complain about our "laws" and most children don't like the "rules" of the family. Most think God, or their parents, are mean because they are not allowed to do what they want to do. But our *good* God gave us *good* laws for our *good*.

1. *The commandments are designed to keep others from hurting or harming us.* When God gave a commandment to people, "Thou shalt not steal," the reciprocal value is that no one would take things that belonged to you. The same with lying, no one would harm you with a lie, nor would anyone murder you. These laws were good laws with good intentions.

When playing football, there is a rule against "clipping" so that the other player can't be harmed. The same in baseball, there is a rule against throwing a "bean ball" so no batter is permanently damaged. In the Ten Commandments, there is a law that says you shouldn't covet the wife of another person, so no one will covet your wife.

2. *Commandments or rules keep us from harming ourselves.* God didn't give the Ten Commandments because He hated us, or He wanted to take away our fun; the Ten Commandments keep us from hurting ourselves. When God tells us to "remember the Sabbath day...," He is telling us we need rest, or we will physically and emotionally wear out. What about the person who refuses to rest at the end of the day? or the end of the week? That person will have a heart attack, a stroke, or will die young. Resting on the Lord's Day can contribute to our health.

In the same way, our society has laws to protect our citizens. We have laws against crossing the street against a red light, lest you get injured and you must wear a seatbelt. We have laws against using illegal drugs, lest you become addicted or suffer physical consequences, death or deformity, such as thalidomide babies who were permanently disfigured.

3. *Commandments are rules that keep us from being punished.* When God gave the Ten Commandments, He didn't want us to make idols, bow down to idols, or have an idol in our possession. God knew that if people worshipped the demonic spirit of idols, eventually they would become influenced by that demonic spirit. So there was an enduring penalty for tolerating idols in your life; God said, "For I, the LORD your God, am a jealous God, visiting the iniquity of the fathers upon the children to the third and fourth generations of those who hate Me," (Exod. 20:5).

In the same way, the pitcher who throws a "bean ball," twice is ejected from the game and the hockey player who illegally "checks" an opponent, is put in the penalty box. Also, there is a "red card" in soccer that gets a player ejected, and anyone who argues too much with an umpire in baseball is thrown out of the game. Living by the rules will keep you in the game.

4. *Commandments and rules tell us how to "play" the game of life.* God gave His people ten commandments for their happiness and health; it was to guide their daily living. Paul describes this process, "(A man) is not crowned unless he competes according to the rules" (2 Tim. 2:5). While the Law never saves anyone, the Law was given to tell us how to relate to God and to one another.

The Ten Commandments give meaning to life, they help guide us to find what God wants us to do. In basketball, there is a net to tell the player if he scored. And in baseball there are bases to tell a player where to run. The same in golf; if there were no holes, the player wouldn't know how to direct his drive, chip, or putt.

We put stripes in the road to keep us in our lanes; that way we don't run into oncoming traffic or crash off the highway. Children who always like to color out of the lines might grow up to be adults who don't like "lines." These are the ones that end up in the emergency rooms, harming themselves and others.

5. *Rules or commandments help people determine how good they really are.* Rules help one player compare himself to another player or compare himself or herself to the record. But in the final analysis, rules help a player compare himself to the standards. What good does it do to be the fastest 80-yd. runner when the record involves a run of 100 yards? Some teens play well for three quarters but lose the game in the fourth quarter. "All runners in a race compete against each other, but only one wins the prize" (1 Cor. 9:24, author's translation).

6. *The rules or commandments reveal God is the rule maker.* When you get halfway through the game, but the rules change, what does that tell you about the rule maker? Suppose you were playing golf and your opponent announces, "I win because I am the first on the green." The rules of golf declare the man with the lowest score, the winner, not the one who gets on the green first. You can't have any credibility if you change the rules during a game.

Look at God the Lawmaker. Every time you apply the Law of Gravity, it always works on every object, every time. But someone asks about a decompression chamber where objects float. There can be a higher power to overcome the Law of Gravity. Those who create a new situation—a decompression chamber—now make new rules. Of course, Jesus walked on the water, defying gravity. Jesus, the High Power, overcame the normal power, i.e., the Law of Gravity. That means you have laws no matter where you live. You live under old laws or new laws, but you still have laws.

The rules or commandments of God always reveal God and how He relates to His created ones. The Bible says, "God is holy, just and good" so you expect God's laws to reflect His nature. Then the Bible says, "Therefore the law is holy, and the commandment holy and just and good" (Rom. 7:12). The laws are an extension of God and reveal God to us.

A good God could not create evil laws, so a perfect God would create what? "The law of the Lord is perfect" (Psa. 19:7).

7. *The rules or commandments point us to* God. God made His rules for us to praise and bring glory to Him. When God says, "You shall have no other gods before Me" (Exod. 20:3), He indicated that our first rule was to put Him first. Jesus reinforces this view when He was questioned, "Which is the great commandment in the law?" "You shall love the LORD your God with all your heart, with all your soul, and with all your mind" (Matt. 22:36,37).

YOUR RESPONSE TO GOD'S LAW (OR COMMANDMENTS)

1. *Keeping the Commandments will not save you.* God gave the Ten Commandments to show how He wanted His people to live together and to serve Him. They were never given for *salvation*. Even if you could keep all the Law—which you can't—you would not earn salvation. "For whoever shall keep the whole law, and yet stumble in one point, he is guilty of all" (Jas. 2:10).

2. *The Law or Commandments point you to God.* Since the Law is an extension of God, and shows us God's nature, this standard point us to God, "For the law was given through Moses, but grace and truth came through Jesus Christ" (John 1:17). Like a teacher who shows a student the truth, "Therefore the law was our tutor to bring us to Christ, that we might be justified by faith" (Gal. 3:24).

3. *Only Christ completely kept the Law, and He fulfilled the demands of the Law in His death.* The only person to keep all the Law was Jesus Christ, and He satisfied its demands. He said, "Do not think that I came to destroy the Law or the Prophets. I did not come to destroy but to fulfill" (Matt. 5:17).

   Because Christ lived a perfect live without sin, He could become our substitute; taking on our sin. Just as a sheep had to be without blemish to become a sacrifice for the sin of an Israelite, so a perfect Christ was our sacrifice for sin. But it didn't stop there, He satisfied both sin and the Law that demanded death for sin. "Christ satisfied the Law, because it was nailed to the cross with him" (Col. 2:14, author's translation).

4. *You still must have a good attitude toward the Law.* Even though the Law has been fulfilled in Christ, still the guidelines of the Law become our criteria for living. We must be like Ezra who was effective in service, a good testimony to others, and walked honestly before God. "For Ezra had prepared his heart to seek the Law of the LORD, and to do it, and to teach statutes and ordinances in Israel" (Ezra 7:10).

5. *Living by the Law or rules will help you get along with others.* Even though we do not keep the Law for salvation, it is a guideline for successful living with other people. "For all the law is fulfilled in one word, even in this: 'You shall love your neighbor as yourself'" (Gal. 5:14).

6. *Living by the Law or rules will help you become successful in life.* Because the Law is good and reflects the attributes of God—Who is the Lawgiver—when I apply His Law to my life, it makes me successful in what I do. "This Book of the Law shall not depart from your mouth, but you shall meditate in it day and night, that you may observe to do according to all that is written in it. For then you will make your way prosperous, and then you will have good success" (Josh. 1:8).

SPECIAL THANKS

No book is a project on one writer. I must thank my Editorial Assistant Linda Elliott for proofing and editing the copy, to Renee Grooms my Administrative Assistant for typing the original copy and laying out the PowerPoint so I could teach these lessons. Special thanks to the ushers, sound technicians, PowerPoint personnel, musicians, radio and television personnel (my Sunday School class televised locally). Thanks to Dr. Jerry Falwell who allows me to teach the Pastor's Bible Class (since 1986). Thanks to the Christian Education staff at Thomas Road Baptist Church that supported me in many ways. Then finally thanks to the class members for listening, asking questions, and giving me support in this project.

For all that is said—and not said—I take responsibility. May God use these lessons to help us all live for Him.

From my home at the foot of the Blue Ridge Mountains,

Elmer Towns
Spring, 2020

PART ONE

THE TEN COMMANDMENTS ACCORDING TO JESUS

Jesus' View on the Priority of People

Jesus taught obedience to the Law was tied to faith in God. People are not just subjects to obey God's law, they are children of the Heavenly Father. Heavenly treasures were better than earthly treasures. The eye was to be single toward God. The Heavenly Father's children mean more to Him than sparrows and flowers, yet the Heavenly Father is concerned about the smallest bird, the lily, and He even counted the hairs on your head. When God's children seek first His kingdom, earthly things are added to them (Matt. 6:19-35; Luke 11:34-36; 12:22-34).

Other gods. Where do other gods come from? Obviously, God did not create them, nor are they eternal. God is the only One that is eternal; He's always been here. So where do false gods come from? Obviously, God *wouldn't* create false gods. Why? Because God cannot make anything false. Also, God *couldn't* create false gods for every false god is a denial of Himself.

People are the ones who create false gods.

Man is an idol-maker. When a man stops worshipping the God in whose image he is made, then he turns to make gods in his own image. All of the man-made gods are not as powerful as the Creator-God, as good as the Holy-God, and surely not as loving as the Savior-God. Ever notice how the man-made gods are not God-like? Man-made gods show the evil side of Man. And when Man turns from worshipping the true God, he then worships a god in his own image. But because Man knows that his god is not real—like the real God—he has to create something to remind him of his god. Man carves a Buddha with a fat belly, or makes an angry looking Baal. Man draws a picture of Ra, the sun god, to coax the sun not to burn up his crops. Or, Man sculpts a bull from clay when he needs fertility for his flock. Man is an incurable "idol maker" because he's rejected the true God of Heaven.

Jesus on Loving God

The Ten Commandments said "You shall have no other gods before Me." That demanded outward obedience. So Jesus dealt with your inward relationship to God. It wasn't enough to kick other gods out of your life. Jesus gave a higher priority to your relationship to God, "You shall love the Lord your God with all your heart, and with all your soul, and with all your mind" (Matt. 22:37). Jesus expected you to give your highest devotion to God, i.e., absolute total love to God.

Every Word is Important

What did God mean when God said *Have*, as in "Have no other gods before Me?" God didn't say you should not *possess* any god. For if God had said you could not *own* a false idol or *have* a false god, many would have looked for the loopholes by worshipping a neighbor's god, or going downtown to worship a public God. It was possible to worship a false god without owning it. So, God said you could not even *have* it in your life.

Also, God didn't say *don't make* any gods. Why? Because people looking for loopholes would have thought they could have worshipped someone else's God. In essence the Living God said don't make false gods, don't allow any false gods, no matter how you may acquire them, don't give them any room in your life.

Also, this First Commandment doesn't say, "Don't worship false gods." A few people might have tried to keep a false God in their house—not to worship—but as a "lucky charm." But God said more than not worshiping it, God said not to have any gods in your life. This is an all-inclusive statement. If you don't have a false god, obviously you won't worship it.

Again, notice the inclusiveness of the word "NO." When God said, "You shall have no other gods," He did not allow the people to worship false gods fifty percent of the time, or even

10 percent of the time. What does the word "NO" imply? It means God wants you to get rid of any false god, anywhere in your possession, or anywhere in your thinking.

Jesus on Inward Obedience

Jesus taught the disposition of the heart concerning the Law, not just outward mechanical obedience to the Law. He taught His followers had a greater responsibility than just obeying the Law, they were "heirs to His kingdom." They were to become salt to others (Matt. 5:13), and the obligation rested on them to let their light shine (Matt. 5:14-16), so people would glorify the Father.

The First Commandment doesn't deal with idols, but they're implied. God said, "You should have no other gods." If God had started prohibiting idols, again people would have looked for the loopholes. They could have worshipped false gods in their hearts, but kept their house free of idols. But, notice the order of these commandments. If you don't have any false gods in your life, (First Commandment) surely you wouldn't have any idols in your house (Second Commandment).

Remember, that an idol is only Man's representation of his ideas about God. When the sun was burning up his crops, Man made idols to Re, the sun god, then prayed to that idol/god to ask for rain and bountiful crops. And when a farmer needed fertility, he made an idol to Baal, the fertility god. And then what did these idols look like? Usually hideous things! Idols looked like the people that made them.

Why Are There Other Gods?

- Because Man is a worshipper.
- Because Man is a compulsive idol-maker.
- Because Man has rebelled against the true God.
- Because Satan has a false religion.

When God told Man not to have other gods *before Me*, what does the phrase *before Me* mean? The phrase *before Me* could mean don't bring false gods in God's face (but the implication is you could keep false gods behind God's back when He wasn't looking). That could be like don't bring heathen idols into a Christian church, i.e., but some would interpret it, you could keep them at home.

In another sense, the phrase *before Me* could mean priority of time, "Don't put any god in line before God." Again, some would interpret it, you can let false gods in line after the true God.

And the phrase *before Me* could also mean God's attention. That suggests that you may have an idol in your life, just as long as God doesn't see it or it doesn't attract God's attention. As an illustration, if God is sitting on the throne, you shouldn't have an idol down in the closet, or in the basement.

None of these loopholes work because the phrase *before Me* is all-inclusive. It means don't have any false gods at any place in your life, at any time in your schedule, for any reason whatsoever. *Put God first*!

How does God feel about idols? He calls them an abomination. As far as God is concerned, an idol is the most wicked thing that you could possess.

If He is not Lord of all,

He is not Lord at all.

PUTTING GOD FIRST IN ISRAEL

The Lord was the center of the camp. When Israel would stop for overnight encampment, the tabernacle was first set up in the middle of the camp. Each of the twelve tribes was assigned a pre-determined place; they were to surround the Tabernacle, i.e., the Lord. This was not encampment to protect the Lord from an enemy attack; "No!" God can take care of Himself. God was at the center of the camp for worship and priority; each of the twelve tribes put God at the center of their lives geographically, which means God was to be placed at the center of their lives in every other way.

The Lord was first in obedience. When God spoke to Israel from Mount Sinai, they were to obey. When God led them from the Shekinah-glory cloud, they were to follow. Wherever God fed in the desert, Israel could eat. They couldn't choose their own way, they couldn't choose what they thought was an enjoyable path, or an easy path, nor could they even choose a safe path. Israel's obligation was to follow the Lord in the Shekinah cloud. And where the Lord leads, He protects and provides.

The Lord was first in danger. When God led Israel to the Promised Land, He didn't bypass danger or trouble. God, who is sovereign, knew that Meribah was a dried-up oasis in the desert. But God led them to Meribah anyway, so there Moses could smite the rock; so He could give them water. God, who knew the future, also realized that when He brought water out of the rock, enemies would come to fight over the water. Water rights are an explosive issue in the desert. So, the attack by the Amalekites didn't catch God by surprise. When Moses extended his arms to Heaven and prayed for military intervention, God gave Moses and the Israelites the victory. When Moses dropped his weary arms in fatigue, the Amalekites won. Didn't God know all this before it happened? Yes!

God did all of this because He wanted to be their leader in battle, but he also wanted Israel to trust Him in the midst of the conflict. Even though we think God leaves loose details around, like small stones on the path to trip us up, God's comprehensive plan always comes back to *Lordship*. We must make Him LORD in the battle, as well as the LORD in planning and victory.

His Lordship involves choice. As God led Israel through the Wilderness, He constantly challenged them to choose Him. The idols of heathen nations tempted Israel to worship them. The daughters of heathen nations tempted the young Israelites to inter marry with them. The devilish practices of heathen religions tempted Israel to worship other gods. A sovereign God knew all these difficulties awaited for Israel, and He allowed it. Why? Because worship always involves choice. If every time God demanded "worship" and the people automatically fell to their face like a robot, then worship would be nothing more than a manufactured product from an assembly line. Our worship would be like playing an audio cassette—all pre-determined and prescribed. But God wanted His people to choose Him, so He said, "You shall have no other gods before Me." The people had to choose God first, and they had to choose to worship God continually. Worship is a choice, and following God is a choice of *Lordship*.

Jesus' View on Conformity To The Law

Jesus taught the essence of true righteousness was not outward conformity to the law, but inner "hunger and thirst after righteousness" (Matt. 5:6). The Pharisees killed "the spirit of the law" with their oral traditions, and outward obedience. Jesus said a sinful thought or desire was the root of sin. Jesus reversed the world's standards that said "outward obedience leads to inner character."

Jesus taught, "righteousness begins with inner obedience" (Matt. 5:17- 48; Luke 6:26-36).

Putting the Lord first is an act of faith. God brought storms into the life of Israel, even when He was in their midst. Israel had to recognize that God was Lord of the storm, long before God dismissed the destructive power of the storm. So often throughout the history of Israel, the people only called on God when they were threatened, or when they were in problems. The Lord wanted first place in their lives on good days *and* bad days. That meant they should have trusted Him each day, before each storm came, not just to save them through the storms. They were to trust Him first in preparation for storms and trust Him in celebration of in victory after the storms. The First Commandment taught Israel to make God first in all of their lives.

Because God is Lord of the storm, He may allow Israel to think that the storm will destroy them. God will let the storms ravage them before He delivers His people from the storm. Why? Because God is Lord of the storms; He is Lord of the calm nights. He is Lord of each day of the week, and He is Lord of each hour of the day. Whether Israel worshipped God, or turned its back on God, God is still the Lord.

Jesus' View of Law Keeping

Jesus demanded total love to God, (Matt. 22:37) and with that love, people could not break God's law, nor trespass against their fellow man. On the night He was betrayed, Jesus gave a third Great Commandment, "A new commandment I give to you, that you love one another; as I have loved you, that you also love one another. By this all will know that you are My disciples, if you have love for one another" (John 13:34, 35). Love is the beginning attitude of the Ten Commandments, demonstrating a positive, not negative, attitude toward life. Because of love, the Ten Commandments are no longer the highest summary of human duty. The new command is to "Love one another," an admonition so profound, yet simple; that even a child can understand and obey.

CONCLUSION

A line has been draw through the ages; it extends from Heaven to Man and reaches around the earth. The line crosses the desert of North Africa and is drawn in the sand at the foot of Mt. Sinai. On one side of the line is God and the blessings of Heaven. On the other side are all the false gods that are found in this world. The line in the sand is the First Commandment that says, "You shall have no other gods before Me."

There is no middle ground. You must worship God, obey God and recognize all that God has done for you. Or, you choose the other side. That choice is God first, or deny God and what He can do for you.

Jesus' View on What's Important

Jesus recognized the preeminence of the First Commandment, not only establishing the Divine order sat down in Exodus 20, but also reestablished the Divine priority of Himself over all of life. Jesus said the two Great Commandments were "You shall love the Lord your God" (Deut. 6:5), and Second, "You shall love your neighbor as yourself" (Lev. 19:18). "On these two commandments," He said, "hang all the law and the prophets" (Matt 22:40).

PRINCIPLES TO TAKE AWAY

- You must choose whether you will follow the true God or false gods in this life.
- You have a choice to put God first in your life.
- You are important to God inasmuch as He has made you *co-workers* and
- *co-rulers* with Him in this worship.
- The best choice you can make with your freedom is to worship God.
- Jesus must have the Lordship of your life.
- There is no middle ground in your relationship to God.

Chapter Two

YOU SHALL NOT ALLOW ANYTHING BETWEEN YOU AND GOD

Second Commandment

"You shall not make for yourself a carved image—any likeness of anything that is in heaven above, or that is in the earth beneath, or that is in the water under the earth; you shall not bow down to them nor serve them. For I, the LORD your God, am a jealous God, visiting the iniquity of the fathers upon the children to the third and fourth generations of those who hate Me, but showing mercy to thousands, to those who love Me and keep My commandments" (Exodus 20:4-6).

FOR the first thirty years of our life, my wife and I had an idol sitting in the corner of our bedroom. But we didn't consider it an idol; it was a nice Oriental piece of artwork. It was a deep rust brown metal color, about fourteen inches tall. Since we like artwork, we had an equally large marble fisherman in our family room, and I had been given a ceramic bust of John Wesley that I proudly displayed in my study.

Back to the idol in our bedroom. I knew I had to do something when I become convinced that this idol was more than a bronze figurine you buy at a gift store to display on a knick-knack shelf. People make idol-shaped statues to appease the power behind the things that control their life. To people living in a heathen culture, the power is usually demonic. When people worship idols, they are worshipping demons, although they don't say it in so many words. They might be horrified if it were even suggested that their idol had ever been used for devil worship.

I told my wife we had to get rid of the idol, but she said, "It's a gift." When I explained my conviction that evil spirits many times reside behind idols, and evil spirits could be brought into our house by the idol; she agreed with me that we had to remove it. We agreed at morning prayer time around the breakfast table, and I took it to work with me. "Where do you throw away an idol?" I didn't want to throw it in my trashcan, nor did I want to take it to a Christian school and deposit it in their trash dump. I didn't want it to end up in anyone else's hand, even if the person were innocent and thought the idol was a harmless piece of art.

Behind a large store I saw a garbage disposal truck backing up to a dumpster. "Aha, I'll put it there." So I threw the idol in the dumpster, and the truck took it to the city dump; it would never be used again.

Why did God tell us not to make idols? The answer is simple. God made us worshippers, but He didn't want us worshipping the wrong thing. God wants each of us to worship Him, that's the dominant thrust of the Psalms.

Jesus' View on Worship

Jesus told the Samaritan woman at the well, "The Father seeks worshippers" (John 4:24). Jesus gives us three insights into worship. First, Jesus gave us a new name for God, He is our Father, and He wants an intimate relationship to us; not just as a king to his subjects, but as a Father to His children. We are to worship our heavenly Father intimately. Second, the Father is seeking our worship; He is not angry and blocking our access to Him. We do not have to overcome His wrath. Third, we can have access to the Father through worship. Jesus taught that the Father wants worship from us, more than anything else.

God doesn't force anyone to worship Him. Think of the angels; they have no free choice. They cry constantly, "Holy... Holy... Holy..." They were created to worship God and can do nothing else. But us? We have freedom of choice. Like our first parents who were instructed to eat the fruit of all the trees in the Garden, but not the one in the center of the Garden. So, we are free to worship God; but God has warned, "You shall have no other gods before Me" (Exod. 20:3). God knows that Man is a worshipper, so He commands us not to have another god, and to not carve another god. "You shall not make for yourself a carved image" (Exod. 20:4).

How should people worship God? The nature of God determines how we should worship Him. Since "God is Spirit," that tells us He must be worshipped in spirit. And what kind of worship is that? Spirit worship is spiritual worship; we should worship Him by the power of the Holy Spirit when we are filled with the Holy Spirit (Eph. 5:17). Be filled with the spirit" (Eph. 5:18). To get the Spirit's filling, you must be yielded to Him. So yield now and worship Him.

Next, you should worship God truthfully because Jesus said you "must worship Him in...truth." How do you do that? You must worship God according to the truth of Scripture; you must worship Him the way God wants to be worshiped. That means you must worship God without the aid of idols because He said "no carved images."

What is wrong with using "idols" to help you worship God? Many people who use a "thing" to worship God say that the "thing" actually helps them picture God in their mind, or helps them focus on the God when they pray. They claim their idol represents the God of their worship. But you don't worship God the way you want to do it, nor do you need something to give you "focus" or more "understanding" to worship God. You just pour out your whole soul to Him in adoration. You just obey the Second Commandment.

The Second Commandment says that an idol should not be represented by an animal, bird, or fish. Those things bring the Creator-God down to the Creation. And what about those whose idol is an image like a man? Every man-made god is limited, i.e., limited in ability, attributes, or limited in what he wants to accomplish for people. Don't let a thing represent God, because nothing can represent God. God is Spirit, so worship Him in your spirit.

Some people ask why can't I see God? Because God doesn't have a corporal body like us, God is an incorporeal being. That means He is a real person with intellect, emotion, and will, He just doesn't have a physical body. The bottom line is that you can't see God because there is nothing there to see. But when you use an idol in worship, you're trying to make God into something you can see.

Jesus' View of God

Jesus taught God is Spirit in nature. "God is Spirit, and those who worship Him must worship in spirit and truth." The woman said to Him, "I know that Messiah is coming" (who is called Christ). "When He comes, He will tell us all things" (John 4:24, 25). The *Old King James* used the phrase "God is a spirit," suggesting God is one spirit among many spirits. The "a" is missing in the original text, so the phrase means "God is spirit," i.e., God is spirit in nature.

But there is a second truth in the above verse. Jesus called God "The Father." This is a phrase not used in the Old Testament. The Jews did not think of God as "their Father." They thought of Him as Almighty God, and the Creator. They knew Him by His three primary names, Elohim, Jehovah, and Adonai. Now Jesus is teaching us that we can have intimacy with the heavenly Father as an earthly child depends on his earthly father.

So what is the positive side of the Second Commandment? When God tells you not to make a carved idol, not to bow down and worship it, God is pleading with you to worship Him. The Second Commandment is about worship. Because people are idol-makers, God says, "Do not make idols of any kind… you must never worship or bow down to them" (Exod. 20:3).

This is not a strange request on God's part. Every mother knows that if you put a four-year-old in a room by himself, and tell the child "don't touch that glass on the table," what will happen? When mother comes back in the room, she will find the child's fingerprints all over the glass. The nature of the human inquisitive spirit is to explore or push the boundary, or do what you've been told not to do. God knows the heart is rebellious, so God can't just say worship Me; God must say, "Do not worship idols."

Why No Idols?

"But be careful! You did not see the LORD'S form on the day he spoke to you from the fire at Mount Sinai. So do not corrupt yourselves by making a physical image in any form— whether of a man or a woman, an animal or a bird, a creeping creature or a fish. And when you look up into the sky and see the sun, moon, and stars— all the forces of heaven— don't be seduced by them and worship them. The LORD your God designated these heavenly bodies for all the peoples of the earth. Remember that the LORD rescued you from the burning furnace of Egypt to become his own people and special possession; that is what you are today" (Deut. 4:15-20, NLT).

God was very specific. His people were not to make idols… keep idols… worship idols … have anything to do with idols. God wanted idolatry completely out of their lives. That is the commandment of the New Testament, "Therefore, my beloved, flee from idolatry" (1 Cor. 10:14). John also warned, "Little children, keep yourselves from idols. Amen" (1 John 5:21).

As a matter of fact, when a person was converted to Christ, they were described as "how you turned to God from idols to serve the living and true God" (1 Thess. 1:9).

EXAMINING EACH WORD IN THE SECOND COMMANDMENT

Thou shall not make. The word "to make" has the idea of "to create," as an artist creating an art form. This could be an artist painting a canvas, carving a sculpture, or creating any art form. God does not want to be represented by an art form. Why? Because God does not have a body. There is no physical substance there. "God is spirit" (John 4:24). Originally, when the Ten Commandments were given, Moses reminds Israel, "You saw no form when the LORD spoke to you" (Deut. 4:15).

The word *make* can also mean to substitute. Anytime you "make a cake," you eat the cake instead of something else, i.e., you substitute cake for bread. A painting of a woman is a substitute for the real woman, and a statue of a man is a substitute of the real man. When Man made an idol, it became a substitute for God. But nothing can take the place of God, so don't have idols.

For yourselves. Notice God understood why people made idols. They were not making idols for God's sake; they were making idols for their sake. Idols were made "for yourselves," which meant idols were made for the human, not God. Don't deceived yourself; when you put something in the place of God, you're not doing it for God, it's a selfish motivation.

Graven. As a young kid, I memorized the Ten Commandments but had no idea what the word *graven* meant. I didn't know it meant "carved." I had heard of people who were gravely ill, so I thought the word *graven* meant something bad or disastrous. Therefore, as a young boy I thought idols were bad because they were *graven*. Obviously, idols are bad; but that's not what the word *graven* means.

Implied in the word *graven* is "your best." A *graven* statue was carved, not poured.

Think of buying a cheap figurine at a gift shop. There are thousands made out of the same mold, just like the one you buy. Therefore, a poured figurine is not expensive; it's probably not artistic, and surely is not unique. A poured idol was never one of Israel's problems. The problem was a *graven* or sculptured idol. These images were something Man did with a hammer and chisel from stone, or Man carved with a knife from wood.

A sculptured statue involves a sculptor's personality, the sculptor's skill and creativity, as well as the sculptor's will and determination. A magnificently sculptured statue is the product of the magnificent sculptor. Idol worshippers are giving "their best" to the spirit represented by the idol.

Years ago in I saw in the summer palace in Moscow, Russia, a Michelangelo sculpture and I was transfixed by its beauty. Technically, the carving was only half done; half of the art was a piece of marble, the other half was a man. But, what was completed was so magnificent I couldn't keep my eyes off. The tour went on without me and my wife had to come back and force me to leave the statue area to rejoin the group. Notice I said, "Michelangelo sculpture." You cannot disassociate the sculptor from his sculpture; and you can't disassociate an idol from the idolater, and when an idol is dedicated to a demon-spirit, you can't disassociate the demon- worship from the idolater.

Image... likeness. God said that we should not make any graven image. Why?

Because we are created in God's image, made by the Divine Sculptor. We are God's creation; He said, "Let Us make Man in Our image, after Our likeness" (Gen. 1:26).

Remember, Man is a worshiper and if he won't worship God in Heaven; he will turn his worship to something else. Second, remember Man is an idol-maker. If Man won't worship God in Heaven, he will make his own idol to worship. The idol became an extension of the idol-maker, i.e., the idol comes from the heart of the idolater.

So, what is the bottom line? Man has become a *god-maker*. Because there is a great vacuum in the heart of Man without God, Man must make his own god, i.e., his own idol.

Not make... My likeness... in Heaven... earth... water. Man is commanded not to make an idol that is like anything in Heaven (sun, moon, stars), the earth (animals, plants, trees), or the water (fish, sea creatures). *The Living Bible* translates these three words, birds, animals, and fish. These are the things that have become the idols of Man. Can you imagine someone falling down to worship a carved fish, or a carved bull, or even a carved eagle? From our enlightened civilization, idolatry appears so foolish; but, how does God see it?

Bow down thyself. God not only prohibited Man from making a *graven* image, but also prohibited him from bowing down to an image. Maybe the prohibition to *bow down* is added because some Hebrews might not carve an idol, but might go next door to worship the neighbor's idol. Worship is reserved for God, and all worship must be directed to God.

JESUS' VIEW ON THE PLACE OF WORSHIP

Jesus taught that the Father seeks people to worship Him everywhere. In Jesus' day, the Father wanted worship, no different than God's desire in Moses' day. Just as Moses instructed the people not to worship idols, so Jesus instructed the Samaritan woman not to worship in her mountain, but to go to Jerusalem to worship, "'Our fathers worshiped on this mountain, and you Jews say that in Jerusalem is the place where one ought to worship.' Jesus said to her, 'Woman, believe Me, the hour is coming when you will neither on this mountain, nor in Jerusalem, worship the Father. You worship what you do not know; we know what we worship, for salvation is of the Jews. But the hour is coming, and now is, when the true worshipers will worship the Father in spirit and truth; for the Father is seeking such to worship Him. God is Spirit, and those who worship Him must worship in spirit and truth'" (John 4:20-24).

Serve them. Not only were people prohibited from worshipping idols, God did not want them serving idols. The idea of serving idols "is giving money or sacrificing things to idols, such as an animal, food or anything." The idea of serving idols was "obeying idols," or "pleasing idols." God did not want His people to do anything that was taught by the priests of Baal, or any other person. They were only to obey the Scriptures.

There are several words in the original language for worship. One of them is *latreuo* which means "to give service to God." The early church "prayed and worshipped" (Acts 13:2), meaning they served the Lord with worship. When the modern-day church meets, it is called by many the "worship service." As a young boy, I wondered why they called it the "worship service." The only people I saw serving God were the ushers, the preacher and some choir members. Most people were just listening to a sermon, some were sleeping. *"How can that be service?"*, I used to think. Now I realize that we are supposed to serve God by worshipping Him. The writer of Hebrews describes this, "Let us continually offer the sacrifice of praise to God, that is, the fruit of our lips, giving thanks to His name" (Heb. 13:15). God must be served with our praise, which is the nature of worship.

The Lord thy God is a jealous God. When God describes Himself as jealous, what does it mean? It means that "He is intolerant of rivalry." God does not want us giving any of our time to a false god. Not ten percent... not fifty percent... nothing! What does God say about those who worship idols? He accuses them of "hating Me." Worshipping an idol is the same thing as hating God.

Visiting. When God talks about visiting the iniquity to the third and fourth generation, what is entailed in a "visit"? The word "visiting" means "charging." God charges to your account, as well as He charges to the account of your children, and your grandchildren. This is like police charging you with breaking a speed limit, and giving you a ticket. This is like you running up a debit on your credit card that must be paid. But, if you're an idolater, you run up a debit on the credit card of your children's, and your grandchildren. They have to pay for your false worship.

Iniquity. The word "iniquity" is *aven* which is "to be bent" or "to control." Idolatry is so bad it becomes a root in the heart that is almost impossible to dig out. There is an old saying, "As the tree is bent, so grows the child." This means that fathers who worship idols, have children who are idolaters. Continuing into the third generation, if the father is an idolater, the grandchildren will also be idolaters. Therefore, be careful of your sin, your sin plants a seed that roots itself deep in the heart. The sin-fruit may be visible for three or four generations.

Them that hate Me. God is so jealous of an idol that He says that those who are idolaters "*hate Me*." Most idolaters say that they don't hate God, but rather they're just honestly searching for God and using a "thing" to find God. However, God has revealed Himself in nature, and people know right from wrong by their conscience. They know in their heart that there is a God, but they usually refuse to worship Him because God demands truth... purity... and commitment. People refuse to live pure lives demanded by God, so they choose an idol.

That's the same as "hating God."

Showing mercy to thousands. To show mercy means "forgiveness." God wants to forgive His children, not punish them. God wants people to repent and turn to Him, then He can forgive them. God will show mercy to thousands, which means to the third and fourth generation. If a person has a normal family of six to twelve children, when that is compounded and multiplied to the third and fourth generations, the result is *thousands* in offspring. So, when God forgives thousands, he will forgive every offspring of an idolater if they will turn to Him.

Love Me and keep My commandments. What does God want from every person He has made? God wants "love." "You shall love the LORD your God with all your heart, with all your soul, and with all your strength" (Deut. 6:5). And the word *obey* simply means "to follow His directions." Moses told the people that God "declared to you His covenant which He commanded you to perform, the Ten Commandments; and He wrote them on two tablets of stone" (Deut. 4:13).

IDOLATRY DEFIES LOGIC

God made people worshipers. God created people to worship Him, have fellowship with Him and to serve Him. God created Adam and Even to meet with Him in the cool of the day.

Since Man is intellect, emotion and will. Man was created intellectually to know and understand God, emotionally to love God and volitionally to serve God with all their heart.

People became God-compromisers. God made people to worship Him, but they end up following their own inclinations, doing what they desire. Rather than obeying God explicitly, people today like Adam and Eve, think they can do it better their own way; hence, they compromise God's standards.

People become God-minimizers. When people refuse to worship and honor God, they bring Him down to their own level. When they make an idol in their own image, they minimize God to their standards.

People become God-makers. When people begin creating images to represent God, that idol has taken the place of God. God originally created people in His image, now people turn around to create something in God's image. But in reality, people create it in their image. People have become *God-makers*.

Our idolatry. Michelangelo looked within the marble to discover what person is there, then chipped away the excess marble, sculpturing it accordingly. The greatest sculptor of all times felt that there was an image of art in each stone, and he went inside the marble to find the image that was there. Don't idolaters do the same thing? They look within their heart, then make a god of what they find. Since we are lustful, our gods are lustful. Since we are rebellious, so our gods violate eternal laws. And because we are limited and finite, our idols cannot compare with God's power in Heaven.

Anything we put in the place of God is an idol. So we become idolaters when we make an idol of our money, as well as we make an idol of our possessions, our hobbies, or our achievements. Anything that takes the place of God, that's an idol. Don't look within to find your "man-made god", rather look within the nature of God to discover who He is. When you discover God, worship and follow Him for His beauty and majesty.

PRINCIPLES TO TAKE AWAY

- An idol is more than a man-made image, it represents the demon-spirit that is represented by the image.
- There is no place in a believers' life for an idol.
- God created people with a thirst to worship, and if they will not worship the true God, they will make their own god.
- Because people are compulsive idol-makers, they become god-makers.
- God says an "idol-worshippers" hates Him.
- God will forgive the idol-worshipper who repents and turns to Him.

Chapter Three

YOU SHALL REVERENCE GOD

Third Commandment

"You shall not take the name of the LORD your God in vain, for the LORD will not hold him guiltless who takes His name in vain" (Exodus 20:7).

"I have the most difficulty with cursing of any thing in my Christian life," a man in my Sunday school class told me recently. He knew it was wrong, but cursed anyway. He explained, "It is so easy to curse, because I get frustrated and angry. Once these curse words get in my mind, it's hard not to use them."

A minister was unloading his furniture to move in to a new house, when he realized the house had a large lawn and he didn't have a lawnmower to cut the grass. Then he was approached by a young boy pushing a lawnmower down the street who said, "Mister, I'll trade you my lawnmower for your bicycle." There was a bicycle on the tailgate of the truck. Since the minister needed the lawnmower, and seldom used the bicycle, he thought it was a good trade. The following day the minister saw the boy and said, "That lawnmower won't start."

The boy explained, "You've got to cuss it to get it going!"

"But I don't cuss," the minister said to the boy. The preacher went on to explain that before he was converted, he cursed but quit.

"You pull on that lawnmower enough, those words will come back to you!"

Why is vile language dealt with so prominently in the Ten Commandments? Why is taking God's name in vain the Third Commandment, before killing, and lying, and adultery?

After all, it's only the words that we speak, and things like murder, lying and adultery are much more important.

God created you to worship and praise Him. In the First Commandment, you are to put *nothing* before God, "Thou shalt have no other gods before Me." And in the Second Commandment, you are to put nothing *between* you and God, "Thou shalt not make any carved idols." Now in the Third Commandment, you are commanded to reverence God. God wants you to reverence Him with your mouth, because your words express your thinking, feeling, and reaction. After all what's in the well, comes up in the bucket. God must rule the center of your life, and when you take His name in vain, you have dishonored Him.

Jesus' View on Positive Speech

Jesus supported the Third Commandment, "You shall not take the name of the LORD your God in vain," when he explained, "But I say to you, do not swear at all: neither by heaven,... nor by the earth..." (Matt. 5:34, 35). "But let your 'Yes' be 'Yes,' and your 'No,' 'No'" (Matt. 5:37). Jesus wants our speech to honestly reflect the positive things of life. Jesus' emphasis was not on stopping negative speech. Jesus taught us to emphasize the positive and we would then eliminate the negative.

VARIETIES OF CORRUPT COMMUNICATION

There are many expressions used by people today of corrupt communication or taking God's name in vain. These include swearing, cursing, blasphemy, filthy language, profanity, and slang. Each of these terms refers to a different aspect of wrong language.

Swearing involves uttering an oath or declaration with an appeal to God or a sacred object. When people swear, they are attempting to direct judgment or anger on people to satisfy unrighteous passions.

Cursing involves asking God to bring harm or evil to a person or object. The result of cursing is to speak blasphemy. In Scripture, a curse carried its own power of execution.

Blasphemy involves directing curses or judgment toward God or His sacred object. The unpardonable sin, blasphemy against the Holy Spirit, involves attributing the obvious works of God to the devil.

Filthy Language is speech described as morally vile. Often it is obscene or nasty language with reference to parts of the body to convey the idea of disgust.

Profanity bridges the gap between swearing and filthy language. Its purpose is to show utter disregard for God.

Slang is language markedly colloquial. It is regarded as generally below the standards of cultural speech. Slang expressions are born into the common language of people when a phrase is coined, having meaning to those within the "in group."

WHAT DOES "IN VAIN" MEAN?

Notice what the Third Commandment didn't say. God didn't say, "You shall not cuss," nor did he say, "You shall not take the name of idols in vain." Nor did God say, "You shall not take the Bible in vain, nor His altar, or His promises in vain." All these things are important, but why was God concerned about the purity of His name? Because *the name of God represents the person of God*. When a person wrongly uses the name of God, they do not reverence or worship the person of God. And what does "vain" mean? It means *to speak of God in a degrading or insulting way*.

There are many ways that people take God's name in vain. Some joke about God or make Him the brunt of their humor. These people who would never curse or swear, actually take God's name in vain when they speak lightly of Him.

When you say God can't do a miracle, technically that's taking His name in vain. You are not demonstrating belief in God's ability, nor are you respecting His person.

Some people ignorantly laugh at the Church's standards, or they laugh at anything having to do with God. They laugh at the commandment prohibiting adultery, and they think Christians are crazy for remembering the Lord's Day. Aren't these people taking God's name in vain when they laugh at things that are holy and pure?

Other Christians trivialize God when they take worship services lightly, or they ignore Bible promises, or they think spiritual things are stupid. Isn't this taking God's name in vain?

Other people take God's name in vain when they make a vow to God, but don't plan on keeping it. The person who fills out a Faith Promise card to impress people with his money, but never planned to give the gift, that person has taken God's name in vain. When people raise their hand in court and promise to "tell the truth, the whole truth and nothing but the truth, so help me, God," but they intentionally lie; they're taking God's name in vain.

Some people repeat Christian expressions or sing hymns of praise to God without heart meaning; is this taking God's name in vain? When people sing Christmas carols about the birth of Jesus Christ, but think only of Santa Claus, are they taking God's name in vain?

When someone angrily curses and condemns a person to Hell in the name of God, they take God's name in vain. When you condemn someone to Hell, you are attempting to use God's authority. When people lightly treat punishment in Hell, damnation, and eternal suffering; they're taking God's name in vain.

Perhaps the most obvious violation is blaspheming God directly, i.e., directing hatred toward God. When people curse God, and/or become angry at Him, they take God's name in vain.

Finally, many people have a gutter mouth, using filthy or nasty expressions. When a person associates filth with God, they have taken His name in vain. They drag His purity into a cesspool. "Put off all these: anger, wrath, malice, blasphemy, filthy language out of your mouth" (Col. 3:8). Paul tells us very distinctly, "Let no corrupt word proceed out of your mouth" (Eph. 4:29).

Jesus Views the Source of Evil Speech

Jesus supported the Third Commandment by examining the sources of evil that corrupt a person's speech. "But those things which proceed out of the mouth come from the heart, and they defile a man. For out of the heart proceed evil thoughts, murders, adulteries, fornications, thefts, false witness, and blasphemies. These are the things which defile a man, but to eat with unwashed hands does not defile a man" (Matt. 15:18-20). The problem of evil speech was not the actual words, but the evil heart that caused the evil words. Since we are defined by the words of the mouth, Jesus taught that evil words were a reflection of an evil heart.

MODERN OBSERVATIONS

As we look at society today, several observations become apparent. One of the most startling is the apparent increase in swearing among women. Men seem to no longer dominate swearing. In previous generations, swearing was looked upon as manly; young boys were especially influenced this way. Today, women are as likely to swear as men. This is one of the results of equalization between the sexes in our society.

A second observation is that more people seem to swear more often than in the past. Swearing is no longer an occasional outburst in anger or frustration. Surveys reveal college students tend to swear at a rate of one in fourteen words. These same studies suggest children swear at the same frequency rate as their parents. As America is becoming less Christian, swearing is becoming more a significant part of the normal speech patterns of Americans.

The third observation relates to the legal arena. Organizations such as the American Civil Liberties Union represent people in court defending their right to swearing under the free speech provisions of the United States Constitution. We not only hear more swearing in public, it's more common in media, i.e., television, movies, and contemporary music.

WHAT IS WRONG WITH CURSING?

When people use God's name with a curse, they reflect their unbelief in God. They have angrily taken the place of God, and they have ignorantly condemned someone to Hell, not knowing the eternal torments that are described in Scriptures.

But cursing also reflects the anger in the curser's heart. Rather than loving your neighbor, one condemns them with a curse. And the person, who is given over to anger, has demonstrated that he cannot control himself, and knows nothing of discipline that comes from being a disciple of Jesus Christ.

Cursing denies God's control over people and affairs in this life. People should recognize the hand of God in life, and that "all things work together for good" (Rom. 8:28).

However, the person who reacts with white-hot hatred denies that God is dealing in his life or the life of the other person.

JESUS' VIEW OF THE CURSER

In the fuller statement of the law in Leviticus, the penalty for the crime of blasphemy was death by stoning. But that was not how Jesus approached cursing. Peter cursed in his third denial of Christ, "Then he began to curse and swear, 'I do not know this Man of whom you speak!'" (Mark 14:71). Nothing was done by those around him to Peter. But the Lord knew, "And the Lord turned and looked at Peter. Then Peter remembered the word of the Lord, how He had said to him, 'Before the rooster crows, you will deny Me three times.' So Peter went out and wept bitterly" (Luke 22:61, 62).

The Scriptures consistently teach the Christian response to cursing. Jesus said, "Bless those who curse you" (Matt. 5:44). The Ephesians were instructed to speak "neither filthiness, nor foolish talking, nor coarse jesting, which are not fitting, but rather giving of thanks" (Eph. 5:4). Paul told the Colossians, "But now is the time to cast off and throw away all these rotten garments of anger, hatred, cursing, and dirty language" (Col. 3:8, LB). Christians should not be guilty of using foul language.

Jesus' View of Your Enemy

Jesus didn't deal with the words of our mouth, but with the attitudes of our heart. He didn't just deal with "cursing" your enemy, but with the hatred of the heart that causes a person to curse their enemy. Jesus wanted to change the heart attitude toward the enemy. "But I say to you who hear: Love your enemies, do good to those who hate you, bless those who curse you, and pray for those who spitefully use you. To him who strikes you on the one cheek, offer the other also. And from him who takes away your cloak, do not withhold your tunic either. Give to everyone who asks of you. And from him who takes away your goods do not ask them back. And just as you want men to do to you, you also do likewise" (Luke 6:27-31).

HOW SOME CHURCH MEMBERS TAKE GOD'S NAME IN VAIN?

Some Christians unknowingly take God's name in vain with their worship. If you worship God each Sunday with singing and praying, yet during the week your life doesn't reflect your lips, haven't you taken God's name in vain?

Jesus' View of Wrong Profession

Jesus again points us to the motives of the heart. Jesus wants more than correct words, he wants us to have the correct heart attitude. "But why do you call Me 'Lord, Lord,' and not do the things which I say?" (Luke 6:46).

And some people falsely use God's name in Christian service. These could be ministers, missionaries, and volunteer workers in the church who have preached in God's name, yet haven't believed the promises of God.

Jesus' View of Empty Words

Notice what Jesus said about empty words. "Many will say to me in that day, Lord, Lord, have we not prophesied in thy name? And in thy name have cast out devils? And in thy name done many wonderful works? And then will I profess unto them, I never knew you: depart from me, ye that work iniquity" (Matt. 7:22, 23).

Some people pray in Jesus' name, yet their mind wanders when they're praying. Other people pray in Jesus' name, yet they treat God like a "rabbit's foot." They hope they'll get lucky and get the request they ask of God. They don't believe in the ability of God to give them what they ask; they have their spiritual "fingers crossed."

Jesus' View of Empty Faith

Jesus reminds us again of the meaninglessness of empty words, "Not every one that calls Me, Lord, Lord, shall enter into the kingdom of heaven..." (Matt. 7:21, author's translation).

WHY DO PEOPLE USE WRONG LANGUAGE?

Studies have been done to determine why people use wrong language. These studies suggest several reasons for this behavior. First, swearing is an expression of rebellion against restraints. It is a way of expressing a desire for freedom or independence from those viewed as oppressive.

A second reason why people swear is to express anger. When a worker hurts himself on the job, it is not uncommon for his first response to be an angry utterance of an oath or curse. A person expresses anger by swearing when injured emotionally.

Swearing has become a tool of feminism to try to make the sexes equal. Also, some young boys perceive being able to "swear like a man" as a necessary step in achieving maturity.

A fourth reason some people swear is to flaunt superiority. In some circles, the ability to swear is valued as a mark of superiority. This is especially true in what would be generally viewed as negative and destructive subcultures.

For many, swearing has become a habit. These people may have begun swearing for other reasons, but they have sworn so much now that it has become an integral part of their normal speech pattern. Sometimes, habitual swearing is the result of years of following poor role models. When a child hears his parents habitually swearing, the child follows his parents' example.

The final reason people swear and use profane language is as an expression of their rebellion against God. When Jesus challenged the scribes and Pharisees of His day for placing their traditions above the clear teaching of Scripture, Jesus reminded His listeners, "Not what goes into the mouth defiles a man; but what comes out of the mouth, this defiles a man" (Matt. 15:11). People who are angry with God and resist His claim on their life often express that anger and rebellion in wrong language.

WHAT DOES GUILTLESS MEAN?

God has said that those who use His name in vain will not be *guiltless*. What does this word mean? When you are guiltless, you are innocent, or without a charge. Suppose you were driving a car and you're involved in an accident. After the police investigate the accident, he gives a ticket to the other person, but not you. You are guiltless; you were not charged with breaking the law, because you were innocent. That's the same meaning for those who use God's name in vain; they are not guiltless or innocent. They shall be charged with a sin-violation, because they are guilty. You can never innocently take God's name in vain.

But why are words important? I have a Christian friend, who claims that he can't break his cursing, but that his words are just a bad habit; they have no meaning to him. My friend goes on to say that he loves God, serves God and tithes in the church. He says his curse words are necessary to keep the men in his shop working diligently, it's a part of his leadership style. He goes on to say that cursing is the only language some vile men understand.

But words are important to God, and they should be important to you. James notes, "Even so the tongue is a little member... it is set on fire of hell" (Jas. 3:5-6). James means the tongue, even though it's a small part of your body, can have eternal consequences. In another place James says, "The tongue... is an unruly evil" (Jas. 3:8). It's not that the physical organ is evil, but it's what the tongue represents.

JESUS' VIEW OF THE SOURCE OF EVIL SPEECH

Jesus taught the tongue represents an evil heart. Jesus said, "Do not ye yet understand... those things which proceed out of the mouth come forth from the heart; and they defile the man. For out of the heart proceed evil thoughts, murders, adulteries, fornications, thefts, false witness, blasphemies: These are the things which defile a man" (Matt. 15:17-20).

Therefore, what your heart thinks, your mouth speaks. So when the Third Commandment says, "Do not take the name of the Lord thy God in vain," it really is saying, reverence the Lord with the words that come from your heart. If you praise God in your heart, you will not blaspheme His name, nor use it as a curse.

JESUS' VIEW OF HONORING GOD'S NAME

Jesus taught us to honor and worship God's name, "Our Father in heaven, hallowed be Your name" (Matt. 6:9). This means we respect God's name.

WORDS HAVE POWER

Why are words powerful? Because they reflect what is in our hearts. Job understood this when he said, "How forceful are right words" (Job 6:25). Our words are so forceful; they give meaning to our life.

Our hearts should remember what God has done for us, and worship Him; for out of our minds and hearts come the emotions of gratitude. So we should not take God's name in vain, but remember God, and be thankful.

JESUS' VIEW OF SPEAKING OUR THOUGHTS

Jesus taught us that we cannot worship God with just our thoughts; God wants us to express our heart with our words. Jesus commands that we "must worship (God) in spirit and in truth" (John 4:24).

Therefore, our thoughts should focus on worship to God and not any negative expression about God or to God.

You should pray daily that your words glorify God. My good friend, Stan Toler, has a prayer he makes every day before getting out of bed. When Stan first awakens, he prays, "Let the words of my mouth, and the meditation of my heart, be acceptable in thy sight, O LORD, my strength, and my redeemer" (Psa. 19:14).

TWELVE STEPS TO PROPER SPEECH

In light of the biblical teaching on language, it is important that Christians seek to clean up their mouths and speak in a manner consistent with their Christian values. There are twelve steps that can help you deal with this problem.

To deal with the problem of wrong language, a believer must *first* realize when his or her language is wrong. The decision to change your speech patterns begins with the conviction that a problem does exist in your mouth.

Next Christians should be careful not to quickly use the negative words of our culture. Language is constantly changing and words that once had certain negative meanings may no longer have those meanings. As society changes the meaning of words, it should not be Christians who are in the forefront of accepting words that previously were rejected. If there is any doubt about the meaning of a word, wait until the transition has been made before you use questionable words.

Be not the first by which the new is tried.

Be not the last by which the old is laid aside.

Anon

Third, try to be proper in all things. If the desire to do the right thing permeates every area of your life, right speaking will come easier. When you strive to use proper language, you will not find yourself constantly struggling to eliminate questionable language.

Fourth, avoid using the language of the world to be accepted by the non-Christian.

While it is important to build relationships with the unchurched as a first step in reaching them for Christ, the use of wrong language may stall your efforts. As you build relationships, "Let your light so shine before men, that they may see your good works and glorify your Father in heaven" (Matt. 5:16).

Fifth, realize wrong language interferes with your growth and testimony. The key to the successful Christian life is to allow the life of Christ to live freely in your life. The use of wrong language places a barrier of sin between the Christian and his Lord. When you slip, sin should be confessed immediately so your fellowship with God can once again be restored (1 John 1:9).

Sixth, when you realize your speech reflects your character and inner discipline, you will be more highly motivated to use correct language. That motivation will help you deal with inner disciplines and develop Christian character.

In his Epistle to the Philippians, Paul wrote, "Finally, brethren, whatever things are true, whatever things are noble, whatever things are just, whatever things are pure, whatever things are lovely, whatever things are of good report, if there be any virtue and if there is anything praiseworthy—meditate on these things. The things which you learned and received and heard and saw in me, these do, and the God of peace will be with you" (Phil. 4:8, 9). These verses identify the seventh and eighth step in cleaning up your language. The *seventh* principle is stop filling your mind with unwholesome movies and exposing yourself to negative media. *Eighth*, pick out a Christian role model that does not have a problem in the area of language. When you have a question about using a word or expression, ask, "Would my role model use that language?"

A *ninth* step in dealing with wrong language is to get smart. Bad language is a dead giveaway of a person's ignorance. By building your vocabulary and expanding your learning, you will have greater resources to avoid using inappropriate language.

Ten, don't just separate yourself from people that curse, but be a testimony in their presence. As you bless those who curse you, they will be impressed by your consistent testimony. Replace evil speaking by being "kind to one another, tender-hearted, forgiving one another, just as God in Christ also forgave you" (Eph. 4:32).

Eleventh, be careful with every word. A good guideline is to "let your speech always be with grace, seasoned with salt, that you may know how you ought to answer each one" (Col. 4:6). Words are like a feather pillow shaken in the wind. It is impossible to collect all the feathers and take back words once they are spoken.

Finally, develop the discipline of memorizing and meditating on the Scriptures. "Let the word of Christ dwell in you richly in all wisdom, teaching, and admonishing one another in psalms and hymns and spiritual songs, singing with grace in your hearts to the Lord" (Col. 3:16). As you consider these twelve steps, may God help you also to speak what is right.

PRINCIPLES TO TAKE AWAY

- There are many different ways to take God's name in vain.
- The issue in speaking is the corrupt heart, not the actual words you speak.
- You can unknowingly take God's name in vain by insincerity or duplicity when you serve or worship.
- Because your words represent your heart, you are not innocent when you use corrupt speech.
- God can help you use correct words when you speak.

Chapter Four

YOU SHALL WORSHIP ON THE LORD'S DAY

Fourth Commandment

"Remember the Sabbath day, to keep it holy. Six days you shall labor and do all your work, but the seventh day is the Sabbath of the LORD your God. In it you shall do no work: you, nor your son, nor your daughter, nor your male servant, nor your female servant, nor your cattle, nor your stranger who is within your gates. For in six days the LORD made the heavens and the earth, the sea, and all that is in them, and rested the seventh day. Therefore the LORD blessed the Sabbath day and hallowed it" (Exodus 20:8-11).

THE Fourth Commandment is a positive admonition. "Remember to keep the Sabbath day holy." This positive commandment follows three negative laws , i.e., (1) you shall have no other gods before the Lord, (2) you shall not make carved idols, (3) you shall not take God's name in vain.

The Fourth Commandment does not say, "You shall not work on Sabbath Sunday." Why? Because God is not primarily interested in what you quit doing, but He is concerned about the positive benefit of *rest and worship*.

The purpose of the Fourth Commandment is not to "stop working," but to start worshipping on the Lord's Day. God wants you to take one day out of seven to worship... serve... sing... fellowship... learn... and minister for God. You should spend the Lord's Day doing the Lord's business.

Jesus' Practice of Observing

As a child—even into adult ministry—Jesus observed the observance of gathering on the Sabbath day for worship. Doesn't this suggest we should follow His example by going faithfully into the gatherings of believers on the Lord's day? Notice Jesus made it a habit, "As was His custom." That became an example to us too. "So He came to Nazareth, where He had been brought up. And as His custom was, He went into the synagogue on the Sabbath day, and stood up to read" Luke 4:16).

The Fourth Commandment begins with remembering. What do we need to remember?

We are to remember how the Lord God celebrated the seventh day; He rested. So as you approach the Lord's Day, go back in your memory to Creation; examine how the Lord rested the Sabbath day, and you'll understand what you should do on His day.

The Lord is our example for work, "For in six days the LORD made the heavens and the earth…" (Exod. 20:11). And what do we know about the Lord's work?

- The Lord did much work.
- The Lord did it all in six days.
- The Lord worked until He got finished.
- The Lord knew when to stop work, i.e., the Sabbath day.
- The Lord rested (the word Sabbath means rest).

Why does God tell us to remember the Sabbath day? Because we are compulsive workers, Man without God works for salvation. Man without hope works continually for money…for promotion…for his boss (that he probably considers a slave driver). If you are a compulsive worker, pause to remember the Lord. (Are you better than the Lord?) He rested.

The Lord tells us to remember His day, because we get caught up in our work and think about our day(s). We think about our work. We think about our accomplishments. On His day, we stop to think about His work and His accomplishments.

But there are some who have no problem stopping their work on Sunday. They're lazy, with no drive or ambition. Those who don't work during the six days of the week should remember that God worked six days. Therefore, God commanded Man to work because some are lazy. God said, "Six days you shall labor" (Exod. 20:8). Some people are so lazy they treat every day in the week like it was God's "rest day."

We should work as our Lord worked. Again, look at the example of how the Lord worked. "Thus the heavens and the earth, and all the host of them, were finished. And on the seventh day God ended His work which He had done, and He rested on the seventh day from all His work which He had done" (Gen 2:1, 2). So how should we work?

How Should We Work?

- Diligently ("Do all your work") (Exodus 20:9).
- Completely ("Made all that is in them") (Exodus 20:11).
- Finish the job ("Were finished") (Genesis 2:1).
- Satisfactorily ("And rested") (Exodus 20:11).

If we learn to work like God worked, we might learn to rest as God rested. However, most Christians chafe under the Lord's Day, not wanting to rest, not wanting to spend the day with God. Perhaps it's because we don't spend the first six days working the way the Lord worked, i.e., we're not motivated to work *for God*, we're not empowered *by God*, and we're not happy in the job because we don't *belong to* God.

Jesus' View of the Sabbath

Jesus supported the deeper meaning of the Fourth Commandment when He said, "The Sabbath was made for man, and not man for the Sabbath" (Mark 2:27). This commandment was not about keeping rules or not working on the seventh day, but rather God had given the Sabbath as a gift to bless Man. The Pharisees put emphasis on the rules and the day; Jesus' emphasis was on people and what the day could mean to people.

Observing the Lord's Day is more than sleeping. Some Christians think Sunday is "nap day" which is all right, but Sunday is much more than taking a snooze. You observe the Lord's Day with the Lord, "partnering" with Him. You enter into His work during the week, and you do His will on His day.

FOUR KINDS OF REST

Sunday means more than physical rest. It means spending time with the Lord, to enjoy the spiritual benefits of the Lord. First, rest is pictured as *eternal* after you die, "Blessed are the dead who die in the Lord from now on... they may rest from their labors" (Rev. 14:13). Next, rest is pictured as *salvation*. Jesus invited us to "Come to Me, all you who labor and are heavy laden, and I will give you re rest" (Matt. 11:28). This rest is from the soul-struggle against sin. When you are born-again, you lay all your sins at the feet of the cross, and rest in Jesus Christ.

The third rest is *victory rest*. "Take My yoke upon you and learn from Me, for I am gentle and lowly in heart, and you will find rest for your souls" (Matt. 11:29). Jesus describes this rest that comes to the child of God who gets victory over the struggles and cares of this world. When we take the yoke of Jesus Christ and learn of Him, we get His victory. This rest is His victory over sin.

And then the fourth rest is *physical rest*. This rest describes sleeping, "Taking rest in sleep" (John 11:13). But it also describes getting away from stress. When the disciples were tired, Jesus told them, "Come... and rest awhile" (Mark 6:31).

Jesus' View of the Lord of the Sabbath

When Jesus approached any of the laws—the Ten Commandments included—He was concerned about heart attitude. He was Lord of the Sabbath and He knew the hearts of people. He wanted people to recognize Him, more than keep outward laws. "Yet I say to you that in this place there is One greater than the temple. But if you had known what this means, 'I desire mercy and not sacrifice,' you would not have condemned the guiltless. For the Son of Man is Lord even of the Sabbath" (Matt. 12:6-8).

WHAT REST DOES FOR YOU?

Rest prepares you for the future. After a difficult day of work, you look forward to laying your head on a pillow. You know that if you could just sleep awhile, you'll be ready for tomorrow. Sometimes in the middle of the day when things are stressful, I close my office door and with a fifteen-minute nap, I'm ready for the challenge of the afternoon. Rest prepares me for my next challenge.

Rest makes you feel good. God is not an ogre who wants to punish you. God wants you to have some enjoyment in this life. Do you know how good it feels to sit down when you're tired? Do you know how good sleep feels when you're weary? Do you know how satisfying rest is when you're physically drained?

Rest restores your soul. The word restores means to bring back to life, or to bring back into operation. When someone faints, and is restored, he is again aware of the world about them. When you wear out the floor tiles, the surface is restored when you add paint or put down new tiles. Sometimes you need rest to restore your soul. Notice what the Shepherd will do for you if you are His sheep. "He makes me to lie down in green pastures; He leads me beside the still waters. He restores my soul" (Psa. 23:2, 3). How does He restore your soul? By leading you into green pastures where you can lie down and rest. He restores your soul by giving you still waters to refresh your parched throat. He restores your soul in the shade that protects from the burning sun. Rest brings restoration; do you need rest?

Jesus' View of Working on the Sabbath

Jesus was confronted by the rulers of the Synagogue because He had healed on the Sabbath. They quoted the Fourth Commandment to Him (Luke 13:14). Jesus pointed out the Sabbath was to bless both people and the animals that worked for them. Jesus said, "Hypocrite! Does not each one of you on the Sabbath loose his ox or donkey from the stall?" (Luke 13:15). He then compared their work to His work, "So ought not this woman, being a daughter of Abraham, whom Satan has bound for eighteen years, be loosed from this bond on the Sabbath?" (Luke 13:16).

Rest makes you obey the Lord. When you learn to rest on Sunday, you become an obedient Christian. We are commanded, "Rest in the Lord, wait patiently for Him..." (Pss. 37:7a). This means when you rest in the Lord, you do as He commands.

Rest makes you forget your failures and problems of the past. When you lie down at night, your aching muscles take over and you go to sleep. In sleep you forget about your worries or about past failures, or about the children. Sometimes worry can keep you awake at night; however, when your body is so tired you can't stand any more pain, rest takes over and you automatically go to sleep. And how do you feel... Good!

Rest gives us an opportunity to worship. We are to "remember to keep the Lord's Day holy." The word holy means to "set apart" or "separate." When we worship God, we are separating ourselves from our six days of secular work. By separating ourselves, we take the first step to becoming holy. But holiness is more than just separation from the secular, it is separation to God. You separate yourself from your secular work, to do your spiritual work.

One word for worship is *liteago*, which is also translated, "to minister or to serve." When you worship God, you minister to Him or you serve Him. Because worshipping is serving God, many churches call it the Sunday morning A.M. service or the "worship service." However, the little boy looked around in church to see only the preacher and the ushers serving. He asked, "Why is no one else serving?" He thought that service was something we did with our hands.

But rather, worship is service with our hearts. On the Lord's Day we separate ourselves to serve the Lord with worship.

Jesus' View on Sabbath Observance

The Jews of Jesus' day made the Sabbath law more important than the people who were to obey the Sabbath. So, Jesus took this occasion as an opportunity to properly interpret the Sabbath and the Fourth Commandment. Jesus said, "Therefore the Son of Man is also Lord of the Sabbath" (Mark 2:28). Because Jesus has the authority over the Sabbath, He could explain how it was to be observed.

What Would the Legalists Have Us Do?

There are some who legalistically observe Sunday as the Sabbath day. (Remember, the Sabbath—7th day—is not Sunday). Saturday was the 7th day of the week; we observe the first day of the week. Saturday and Sunday are different days. The Old Testament prohibited the Jews from lighting a fire, or fixing a meal; so some legalists today will not prepare a meal on Sunday, nor will they go to a restaurant to purchase a meal. What is the motto of the legalist?

No work.

No job.

No hope.

Punishment, if you do.

As a little boy, my mother and father were not Christians. But they had been raised under the influence of the Protestant-Puritan ethic where the Sabbath had been observed. Their parents taught them what to do on Sunday and what not to do. So, my mother had rules for me. I could play in the backyard where no one could see me, but I couldn't play in the front yard. I could play quiet games, but nothing that got me dirty, or made me sweat. As an illustration, I remember digging WWII foxholes in the neighboring field. I was playing GI Joe or soldiers.

Mother told me I couldn't dig or play in my foxhole, because I would get dirty. However, I could swing, ride my bicycle, and do things that weren't "extreme." I obeyed Mother, but in my heart I wanted to get dirty and sweat. I had not learned the meaning of Sunday.

We never went out for a meal on Sunday because we didn't want to make other people work. However, Mother always put a roast in a large pot, and included all the vegetables, i.e., celery, potatoes, carrots, onions, etc. That didn't take work because she put it on the stove to let it simmer the whole Sunday morning. Then at dinnertime, Mother would say, "I'll just make some rice to go with the roast," my mother would justify adding, "It's not work."

I've already said we didn't go out to eat when I was a little boy, not once. But several times we went out to buy ice cream at a store called "The Double Dipper." According to my recollection, it was the only store open anywhere in Savannah, Georgia. Then came WWII when President Roosevelt allowed movies to be opened on Sunday for the servicemen who didn't get to see them through the week. And after the movies opened, other forms of recreation were available to the servicemen. Once the doors were opened in our society, everything else came stampeding through.

Jesus' View on Observing the Sabbath

Jesus recognized that it was necessary to work, even under the Old Testament Law. Since "The Son of Man is also Lord of the Sabbath" (Mark 2:28), it is conclusive Jesus would know when it was proper to work on the Sabbath. Doesn't this suggest Jesus knew how we should observe the Lord's Day in our modern times?

"Now it happened on the second Sabbath after the first that He went through the grainfields. And His disciples plucked the heads of grain and ate them, rubbing them in their hands" (Luke 6:1).

Then Jesus said to them, "I will ask you one thing: Is it lawful on the Sabbath to do good or to do evil, to save life or to destroy?" And when He had looked around at them all, He said to the man, "Stretch out your hand." And he did so, and his hand was restored as whole as the other" (Luke 6:9-10).

The names for the days of the week. Where do the names of each day of the week come from? Romans adopted the Egyptian week of days, and named Sunday after the Sun God, Monday after the Moon God and the rest of the days of the week were named after planets.

Tuesday got its name after the Norse God, Thor, and so forth. However, the word Sabbath (means rest) got its name from God. Therefore, when you celebrate Saturday, remember, it is really the Sabbath designated for rest. Today, we celebrate the Lord's Day, because it's a day we give to the Lord.

Most people recognize the need for one day in seven for physical and mental rejuvenation. People need a time to get spiritually recharged, because they have devoted themselves to working throughout the week. They want to emphasize the spiritual over their preoccupation with money and hard work. The Lord's Day is a time for introspection, and communion with God. Specifically, a person ought to examine his walk with God, as well as a time to converse with God.

Many people see the need for ecological focus on the Lord's Day. They go for a drive in the woods, they jog on a nature trail, or some other form of exercise to renew their strength.

Whatever people do, it's a time of recreation, a day of rest, or diversion out of what they've been doing the other seven days. It is a time for physical and mental rest.

Jesus' View on Sabbath Observance

Jesus knew that the Sabbath was a day to do God's work, i.e., healing the sick and hurting. "Now it happened, as He went into the house of one of the rulers of the Pharisees to eat bread on the Sabbath, that they watched Him closely. And behold, there was a certain man before Him who had dropsy. And Jesus, answering, spoke to the lawyers and Pharisees, saying, 'Is it lawful to heal on the Sabbath?' But they kept silent. And He took him and healed him, and let him go. Then He answered them, saying, 'Which of you, having a donkey or an ox that has fallen into a pit, will not immediately pull him out on the Sabbath day?'" (Luke 14:1-5).

The meaning of Genesis 2: 1, 2. Look at God's activity on the Sabbath day to learn principles for observing Sunday. First, remember that God is the Creator; hence, depend on God for everything. Second, the Lord's Day reminds you to rest physically (remember that God wants you physically fit). Also, you rest spiritually and depend upon His grace to keep you spiritually fit. Next, the Lord's Day should make you grateful for His creation of life. Because God rested from all He did, i.e., His creation of people; we ought to be thankful that God has created us and gave us physical life.

Fourth, the Lord's Day is a time for celebrating what God has done. Just as God celebrated what He did, so we celebrate His plan for our life, including our forgiveness of sins, and our ability to work and make money.

In the fifth place, the Lord's Day is a time of thinking differently than we have during the week. Obviously, during the week we think of making a living, earning money, protecting our family financially, and for our physical necessities. Then comes Sunday. Now we should rejoice in all of the physical and temporal things God has given to us. Sunday is a time to rejoice, a time to be thankful, and a time to praise God for His goodness.

In the sixth place, the Lord's Day is a time to look beyond our present circumstances by looking to the future. Inasmuch as God rested on the Sabbath Day (the Bible says He only did this once), we too will have our final rest. We will receive our resurrected bodies and enjoy eternity forever. Therefore, on our present Sundays, we should look forward to the "rest" that we will have in the future.

On the other hand, there are some with extreme interpretations of Sunday. They don't make Sundays special. They point to Colossians 2:16 to justify just about any kind of activities on Sunday. "So let no one judge you in food or in drink, or regarding a festival or a new moon or sabbaths, which are a shadow of things to come, but the substance is of Christ" (Col. 2:16, 17). The church at Colosse apparently had some who were strictly observing the Sabbath day according to the Old Testament, and perhaps others who were teaching even stricter obedience to the Old Testament Sabbath. Paul was not saying a Christian could do anything on "the Sabbath," which probably referred to our Sunday. Also, some Christians in Colosse were demanding an outward conformity to the Law in regards to meats, drink, and holy days (Passover, Pentecost and the Day of Atonement).

Jesus' View of the Sabbath

Because Jesus was the Lord of the Sabbath, He could interpret every observance of the Sabbath and tell people how to observe the Sabbath. "But the ruler of the synagogue answered with indignation, because Jesus had healed on the Sabbath; and he said to the crowd, 'There are six days on which men ought to work; therefore come and be healed on them, and not on the Sabbath day.' The Lord then answered him and said, 'Hypocrite! Does not each one of you on the Sabbath loose his ox or donkey from the stall, and lead it away to water it? So ought not this woman, being a daughter of Abraham, whom Satan has bound—think of it—for eighteen years, be loosed from this bond on the Sabbath?' And when He said these things, all His adversaries were put to shame; and all the multitude rejoiced for all the glorious things that were done by Him (Luke 13:14-17).

Paul told the Colossians that they must observe the Lord's Day internally, i.e., in their hearts. He reminded the Colossians that their legalism resulted in their "not holding fast to the Head (Christ), from whom all believers get their spiritual life, which they enjoy with other believers" (Col. 2:19, author's translation). Paul was telling them they didn't get their legalism from Jesus. Paul wanted them to remember that they were members of Christ's body, and that "the body is of Christ" (Col. 2:17). They were to join with other believers on the Lord's Day for worship, Christian fellowship, preaching, teaching, and a renewing of their spiritual life.

Almost all of the early church fathers recognized Sunday as the day of rest. However, there were some groups during the 4th and 5th centuries (the Eastern Orthodox and Irish Church) that celebrated both Saturday and Sunday, giving both days equal recognition. Perhaps that is why in America we have two days of rest, i.e., Saturday and Sunday.

The Christian church has never made Sunday observance a basis for one's fellowship with God, nor a basis for salvation. However, there have always been a few who sincerely believe in Saturday (Sabbath) worship, but they have always been in the minority. However, even those Sabbatarians who believe in Saturday worship never made it a basis for one's spirituality, i.e., those who broke the Sabbath were not considered vile sinners. Remember, salvation is always based on the grace of Christ alone (Eph. 2:8, 9). So what does that mean? We can never be saved by any effort of our own, especially by how we observe Sunday.

PRINCIPLES TO TAKE AWAY

- The primary purpose of the Lord's Day is worship.
- The Fourth Commandment also teaches the dignity of work.
- You should observe the Lord's Day the way Jesus taught because He is the Lord of the Sabbath.
- You will observe the New Testament Lord's Day in different ways from the Old Testament, but you will still set one day aside to God.
- Today's people celebrate the Lord's Day in many different ways.

Chapter Five

HONOR YOUR PARENTS

Fifth Commandment

"Honor your father and your mother, that your days may be long upon the land which the LORD your God is giving you" (Exodus 20:12).

THE Fifth Commandment has perhaps the most important influence on the future of Christianity, because how people treat their children, determines how the Church will exist and minister in the future. A few years ago a denominational official challenged its national convention: "Our denomination can double in the next 20 years if we don't win another soul to Christ, and all we do is *Christianize* the young people born into our families, teaching them, keeping them, and making sure they follow Jesus Christ."

What a great challenge... every church... every denomination... the entire Christian population in every nation could double every 20 years if we could just *Christianize* our young people born into our families.

Jesus' Taught the Fifth Commandment Was Still Valued

Jesus Christ declared that parents should be honored. There was no doubt about His view of this commandment, or that the commandment was still applicable. "For God commanded, saying, 'Honor your father and your mother'; and, 'He who curses father or mother, let him be put to death'" (Matt. 15:4).

"You know the commandments: 'Do not commit adultery,' 'Do not murder,' 'Do not steal,' 'Do not bear false witness,' 'Honor your father and your mother'" (Luke 18:20).

WHAT THE FIFTH COMMANDMENT LEAVES OUT

No commandment to parents. The Fifth Commandment is not directed to parents to love their children or to respect them. Why? Because it is natural for mothers and fathers to automatically love their children. When God created human beings in the Garden of Eden, He gave them a command to "reproduce themselves." And with this command to reproduce children is God's plan to make it happen. God built within fathers and mothers a deep love for their children to protect their children and to reproduce themselves in their children.

What about the parental child abuser? Yes, there have been parents who have sexually abused their children, but that is not natural. This is satanic and evil. What about the mother who drowns her children in the bathtub? Yes, there have been parents who kill their young, but that is not natural. That's also satanic. These parents for various evil purposes have violated the love that God originally placed within their hearts for their children.

Parents reproduce themselves in their children. There is no command for parents to reproduce themselves in their children, because that is a God-given desire. Every parent wants the child to do what they've done to experience their experiences. God doesn't have to command parents to pour themselves into their children. God gave a consuming desire to parents to love their children and to reproduce themselves in them.

No diverse family styles. Notice God told children to honor one's father and mother. Note: God included a male and female. That leaves out the diverse family styles of lesbian women who want to adopt a child, the same with homosexual men. God's natural plan is one man, for one woman, so that they might have children. Anything less than that is unnatural.

One man, for one woman, for one lifetime.
—Jerry Falwell

Honor is the greatest characteristic of all. Notice God didn't tell children to obey their parents. Why? Because when you honor a parent that is higher than just outward obedience. Honor comes from the heart of a child. Honor is the highest positive affirmation you can give to parents. Honor includes listening to them, following their direction, and loving them. To honor parents is the greatest commandment, and this includes obeying parents.

JESUS' VIEW OF HONORING PARENTS

Jesus re-affirmed the Fifth Commandment when rebuking the Scribes and Pharisees when He said, "For God commanded, saying, 'Honor your father and your mother'; and, 'He who curses father or mother, let him be put to death'" (Matt. 15:4). The Jewish ruler had found a loophole in the Law where they didn't have to honor or obey their parents. Jesus noted, "Thus you have made the commandment of God of no effect by your tradition" (Matt. 15:6).

WHY OBEDIENCE BRINGS LONG LIFE

You will have good children. When you honor your parents, you become a role model to your children who in turn, will honor you. When you give your greatest allegiance to your parents, i.e., honor; your children see what you do. It becomes a lesson *caught, rather than taught* with words.

Why will you live longer? If you honor your parents, your children will honor you and take care of you. Your children will supply money, physical necessities, health and protection when you get old. And your kids will help you live to a ripe old age, just as you helped your parents live to a ripe old age.

Stress won't shorten your life. When children rebel against their parents, their rebellious lifestyle shortens their life. But "honor" reduces the stress of life, then both children and parents live longer.

The key is authority. God wants you to obey your parents' authority, as they obey God's authority. Rebellious young people against their parents are also lawless against other standards in society. If they rebel against their parents, they'll probably rebel against Christianity itself, and their rebellion will feed over into other areas of life. They will rebel at work, school, and against the government.

Ulcers shorten your life. When the body is under tension, the stomach muscles stretch themselves dangerously thin. When the thin membranes of the stomach are stretched beyond the norm, blood seeps through and dries on the stomach lining, causing ulcers. So, it's only natural to conclude that a *peaceful lifestyle* will help reduce ulcers. As ulcers will shorten your life, so will a number of other physical problems that come from stress. So there is physical longevity where you honor your parents, because you're living a peaceful life.

Learning from rats. American scientists who used experimental rats realized that American rats live 700 days. However, Japanese scientists using the same strain of rats lived 900 days. This difference in lifespan puzzled scientists. They traded rats, but still Japanese rats outlived American rats. As they observed the care of rats, they noticed in Japan that when cleaning out a rat's cage, the rat was placed on the shoulder of the scientist cleaning the cage, and was given warm affectionate strokes. In America, the rat was placed into a different cage, and not shown any affection. Scientists concluded that affectionate stroking of the rats, plus constantly being returned to the protective environment of the same cage each day, produced longer life. In the same way, the scientists determined that children who are warmly handled by parents... hugged... hugged... and shown affection, these babies live longer than those who are treated antiseptically... impersonally... and mechanically. Can we not conclude that children who obey their parents have a warm protective environment and receive emotional "strokes," hence they live longer.

Talking builds a relationship. Again, scientists indicate that babies whose mothers talked to them achieved more in life. These babies had higher vocabularies, higher IQs and went farther in education. Now these environmental items measure the relationship of child to parent but the conclusion is that children who have a good relationship to their parents are higher achievers.

In May 2002 *The New England Journal of Medicine* reported that babies that were breast-fed had higher IQs than those babies that were formula-fed. Again, the relationship between mother and child determines advancement of the child. Since relationship governs every area of life, could we not conclude that children who obey their parents have a better relationship with them than those who don't?

Social protection. Those children who obey their parents learn to obey the rules of society. They would not as likely get killed in an accident, or be hurt in other unfortunate ways, simply because they are more obedient to our laws. (Remember, laws are for our protection). Hence, obedient children are not likely to be killed, maimed, or harmed as those who are less obedient to their parents.

Spiritual reasons. Beyond all the natural reasons why children who obey their parents live long, look at the guidance and sovereignty of Almighty God. God has promised that those children who obey parental authority live longer lives. Hence, God can put a "hedge" around children to protect them from the Enemy, helping them live a longer life (Job 1:10).

Suppose you get 10 percent longer life from obeying your parents, isn't this enough reason to obey your parents?

Americans have discovered that people, who do not smoke, live approximately 6-10 years longer than those who do smoke. The tar from nicotine does not destroy and coat their lungs, hence a person lives longer who does not smoke. Because of this, America has gone to enormous extremes to prohibit cigarette smoking from airplanes, public buildings, and in most states; you cannot smoke in a restaurant. All this for longer life. Why won't America recognize God's promise, and support legislature that gives parents the right to expect obedience from their children.

WHAT DOES HONOR MEAN?

When you are asked to honor your parents, what does honor mean? Of all the affirmative words, honor is the highest. In the original language it means "heavy" or to "sit heavy." When something is heavy on your shoulders, you know it's there. It is not always easy to honor your parents. Sometimes you have to go against your selfish desires. Sometimes you sacrifice your time, money or resources. When you put your parents first, it means you are second.

When you pick up a concrete block, you eventually have to put it down. It's heavy. It's a burden. It's not always easy to honor your parents, but it's a burden worth doing. You put them in the correct position in your life. And when you do it, you recognize that you've done the right thing.

Youth's Response to Authority:

Don't trust anyone over thirty.

I want to do it my way.

You don't know what it's like being young.

Authority. Why should you honor your parents? We do not honor them just to show our gratitude, although showing our gratitude to them reflects the character they have put within us (character is habitually doing the right thing, the right way). When you honor your parents, it's about *authority*. The child is recognizing the authority of his parents over his life, just as parents recognize the authority of God over their life. Therefore, when the parents teach their children to honor them, they are ultimately teaching their children to be submissive to authority.

Notice how Paul adds to the concept of honor. "Children, obey your parents in the Lord, for this is right. Honor your father and mother, which is the first commandment with promise" (Eph. 6:1, 2). Paul adds obey to honor. In one sense the word *honour* is an Old Testament concept, and the word *obey* is a New Testament duty.

JESUS' VIEW OF HONORING PARENTS

Jesus revealed a new name for the first human person of the Trinity, i.e., Father. The Fifth Commandment had prepared God's people to honor the heavenly Father—the heavenly prototype—by honoring His earthly representative, i.e., parents. Everything in Jesus' earthly ministry honored the Father, "I honor My Father" (John 8:49). He wants us to follow His example by honoring our earthly father.

HOW LONG SHALL WE OBEY?

Some people feel that you only obey your parents when you are children. But when you get married and start raising a family, you no longer have to obey them because you are now parents of your children. Also, some feel you only obey Christian parents, or you only obey parents when they tell us the Christian thing to do. That means the Christian child doesn't have to obey the non-Christians parent. Let's look at the above implications.

Does the statement, "In the Lord," refer to children? to parents? Does this mean children who are in the Lord should obey their parents, but children who are not in the Lord do not need to obey their parents? There are some that say that the Ten Commandments only pertain to Christians, so the unsaved don't need to obey them.

The phrase in the Lord does not apply just to children. Obviously, Christian children should honor their parents and obey them; but so should all other children. Why? Because it's about authority; every child should be under authority of their parents, just as their parents are under the authority of government, the workplace, and society in general.

Do the words "in the Lord" relate only to Christian rules? Some feel that we only obey "in the Lord," i.e., we only obey Christian commands from Christian parents. This means that if our Christian parents tell us we must go to Sunday school, then we must obey. If the Ten Commandments are only for Christians, and the Fifth Commandment applies only to Christian parents, then what would happen in non-Christian homes?

But the issue always comes back to authority. You're not just obeying Christian principles; you're obeying the general principle of authority that is necessary to hold all society together. Christians believe all authority comes from God, and when children obey their parents, they ultimately come under the authority of God. When parents obey the government, they ultimately are obeying God. So, no matter what authority a child is obeying, ultimately; it's God's authority!

Jesus' View on Honoring Parents

Jesus taught that parents received great honor on this earth, but He also taught that one's relationship to God was greater than one's relationship to parents. For Jesus declared that the person who loved his parents or anyone else in his family more than himself, was not worthy of Christ. "He who loves father or mother more than Me is not worthy of Me. And he who loves son or daughter more than Me is not worthy of Me" (Matt 19:37).

Then Jesus taught that one's love to Him could be so great that it seemed like *hatred* in comparison. From the other places where Jesus taught people to *honor* parents, we know He did not mean to hate one's parents. But if your love for Him were supreme, your relationship to others would seem to be *hatred*. "If anyone comes to Me and does not hate his father and mother, wife and children, brothers and sisters, yes, and his own life also, he cannot be My disciple" (Luke 14:26). A modern paraphrase translates it this way, "If you want to be my follower you must love me more than your own father and mother, wife and children, brothers and sisters—yes, more than your own life. Otherwise, you cannot be my disciple" (Luke 14:26, NLT).

TWO PROMISES FOR OBEDIENCE

Paul has said two things will happen to you if you honor your parents and obey them.

First he promised, "that it may be well with thee" (Eph. 6:1). That means your present life will be better if you honor and obey your parents. But there is a second promise that deals with the future. This is called *the first commandment with promise*. And what is the promise? You are promised long physical life if you obey your parents.

My mother lived to be 95 years of age, and she credits it to obeying her mother when she was a small child growing up. I obeyed my mother, and I plan to live a long time, barring accident or other Divine intervention.

CHALLENGING THE PARENTS

The Fifth Commandment is a challenge for children to honor and obey their parents, but what about the backhanded "challenge to parents"? What must they do about this commandment? Simple, parents must be *honor-worthy*. If children are to honor their parents, they must be worthy of the honor given to them. Parents must be loving, kind, protective, and they must be spiritual. That means parents who want children to honor them, must honor God. The Fifth Commandment is about authority, everyone is under some authority, from somewhere, and all authority comes from God.

JESUS' VIEW OF HONORING THE FAITH OF PARENTS

Jesus taught people to obey the Fifth Commandment they must honor their parents. The Old Testament required the parents to teach children faith in God (Deut. 6:5-13). The spiritual teaching of children was not the responsibility of priests (the Temple), prophets (spoke the words of God) or the king (ruled for God). The responsibility was never given to the Synagogue; it was given to parents. Therefore, when children honored their parents, they honored the faith of their parents. In this sequence faith in God was taught from generation to generation.

WHY PARENTS SHOULD RECEIVE HONOR?

Physical life. Father and mother have joined together to pour their soul and physical life into a *human baby*. Everything that baby has in life comes from father and mother—equally.

The mother cannot do it alone, neither can the father. And as you examine young babies, you're not sure they have the personality of the father or mother, or both. They get their physical life from their parents.

Shelter, clothing and food. There are three basic necessities that a child must have, and without these necessities the child will die. They must have shelter from the elements to remain healthy. They must have clothing and they must have food to make them strong and healthy, or they will perish. While there are stories of animals that protect children, God has given children to a husband and wife, so they can take care of all the natural needs of that child throughout his/her growing life. As a matter of fact, when comparing human babies to the offspring of animals, most newborn animals can make it in life without parents much quicker than a human baby.

In God's plan, God wants parents to have a long time to influence their baby, but not just physical influence. God includes spiritual influence.

Education. Father and mother are responsible for teaching the baby to crawl, recognize objects, stand, repeat words, run, put sentences together, and express their needs and feelings. The entire education of a child is dependent upon another person. This is done primarily by parents.

Protection. The child faces a world of disease. Without protection from a parent, the child can become sickly and die. There are other dangers such as crime, predators, drugs, and rapists. All of these can prey upon a little child, who needs a parents to protect him/her from dangers yet unknown.

Direction. Every child needs direction in life. This involves giving him counsel, suggestions, role modeling and warnings of dangers.

Correction. Part of learning how to live is knowing what not to do. Therefore the child needs loving parents to teach him the dangers of stairs, the Interstate, and deep water in a swimming pool. The child needs physical, emotional, mental and spiritual protection.

Love and support. Of all the needs of a child, love is the greatest. And since it is natural for a father and mother to love a child, God has given them a child to receive their love. And at the same time, the child reciprocates their love. Think about it, the little baby can give almost nothing in return for what it receives. Yet, it gives the greatest gift of all to the parents; the child allows parents to love him, and in so doing, fulfills their life. Christian comedian Jerry Clower was watching a high school football game; his son was the field-goal kicker. Clower enjoyed the entire game, even though his son only had a few seconds of action in each game, i.e., to kick field goals or point after touchdown. Toward the end of the game, a field goal was needed to win the game. Jerry Clower's son waited, the ball was snapped; and he kicked the ball as he had done on many occasions. But the ball went wide left.

Two or three rows in front of Jerry Clower, a man began to ridicule, shout curses, and heckle the boy for missing the field goal. Clower went down and sat next to him and said very kindly, "You need to thank Jesus that you're alive."

"Why," the man said.

"That's my son, and if I weren't a Christian I'd kill you for heckling him."

Jesus' Taught the Consequences of Not Honoring Parents

Jesus taught that it is wrong to break God's commandment and not honor your father and mother. "He answered and said to them, Why do you also transgress the commandment of God because of your tradition? For God commanded, saying, Honor your father and your mother; and, He who curses father or mother, let him be put to death. But you say, Whoever says to his father or mother, Whatever profit you might have received from me is a gift to God—then he need not honor his father or mother. Thus you have made the commandment of God of no effect by your tradition. Hypocrites! Well did Isaiah prophesy about you, saying: These people draw near to Me with their mouth, And honor Me with their lips, But their heart is far from Me. And in vain they worship Me, Teaching as doctrines the commandments of men" (Matt. 15:3-9).

PRINCIPLES TO TAKE AWAY

- Jesus reaffirmed the command to honor your father and mother.
- The key to honoring father and mother is the authority given them over you by God.
- Parents must be honor-worthy.
- Parents can make many positive contributions to their children.
- Those who don't honor their parents usually have difficulty with authority in other areas of their life.

Chapter Six

YOU SHALL PRESERVE THE LIFE OF YOUR NEIGHBOR

Sixth Commandment

"You shall not kill" (Exodus 20:13).

Jesus' View of Murder

To understand why you must not murder anyone, study reasons Jesus gave for the purpose of people on this earth. The Lord created people in the first place to worship and praise God. Jesus reminds us, "God is Spirit, and those who worship Him must worship in spirit and truth" (John 4:24). This means every one must worship the right object, i.e., God, and must worship correctly, i.e., with the right knowledge (*truth*) and right expression of passion (*spirit*).

And why must each person worship God? The Bible says, "The Father seeks worshippers" (John 4:24, author's translation). Above anything else, God wants worship from his people. More than holy living, more than giving money sacrificially, more than dedicated service, even more than evangelism, God wants His people to worship Him. When a person is killed, he/she cannot worship God, nor do they motivate others to worship God. Murder destroys the whole purpose why people are put on this earth.

WHAT HAPPENS WHEN SOMEONE STOPS WORSHIP

When someone steps between worshippers and God, they are treading on holy ground. They have violated the very reason for which God created Man. When someone kills another, that person can no longer worship God, nor is praise brought to God from that person's life. If you kill someone, he can no longer worship God, nor do His will. How do you think God reacts when you cut off His worship? How does God feel when you take away the thing He wants most? When you answer that question, you understand that murder is not primarily a sin against a person, *it is a sin against God*. God is angry with murderers. He puts a murderer in the same category with demon worship and devilish activity. "Murderers, sexually immoral, sorcerers, idolaters, and all liars shall have their part in the lake which burns with fire and brimstone" (Rev. 21:8).

Jesus' View on the Source of Murder

Jesus taught that Satan is the source of murder, that he is the arch-enemy of God and man. Satan was a murderer from the beginning and is back of all murder today. "You are of your father the devil, and the desires of your father you want to do. He was a murderer from the beginning, and does not stand in the truth, because there is no truth in him. When he speaks a lie, he speaks from his own resources, for he is a liar and the father of it" (John 8:44).

WHY THE SIXTH COMMANDMENT?

Murder destroys God's image in people. There are many reasons why it is wrong for one person to murder another. Look at some reasons why society— even secular government— punishes murder. God originally gave human government the authority to punish those who murder. God said, "Whoever sheds man's blood, By man his blood shall be shed; For in the image of God He made man" (Gen. 9:6). Each human being reflects God. When we look in the mirror each morning, we see our image looking back at us. When we comb our hair, we are improving our image into what we want to be. Remember, just as you look in the mirror to see yourself; so God looks into our face to see Himself. We are a mirror that reflects God's image back to Himself. So, the primary offense of murder is that it is an attack on God, not just an attack on the person.

Let's look deeper at the image of God. Since God is love, when you love someone or love your children you're reflecting that passion of love that you got from God. But God also hates sin, and when you get angry, you are reflecting that passion that you got from God. While God's justice is against sin's rebellion, He expects you to get angry, but to not sin with your anger. "Be angry, and do not sin" (Eph. 4:26). When you use your mind to think, you are reflecting the Personhood of God, for God has rational ability and has been expressing Himself throughout eternity as the Trinity talked among Itself. Just as a person is intellect, emotion and will, so you reflect the power of choice you got from God.

God did not want "Barbie dolls" sitting in a row to praise Him. No! Praise to God is empty when God presses a button, and you mimic the words "I love you," or "I worship you." Is God pleased when He presses a different button and you shout "Hallelujah!"? No! Worship must spring from the choice of the worshipper. You must choose to worship God with all your heart because of what He has done for you. Worship is choice. You must worship God *knowingly* with all your mind. You must worship God *willingly* from free choice. You must worship God *passionately* from a heart filled with gratitude.

Murder cuts you off from God. No only has the murderer cut off worship to God, the murderer has cut himself off from God; for in choosing to murder someone, the killer has chosen to reject God. In return, God can only reject him or her. "But the cowardly, unbelieving, abominable, MURDERERS, sexually immoral, sorcerers, idolaters, and all liars shall have their part in the lake which burns with fire and brimstone, which is the second death" (Rev. 21:8, emphasis added).

Murder is a crime against society. Lawmakers have made laws to make murder a crime.

Why? Because the lawmakers do not want to be murdered, nor do they want their family murdered. Those who enact laws against murder, do so because of self-protection. So, voters usually approve of lawmakers and judges who protect them from murderers. A civilized voting public usually rejects those who allow murderers to roam free. When a government makes laws to punish murderers, this is called a social contract. America originally made civil laws outlawing murder because it violated the *moral law of God*. But today, our nation has secularized its laws; we have made murder a violation of *constitutional law*.

First-degree murder is when someone intentionally plans to kill another person. In most societies, first-degree murder receives the most severe penalty, i.e., usually capital punishment. Not long after Man sinned in the Garden (Gen. 3:3-24) that the first children were born into the world, i.e., Cain and Abel. However, the story is well known that Cain kill Abel, i.e., he murdered him. This apparently was an intentional murder, i.e., it was murder in the first degree.

First-degree murder was punished by death, "An eye for an eye; tooth for a tooth" (Exod. 21:24, Deut. 19:21). The commandment against murder is repeated several times in the New Testament, (see Matt. 19:18, Luke 18:20, Rom. 13:9). There was another kind of murder, i.e., when one person unintentionally killed another person. Our law today may call this murder in the second degree or *manslaughter*. Our society has a lesser punishment for those who unintentionally commit this crime. During Bible times, when a person accidentally killed another person, he could flee to a city of refuge for safety and protection (Josh. 21:1-45). That killer was not executed for killing another.

Jesus' View of Murder

Jesus deepened the meaning of murder by giving it a spiritual dimension. He said whoever harbored hatred or anger against anyone was in danger of God's punishment (Matt. 5:21). A person was guilty of murder if he were so angry with a person that he wanted to kill him, or he intended to kill him (premeditated), but did not carry out the act. Jesus said that murder began in the thoughts of the heart (Matt. 15:19, Mark 7:21). However, even murder can be forgiven by God. If a person has murdered another, God will forgive Him (Matt. 12:31; Mark 3:28).

Perhaps the greatest murderer of all was Saul of Tarsus who went throughout Jerusalem with "threats and murder" (Acts 9:1). He was guilty of a greater crime than just taking a life. Saul (who later became Paul the Apostle) was guilty of murdering Christians, which implied hatred toward the God they served. But in the mercy of God, Saul was converted, called into ministry, and became the greatest Christian worker of all time. Those who have been guilty of any kind of murder, can receive forgiveness and

You Shall Preserve the Life of Your Neighbor

can experience the love of God. (Their sin is forgiven by God, but they still have a legal debt to pay to society).

JESUS' VIEW ON THE PUNISHMENT OF MURDERS

During Jesus' day, murder was a crime against society and against God. Society punished the murderer. But, Jesus recognized the legitimate authority of divine punishment when He said the murderer "shall be in danger of the judgment" (Matt. 5:22). This was judgment by God in the last day for those who committed murder.

The Sixth Commandment prohibits anything that shortens or snuffs out life. You don't have to pull a trigger to actually murder someone. Any act against another person that terminates or cuts short their life is murder. When someone in World War II told the Germans where Jews were hiding, and those Jews were executed, the betrayer was guilty of murder. If you helped to plan a bank robbery, and guards were killed in today's society, you are guilty of murder, even though you were not present when the crime was committed.

You can also be guilty of murder by inaction or choosing not to rescue someone. If someone were drowning in the lake and you had the ability to save them, but you refused to throw them a life preserver, isn't that taking a life? If a person were suffering a severe heart attack and couldn't reach his nitro-glycerin tablets that could save him, and you made a choice to let him die; aren't you responsible for his death? So murder doesn't mean pulling the trigger; you can kill someone by evil plans, inactivity, or choice, i.e., choosing not to save a life when you could.

JESUS' VIEW OF MURDER

The act of murder was prohibited in the Sixth Commandment. It was, among other purposes, to keep society safe. However, Jesus imposes a new standard about murder. He dealt humanly with the heart motive of murder. Inward anger was the same to Jesus as outward murder. "Whoever is angry with his brother...shall be in danger of the judgment" (Matt 5:22). But in introducing "motive" to determine the guilty of a murderer, Jesus was also introducing a new and higher reason to keep society safe. If people didn't get angry, they obviously wouldn't kill.

Other acts that are certainly murder. There are certain acts that fall within the limits of murder, i.e., *euthanasia*, when you take the life of an elderly person either by giving him a lethal injection, or refusing him the means of life. Also, *genocide* is murder, the elimination of a targeted group of people. *Suicide* is a form of murder; even though suicide is not killing another person, it is taking your own life. It's wrong to take any life, even your own. What have you done? You've pushed God aside, and taken God's decision to terminate a life. Likewise, terrorism is murder. When terrorists intentionally crashed a plane into the New York City World Trade Tower and the Pentagon, they murdered innocent victims.

Are self-destructive acts considered murder? What about the person who continues to smoke a cigarette, knowing that cigar tar and nicotine will shorten his or her life? Is that person guilty of some form of suicide? Medical research has demonstrated that smoking cuts short the average life by seven to ten years. If a person knows he or she is terminating his or her life early, and continues to smoke, has he committed murder by suicide? Could that person not have praised God for an additional seven years, or served God effectively an additional ten years?

Doesn't alcohol consumption have the same accountability as cigarettes? Those people who die of cirrhosis of the liver have shortened their life by alcohol addiction. And what about drug addiction? Isn't the person taking dangerous drugs shortening his life? And what about the homosexual? The average actuarial tables for insurance companies reveal AIDS victims live approximately 45 years of the 72 years of normal life expectancy. When the Center for Disease Control says that over 80 percent of homosexual men have AIDS, whether active or inactive, shouldn't that be warning enough to stay away from homosexual acts? If a young man knows he is exposing himself to AIDS through homosexual activities, isn't that breaking the Sixth Commandment? It seems that any act that intentionally shortens a life, is an act of suicide.

What about unintentional acts that shorten a life? Sometimes our actions shorten a life, but we never intend it. What about the person who withholds food with the intent to become slim or the young girl who wants a "model-like" appearance? What happens when she becomes anorexic? She probably became anorexia in desire, long before it affected her body. If she shortens her life, has she not broken the Sixth Commandment? What about those who drive dangerously? Are they not threatening their life, or the life of another? What about other dangerous habits? If someone is involved in life-threatening acts or habits, how guilty is that person of breaking the Sixth Commandment? And then there is the sin of overeating. The Bible warns us against gluttony, "For the drunkard and the glutton will come to poverty, and drowsiness will clothe a man with rags" (Prov. 23:21). Is the person who constantly overeats, coming dangerously close to breaking the Sixth Commandment?

Jesus' View of Murder

Jesus taught that religious hypocrites of His day were related to those who murdered God's prophets in the past. Even though the hypocrites didn't commit the actual crime, Jesus said of them, "You murdered."

"Woe to you, scribes and Pharisees, hypocrites! Because you build the tombs of the prophets and adorn the monuments of the righteous, and say, If we had lived in the days of our fathers, we would not have been partakers with them in the blood of the prophets. Therefore you are witnesses against yourselves that you are sons of those who murdered the prophets. Fill up, then, the measure of your fathers' guilt. Serpents, brood of vipers! How can you escape the condemnation of hell? Therefore, indeed, I send you prophets, wise men, and scribes: some of them you will kill and crucify, and some of them you will scourge in your synagogues and persecute from city to city, that on you may come all the righteous blood shed on the earth, from the blood of righteous Abel to the blood of Zechariah, son of Berechiah, whom you murdered between the temple and the altar. Assuredly, I say to you, all these things will come upon this generation" (Matt. 23:29-26).

PHYSICAL LIFE IS A TREASURE FROM GOD

Jesus' View of Murder

"Jesus said unto him, Thou shalt love the Lord thy God with all thy heart, and with all thy soul, and with all thy mind. This is the first and great commandment. And the second [is] like unto it, Thou shalt love thy neighbour as thyself" (Matt. 22:37-39 KJV). Any who murders another is breaking the second great commandment. No one wants to kill himself, so how can they love another person as themselves if they desire to murder them, or they actually commit the crime?

Obviously, the Lord wants us to love Him with all of our hearts, but we can't if we don't have a physical body through which we can manifest that love. So, the bottom line to judge our actions is, "as you love yourself." God knows each person loves himself. So, you must love other people, just as much as you love yourself. Can you really love your neighbor if you want him dead or try to kill him?

Don't ask who is your neighbor, thinking this only applies to the people who live next to you. When the lawyer asked the question, "Who is my neighbor?" (Luke 10:29), Jesus gave him the parable of the Good Samaritan.

A man went down from Jerusalem to Jericho, but thieves robbed him, mugged him and left him to die. First, a minister came by, but didn't help him. Next, a religious person came by, he also didn't help him. (Did they break the Sixth Commandment by withholding life-giving aid?) Then, a Samaritan—a different ethnic group—helped the wounded man. He bandaged up his wounds, took him to an inn where he gave him food, shelter and healthcare. Then Jesus asked, "So which of these three do you think was neighbor to him who fell among the thieves?" (Luke 10:36). The answer was obvious; it was the one who "showed mercy." So the answer to who is your neighbor—anyone who has need.

Jesus' View of Murder

"For out of the heart proceed evil thoughts, murders, adulteries, fornications, thefts, false witness, blasphemies" (Matt. 15:19, emphasis added).

"You have heard that it was said to those of old, You shall not murder, and whoever murders will be in danger of the judgment. But I say to you that whoever is angry with his brother without a cause shall be in danger of the judgment. And whoever says to his brother, 'Raca!' shall be in danger of the council. But whoever says, 'You fool!' shall be in danger of hell fire" (Matt. 5:21, 22).

Since Jesus said hating a person was murder, and murder came out of our hearts; then we must not hate a person. Rather, we are to love them. We can't hate any, nor can we harm them physically; we must love them all.

No second chance. You are never given a second chance in physical life. You live once, then die. Therefore, you should joyfully receive life, and use every ounce of energy to love God, in every way possible. Then, you are to love your neighbors, just as you love yourself. *Love is the ultimate expression of the Sixth Commandment.* If you loved people, you could never think of hating them or killing them.

Our ultimate love is God. Because our ultimate obligation is love to God, we must always think, "What is best for God?" And when we do that, we will love other people with the same love that we have for God. Today, there seems to be so much hatred in the world; why can't we love one another? While love will never rule this world—until we get to Heaven—we must let love rule our heart and we must attempt to let love rule the world in which we live.

Jesus' View on the Motives of Murder

When the rich young ruler claimed to have kept all the commandments, Jesus repeated the Sixth Commandment, "You shall do no murder" (Matt. 19:18). While Jesus didn't apply this commandment to his inner motives, at other places Jesus dealt indicated heart attitudes were responsible for murder (Matt. 5:22).

Review: Why Murder Is Wrong

Murder is wrong because it destroys a person's worship-relationship to God. How can God get praise from a person who is murdered? Therefore, murder is not between the killer and his victim, nor is murder between the killer and law; murder is between the killer and God.

While the law may put a murderer in prison, or even execute him; that punishment is nothing compared to God's punishment—if the murderer doesn't repent and ask for God's mercy.

When a nation forgets about God, and the moral laws of God, but writes God out of its constitutional law; that nation will probably suffer more and more lawlessness. There will be more and more murder in the land (Prov. 14:24). However, when a nation accepts the moral law of God, i.e., that murder is against God; that nation can build internal restraints into its citizens; and the incidence of murder will probably go down. But, when murder is just against a social contract, i.e., for the protection of people; then the killer will kill when he feels it is to his advantage.

But God forgives murder, all murder. Just as God forgave Saul of Tarsus, then called him into ministry and used him greatly; so any person can become a "Paul"; they can be used of God, no matter what they have done.

Principles to Take Away

- Murder is a crime against God because the victim had the image of God and now the victim cannot worship or bring glory to God.
- A person murders because of the anger in his heart.
- There are many ways to take the life of another.
- You cannot obey God's commandment to love your neighbor as yourself when you murder.
- Even though murder is a great crime, God will forgive the murderer.

Chapter Seven

YOUR BODY SHALL BE MY SANCTUARY

Seventh Commandment

"You shall not commit adultery" (Exodus 20:14).

EARLY one morning, Jesus was sitting near the temple. He was just beginning to teach those that were gathered. He heard the shouts of a small angry mob dragging a disheveled woman. She was thrown to the ground in front of him, in the center of a gathering circle. Angry shouts of the men were mingled with whimpered crises of a terrified woman.

The face of the men standing over her were contorted with rage, their eyes widened with hate. Some shook their fist, some pointed toward her.

Most of the crowd were Pharisees, honored students of the Old Testament law, proud and persistent in their attempts to please God by keeping the commandments. They attracted a crowd of early worshipers to the temple. They were watching to see what was going on.

"Please don't hurt me!" the woman begged. She crossed her hands and covered her face in fear.

One man stepped toward her, shaking his fist. "You deserve dearth!" He looked toward Jesus and snarled, "Isn't that right?"

Without giving the Master an opportunity to answer, someone shouted, "Stone her!"

"She deserves to be stoned!"

"That is what the Scriptures demands, and that is exactly what we intend to do... "Stone her."

The guilty woman now lay face down on the ground; her head cradled in her arms.

The Pharisees who had demanded the death sentence began an agitated explanation toward Jesus, "She is a common whore! This woman was found in bed with the husband of another.

Someone yelled, "We caught them in the very act of sin!"

"Stone her!" another Pharisee screamed, "Stone the adulteress!"

The woman sobbed, her body trembling with fear – and the shame of the discovery.

The Master turned toward the woman. Stillness replaced their shouts. They watched His every move. They listened for any word from Jesus. Perhaps this would be their opportunity to catch the Galilean in an act of denying the seventh commandment. This was their opportunity to forever slam the door on His claims of being the Messiah.

Jesus knelt to look at the fallen woman.

"Pick up a stone, Jesus!" One yelled toward Him. "If You are God's messenger that You claim to be, You cast the first stone."

Instead of reaching for a stone on the ground, Jesus began to trace something in the sand near her – was He forming words?

What was He going to write?

Was it a list of sins perhaps? Her sins? Or the sins of her accusers."

Names perhaps? A rap sheet of the men standing in the tiny crowd who had also committed the act of adultery. Now they were the hypocrites, trying to get the woman stoned to death.

"You throw the first stone" Jesus said. "If you have not sinned, this very same sin."

Jesus looked down and continued scribbling on the ground.

His tracings caused a grim reaction among the angry accusers. Their haughty looks changed. Their jaws dropped. Their eyes fell—looking away from the woman on the ground. First, the eldest Pharisee; the leader of the mob steeped back and began to walk away. Another stepped back to follow him. And then another, until only a few stragglers remained.

She slowly raised her head and looked for the circle of accusers. Puzzled, she turned toward the Master. "You're Jesus?"

He responded, "And where are those who accused you?"

She looked around to see all who were accusing her were gone.

"Now go as well," the Master said, "And be done with your sin."

Jesus added, "I don't condemn you. I forgive you."

SIN'S SCARLET LETTER

Hester Prynne, the adulteress who bore the illegitimate child in Nathaniel Hawthorne's 19th century classic writing about Puritan life, was forced to bear the shame with a scarlet reminder "A" that was sown to her clothing. Her legendary struggle for acceptance among a people not unlike the Pharisees of Jesus' time was a lesson in passion, pain, and persistence.

Webster defines adultery as a "willful sexual intercourse with someone other than one's husband or wife." Adultery is more than a physical act; it includes the whole person: First, it includes the *mind*, because you know that the other person is someone's spouse. Second, it includes the *emotions*, it is done for personal pleasure. And third, it involves the *will*, because it is a willful act, the person decided to commit adultery.

Adultery may also include rape, homosexuality, or incest. In each instance, a law of God is broken— the Seventh Commandment, "You shall not commit adultery."

Adultery specifically relates to sexual relations between people who are married to another spouse. Sex between unmarried persons, or between a married person and a single person, is called *fornication*. Notice that God puts adultery and fornication together on the same level of evidence when He pronounces judgment on those who break His law, "Fornicators and adulterers God will judge" (Heb. 13:4).

Adultery or fornication is like taking poison willfully. And the result is just as deadly. *Physical* death will probably not result from the incident. But other forms of death stalk the unruly hearts like a starving predator.

Emotional death. Relational death. Spiritual death.

Sin casts a permeant shadow over those who trade a lifetime of commitment for a few minutes of pleasure. And the shadow ever widens—to family members or friends, sometimes to the larger community.

In an age when *absolutes* are often ridiculed, adultery is absolutely wrong for many reasons:

It is wrong because God's Word says it is.

It is wrong because it breaks the marriage bond that God blessed. It is wrong because it is personally and socially destructive.

It is wrong because it blasphemes the Holy Spirit.

It is wrong because it can destroy a person's lifework or influence. It is wrong because it enslaves a soul that Christ died to make free.

When the apostle Paul wrote to Christians in Corinth about sexual sins, he reminded them, "Do you not know that your bodies are members of Christ? Shall I then take the members of Christ and make them members of a harlot? Certainly not! Or do you not know that he who is joined to a harlot is one body with her? For 'the two,' He says, 'shall become one flesh'" (1 Cor. 6:15-16).

What does Paul mean by "one flesh"? It could mean *physical union* in that two people who commit adultery experience physical and emotional oneness. But perhaps it is much deeper. When sexual union produces a child, *two people become one in that child*. A child conceived has the nature of both father and mother.

Sexual union that produces a child produces a soul that has an eternal destiny—one that will live forever in heaven or hell. Rick Warren said, "Every act on earth will strike some chord that will vibrate in eternity." Adulterous relations "for the fun of it" can result in a sobering reality, adultery can produce a child that demands serious nurture, provision, and guidance. Add to that resulting family problems, continuing financial obligations, or long-term societal care; one fleeting and selfish act may result in a child that must be supported for eighteen years or more.

A SANCTUARY OF GOD

Jesus offered the adulteress woman an opportunity to see herself in different light. "Go and sin no more" (John 8:11). He wanted her to understand that her actions betrayed the inner attractiveness that God had intended for her to display. Her body was to be God's sanctuary— His dwelling place.

The concept of "sanctuary" is one of the most beautiful in the Bible. A sanctuary is a place where you enter the presence of God. It is where He lives.

Originally, created human beings worshipped their creator in open sky sanctuaries. In the outdoor beauty of God's creation, His people built altars, and sought to restore broken relationships with Him through their blood sacrifice offerings.

But when God led His people out of Egypt, He said to them, "Make me a sanctuary that I may dwell among you" (Exod. 25:8, *Author's Translation*). Israel could have continued worshipping God, as did their fathers, i.e., making an altar anywhere. But now God wanted to live *among* His people; He wanted to demonstrate His love and power through them—in a specific place. Before the magnificent temple was built in Jerusalem, God met with His people in a more humble setting.

He told them to make a tent, a portable sanctuary. As Israel moved from country to country, they took the tent down, carried it on the back of the priests, and pitched it at the next place. By taking the tent with them, they took *God's presence* with them.

When the sanctuary tent was pitched, a *Shekinah-glory* cloud loomed above it. The wanderers only had to look up to the cloud to know that God was with them. (See Exod. 40:34-35.) The tent was a place where God *dwelled*, a place where He met with His people in times of worship. The articles and furniture in the tent—such as the brazen *altar*, laver, or the Ark of the Covenant—were not just for the worship ceremony, they were further reminders of God's desire for a relationship with His people.

Whether a temple or a tent, the *sanctuary* was a symbol of God's indwelling greatness. David said, "Strength and beauty are in His sanctuary" (Psa. 96:6). As God's people entered the sanctuary, they sensed His greatness. They were instructed, "Lift up your hands in the sanctuary" (Psa. 134:2), and they did—symbolically lifting up their hearts to God. In the process of worship, they developed strength of purpose and character.

It's the same today. When you lift up your heart to God; when you acknowledge His greatness and holiness; and when you give allegiance to His Word; you are developing inner strength and character. Additionally, when you give up yourself to God, He enters your life and His power flows through you. Your body is God's sanctuary, that's why adultery is so wrong. Adultery turns worship into lust.

The tent or temple sanctuary was also a place of beauty. Gold overlay covered furniture or utensils, and other ornaments were covered with silver. When the priests who served God entered the sanctuary, they were dressed in ornate and colorful robes, made with the finest of material—and appointed with precious stones. Magnificence was everywhere: the golden laver (giant golden bowl), a golden altar with incense burning, the golden Mercy Seat on top of the Ark of the Covenant.

But the most beautiful thing about the sanctuary was the presence of God Himself. As people worshipped Him, they were conformed into His image. They assumed His attributes. They were strengthened and changed by His presence.

Sex is a thing of beauty; it was designed by God to be used in the temple of the body.

But when someone commits adultery, they turn the beauty of sex into an ugly thing.

God still meets with His people. People are still strengthened in character and filled with awe at His majestic presence. But God doesn't indwell just one church. He indwells each church where His people assemble. But also, he indwells each believer. Paul the apostle said, "Do you not know that your body is the temple of the Holy Spirit who is in you, whom you have from God, and you are not your own? For you were bought at a price; therefore, glorify God in your body and in your spirit, which are God's" (1 Cor. 6:19-20). The Seventh Commandment is about keeping your physical body a holy sanctuary as God's dwelling.

God indwells His people. He lives in them by His Holy Spirit. (Rom. 5:5). In one sense, He *paid cash* for the residence. The currency was the blood of His only son, the Lord Jesus Christ. And when He moved in, He did a master home improvement. He decorated the residence with His very character: Holiness. So, His place is a place of purity. A place of beauty. A place of grace. A place of emotional, physical, and spiritual wholeness.

Though believers are urged to meet regularly for worship, encouragement, and instruction (Heb. 11:25)—and God meets with them—nothing is said in the Ten Commandments about the facility where God is worshipped. There is no commandment, "You shall worship in your church." While the Seventh Commandment doesn't mention worshipping God in a physical location, it does suggest that we honor/worship God at home—in our physical bodies— His dwelling place—our lives.

JESUS AND THE SEVENTH COMMANDMENT

Jesus came to earth to give us abundant—full and meaningful—life (Jn. 10:10). So His opinion about the seventh commandment was not just about the sin of adultery, it was also about personal wholeness. When the rich young ruler came to Jesus and asked the secrets to life, Jesus instructed him to keep the commandments, and repeated the sacred law, "You shall not commit adultery" (Matt. 19:17-18). But as with the other commandments, Jesus was just as concerned with the spirit of the law as He was with its letter.

Jesus wants us to avoid adultery, first, because of what it does to us physically. The pain and death of others, whether physical or spiritual, is an arrow to His loving heart. That was plainly seen throughout His earthly ministry.

Jesus has a personal stake in providing a fulfilling and whole life for each of us. Adultery was one of the awful acts of rebellion that Jesus saw in that cup of grief handed to Him by His father in the agonizing hours of Gethsemane. Thankfully, Jesus considered its terrible ingredients. And then in an act of consummate mercy, He bore their consequences—and our guilt—on the Cross.

He also wants us to avoid adultery because of what it does to us socially. Answering the Pharisees questions about the "No-fault Divorce" policies of their day, Jesus established a scriptural boundary for marriage. Adultery leads to broken spirits and to broken homes. Matthew 19:8-9, "He said to them, 'Moses, because of the hardness of your hearts, permitted you to divorce your wives, but from the beginning it was not so. And I say to you, whoever divorces his wife, except for sexual immorality, and marries another, commits adultery; and whoever marries her who is divorced commits adultery.'"

Jesus taught that we are made in the spiritual image of God. We are visible expressions of His invisible being. We carry character credentials that He gave to us. So a spirit of bondage to anything—including our own passions—is contrary to His purpose for us.

Jesus loves us so much that He wants to keep us from anything that would bring harm to us personally, or to our family or friends. Though He was sinless (Heb. 4:15), He knew full well the consequence of breaking God's law; and He was acquainted with its penalty. As He faced the agony of Calvary, He said, "My soul is exceedingly sorrowful, even to death" (Mark 14:34).

He also knew of the wide, ripple effects of sin. For example, though He never had a home, He looked down the road of the ages and saw the homes that would be broken by adultery. And though He enjoyed the love and trust of His followers, He could see a time when He would experience their shattered vows.

Third, He wants us to avoid adultery because of what it does to us emotionally. Since Jesus created us (Col. 3), He understands the correlation between our body and mind. With a much wider view of adultery, He taught that adultery was more than a physical act. He taught that it is birthed in the mind and heart. In His classic Sermon on the Mount, Jesus moved adultery from *behavior* to *attitude*, "You have heard that it was said to those of old, 'You shall not commit adultery.' But I say to you that whoever looks at a woman to lust for her has already committed adultery with her in his heart" (Matt. 5:27-28). He understands that the enemy of our faith can work on our emotions—tearing away at our resistance, making us vulnerable to attitudes that would enslave us, and eventually destroy us.

As with every law of God, Jesus knew that the Seventh Commandment was given for our benefit. And as with every other commandment, He offered a reasonable remedy. In this case: marriage.

THE MARRIAGE REMEDY

In a teaching that would fly in the face of modern debate over marriage, Jesus reinforced its sanctity. "'Have you not read that He who made them at the beginning "made them male and female". 'For this reason, a man shall leave his father and mother and be joined to his wife, and the two shall become one flesh'? So then, they are no longer two but one flesh. Therefore, what God has joined together, let not man separate'" (Matt. 19:4-6).

Though the marriage relationship is always a work in progress (and will not be experienced by everyone) it provides proven safeguards against breaking God's Seventh Commandment.

1. *Marriage provides a partnership of spirit.* With all of the technology that links our world, loneliness is still one of its most common maladies. And marriage is one of God's cures. When God looked at Adam tending the Garden of Eden by himself, He responded, "Adam gave names to all cattle, to the birds of the air, and to every beast of the field. But for Adam there was not found a helper comparable to him" (Gen. 2:20). So, God provided a helper—a life partner: Eve; someone who would share the duties and delights of the Garden. Jesus intended that an earthly partner would bridge the loneliness of life—even when it was at its worst or best.

2. *Marriage provides physical intimacy.* Jesus' first miracle was performed at a marriage celebration (Jn. 2). His presence at the wedding at Cana was a blessing on the marriage state and a respect for its biblical boundaries.

    One-night stands were never God's plan. The desires that He implanted in us were meant for a much deeper relationship than casual or careless sex; they were for physical intimacy that deepens with time. There is a tender scene in the Old Testament account that describes Adam and Eve's relationship, "They were both naked, the man and his wife, and were not ashamed" (Gen. 2:25). They were physically and emotionally attracted to one another—comfortable with each other's unclothed body and vulnerable to each other's feelings.

3. *Marriage provides a family setting.* When Adam saw Eve, he said, "This is now bone of my bones, and flesh of my flesh" (Gen. 2:23). God's love for this first family looked beyond their first meeting. It saw their first child as well. The daily joys (and challenges) of raising children are God-given. They strengthen. They bond. They provide a setting where truthfulness and trust can be gloriously displayed. The comfort Adam and Eve enjoyed in their own relationship would be shared with their children.

Jesus' formative years were spent in a family setting. Joseph and Mary modeled the best of marriage in His eyes. The struggles and successes of His earthly guardians would influence His teachings on the importance of family.

In spite of the painful agony of the Cross, Jesus made sure that His mother—perhaps a widow—was cared for. Surely that concern was learned by the lessons He practiced in His own home.

4. *Marriage provides physical pleasure.* Sexual bonding in marriage is not accidental, nor is it incidental, to God's plan. He gave us a pre-determined, safe place where we could express our sexuality—a place of personal and social acceptance. Hebrews 13:4, "Marriage is honorable among all, and the bed undefiled." The wisdom writer advised, "Drink water from your own cistern, running water from your own well" (Prov. 5:15). Jesus intended that marriage would be a place where its partners could freely—and fully—express themselves sexually; a place where physical appetites could be satisfied without fear of spiritual consequence.

CLEANLINESS IS NEXT TO GODLINESS

In a spiritual sense, the adage "cleanliness is next to Godliness" has a much deeper meaning. When you make a life commitment to Jesus, you no longer have control over how clean you want the *house*. Since your body is His residence, and since you have given Him the right to make the *house rules*, every function of the house/heart falls under His supervision. That includes your sex life. You are a sexual being. You were gifted by God with sensations, emotions, and motivations that are meant both for personal pleasure and for the population of the world.

The question is not whether *you* think a sexual activity is all right, but what does *God* think about it. Does it fit within the framework of biblical principles? Does it honor rather than *dishonor* you? Does it bring emotional, physical, or spiritual harm to another? Does it glorify God, and His plan for your life?

How clean does Jesus want my body to be? The answer: Clean enough to keep the *sanctuary of God* (your body) holy, and wholly in order.

Addictive sexual activity, outside the parameters that God has set for you, is one that will not only bring disorder but uncleanness to you. Sexual unfaithfulness to your spouse, as an added example, may result in a sexually transmitted disease that will infect your body and your spouse's body as well. One study indicated that "56 million Americans (more than one-fifth of the population)... may be infected with incurable STDs — afflictions that cause more serious complications among the nation's women and children. Unborn babies who contract STDs risk neurological problems, pneumonia, congenital abnormalities, low birth weight and spontaneous abortion. Herpes in infants can result in brain damage or death."[1] Promiscuous sex dishonors God, creates disease in your community, creates disorder in your family life, and is also in direct disobedience to the Word of God.

Conversely, sexual cleanliness (sexual behavior within the boundaries of biblical principle) actually expresses your godliness. Christ wants to manifest His glory through your body; He wants you to be an example of self-control, sacrifice, and spiritual surrender. Jesus said, "You are the light of the world. A city that is set on a hill cannot be hidden. Nor do they light a lamp and put it under a basket, but on a lampstand, and it gives light to all who are in the house. Let your light so shine before men, that they may see your good works and glorify your Father in heaven" (Matt. 5:14-16).

The true follower of Christ has abandoned his or her "rights" (self-direction) for the greater cause of "righteousness" (spiritual and relational right-ness with God). A best-selling, secular book of years back proclaimed, "Our Bodies, Ourselves" as its title and its decree. The life of Jesus was a direct contradiction. Paul wrote about it in Galatians 3:13-14: "Christ has redeemed us from the curse of the law, having become a curse for us (for it is written, 'Cursed is everyone who hangs on a tree')." Christ made a decision in the Garden of Gethsemane that forever sealed His surrender to God's will. He decided to offer His own body as a sacrifice so that we might be free from slavery to sin and its consequences.

The woman taken in adultery was not free. She was a slave to her passion—and subsequently a slave to the passions of another. But Jesus offered her the opportunity of a new commitment. A commitment of love not lust. Of faith, not fear. A commitment filled with grace, not guilt.

In a faith-based world, our bodies are no longer ours. We believe what Paul wrote in the Scriptures, "Your body is the temple of the Holy Spirit... you are not your own" (1 Cor. 16:19). And again, "Do you not know that your bodies are members of Christ? Shall I then take the members of Christ and make them members of a harlot? Certainly not! Or do you not know that he who is joined to a harlot is one body with her? For 'the two,' He says, shall become one flesh.' But he who is joined to the Lord is one spirit with Him. Flee sexual immorality. Every sin that a man does is outside the body, but he who commits sexual immorality sins against his own body" (1 Cor. 6:15-18).

THE PRACTICE OF THE SEVENTH COMMANDMENT

Recognizing that your body is a sanctuary where God dwells. This is a faith-based commitment that makes you a fitting and holy "sanctuary" to God.

First, let the Holy Spirit help you control your physical appetites. You are living— and loving—in a society that has seemingly abandoned a code of moral behavior. "Everyone for themselves." "Anything goes." "Live and let live." "If it feels good, do it." seems to be the theme of the world's every movie, TV sitcom, or song.

God not only wants you to be holy, He wants you to be whole. And He has promised to deliver the goods. Galatians 5:16, "Walk in the Spirit, and you shall not fulfill the lust of the flesh." Spiritual power is available to help you stand against the winds of the time.

Avail yourself of God's power. "Walk in the Spirit"—make Him your daily companion and supply:

1. In prayer
2. In the reading of God's Word
3. In mentoring and friendships with people of faith
4. In preferring faith-based activities over world-based activities
5. In filling your mind with eternal rather than earthly "stuff"

Second, recognize how vulnerable you really are. Someone said it right, "To err is human." As long as you are human (and you will be for a good while!), you will be subject to human wants and weaknesses—and errors. The antidote for human fear or failure is spiritual fortitude (See 2 Tim. 1:7).

Strengthen yourself against the world's "inevitable." James, the brother of Jesus, wrote, "Blessed is the man who endures temptation; for when he has been approved, he will receive the crown of life which the Lord has promised to those who love Him" (James 1:12). Did you catch that? "Endures." Just as you would practice strength training for an athletic competition, you develop a system of endurance training for spiritual competition.

Actually, you're in a marathon-wrestling match against the enemy of your character and your influence that would make a *WWF* competition look like a Cub Scout camp out.

Ephesians 6:12, "We do not wrestle against flesh and blood, but against principalities, against powers, against the rulers of the darkness of this age, against spiritual hosts of wickedness in the heavenly places." An unseen enemy is seeking to beat the "spiritual stuffing" out of you, and to lead you by the nose into places and situations that will destroy you personally—as well as destroy those who trust you.

Put up a fight. There's a medal waiting: "You will receive a crown of life." Here's your game plan:

1. Resist the enemy with your *attitudes*. Defy him in your thought life.
2. Resist the enemy with your *activities*. Choose the wholesome.
3. Resist the enemy with your *affiliations*. Choose spiritually supportive friends.

Third, guard your heritage. You have something more to leave your family than an inheritance of stocks, bonds, real estate, or bank accounts. You can leave them wonderful memories of a noble life. You can bless the lives of your friends and family with your personal integrity. "Integrity comes from within. It's the result of focused faith, godly choices, right associations, and a tenacious commitment to truth. When it's there, in the life of God's servant, it's beautiful. When it's missing, it's messy!"[2] You can leave spiritual, moral, and ethical character traits on which others can pattern their lives—and arrive at their own wholeness.

1. Determine to live a cut above the crowd.
2. Determine to stand by your belief system.
3. Determine to make public displays of affection toward God.
4. Determine to depend on the resurrection power of Christ.
5. Determine to think about your short-term actions in relation to their long-term effect.

Rick Warren said in his bestselling book, *The Purpose Driven Life*, "When you understand that life is a test, you realize that nothing is insignificant in your life. Even the smallest incident has significance for your character development. Every day is an important day, and every second is a growth opportunity to deepen your character, to demonstrate love, or to depend on God. Some tests seem overwhelming, while others you don't even notice. But all of them have eternal implications."[3]

Fourth, commit to your marriage relationship. Marriage is more than a ceremony of "I Do's." It's a series of "I Will's." Every single day—in the home, on the job, in the classroom, in places of entertainment—you will have an opportunity to willfully protect or renew your marriage commitments.

There are some important steps:

1. Confide in your spouse.
2. Avoid intimate friendships with the opposite sex.
3. Express your sexuality within your marriage.
4. Spend quality time with your spouse.
5. Put your spouse first—above the rest of your family or friends.
6. Practice random acts of love to your spouse.
7. Don't look for a way out of relationship problems; look for a way through.

One of the most infamous incidents recorded in the Scriptures didn't have a happy ending—at least not in a Hollywood sort of way. After the adulteress woman was restored, there was no cut to a loving and forgiving embrace. No letters of apology scrolled across the screen. We don't know if the home that was broken by adultery was ever put back together. There was no love song playing underneath a scene of a healed person walking toward a beautiful and hopeful horizon, with her head held high. There's much that isn't scripted.

But it doesn't need a *Hollywood ending*. We do know this. God in Christ forgave her. In heaven's eyes, she was as if she hadn't sinned. The Bible says it's so. Mercy was complete for her. And it is for you as well. You may have broken the Seventh Commandment. Or you may have made an emotional commitment that is leading you in that direction. The good news is that you can have a happy ending. Grace can restore.

What you have already done has already been nailed to the Cross. Christ died to forgive the sin that you acknowledge and abandon. And Christ ever lives, sitting at the right hand of God in heaven, praying for your strength to overcome the traps this world sets along your journey. His Holy Spirit turned a tomb into a triumph, and that same power will help you live a faith- based life in a self-centered world.

ENDNOTES

1. Scott DeNicola & Jeff Hooten, "Women at Risk" (12 December 03) <http://family.org/cforum/citizenmag/features/a0001074.cfm.
2. Stan Toler & Jerry Brecheisen, *Lead to Succeed: New Testament Principles for Visionary Leadership* (Kansas City: Beacon Hill Press of Kansas City, 2003), pp. 30-31.
3. Rick Warren, *The Purpose Driven Life* (Grand Rapids, MI: Zondervan, 2002). p. 43.

Chapter Eight

RESPECT THE "STUFF" OF OTHERS

Eighth Commandment

"You shall not steal" (Exodus 20:15).

H AVE you ever had something stolen from you? How did you feel?

How a Victim of a Thief Feels

Angry, it was yours.

Defrauded, you don't have it.

Powerless, you can't use it.

Deflated, you lose face.

On the day that I was to graduate from Dallas Theological Seminary, someone broke into my house and stole several items, i.e., fourteen white shirts, freshly laundered and packaged along with my graduation robe that was in a suit box. The thief must have thought the suit box had a new suit, and that the package of new shirts was a graduation gift. I lived across the street Faith Bible Church where I was pastor. Everyone in the community knew that I was graduating that day. Also, everyone knew no one was home during church service. When I phoned Dr. Don Campbell, Registrar of Dallas Theological Seminary, to tell I didn't have my graduation gown, he indicated I couldn't walk in the processional without it. But he told me not to worry, "You'll still graduate and get your degree." But I had spent four years studying for that degree and I wanted to end it with a celebration. I wanted to walk across the platform to actually have the president place the piece of paper in my hand.

The thief had not just stolen a graduation gown, the thief had stolen the crowning achievement of four years of tedious work. I didn't get angry, but was deflated. The thief stole my happiness.

The registrar of Dallas Theological Seminary suggested that I phone the registrar of Southern Methodist University because it had a vault of extra graduation gowns. I was able to find a graduation gown and actually walk across the aisle and receive my diploma.

It took a long time for me to get over losing my white shirts and stolen graduation gown.

It was more than property; they hurt me and almost made me miss a ceremony I had looked forward to for four years.

As I grew older, my attitude toward a thief changed. Recently, I had some of my books for sale in the church lobby after preaching a sermon. I had reduced them from $14.95 (bookstore price) to $10.00. A man was thumbing through the book and asked if I would autograph it to his wife and daughter who were not with him. When he looked in his wallet, there was no money. He asked if he could go to his car and bring back a check. "Sure," I said. After I packed up the books, I was waiting for him to return. It was then an usher told me he saw the man run to his car and drive rapidly out the back drive. I laughed... and laughed... and laughed. I was laughing out of pity for the "thief." I would have been delighted to give him the book, if he asked. Then I thought, how can he enjoy a book on "spirituality" after stealing it.

Some lives have been destroyed when something was stolen from them. But the thief's character has also been destroyed. Movie stars are scandalized when caught shoplifting. Executives go to prison for fraud when they misappropriate a corporation's funds.

Treasurers of a church are humiliated for stealing from the church bank account, and cadets are kicked out of West Point for stealing grades from others.

Jesus' View on Getting Money

Jesus was not against ownership of property or possession. He commended the two diligent workers who doubled their five talents and three talents (Matt. 25:14-30). Jesus rebuked the worker who refused to work wisely. Jesus commended laborers working for money (Matt 20:1-16), and the woman with a possession of silver coins (Luke 15:8-10). However, Jesus never measured a person by how much money they had. He commended the poor widow who gave all her money in the offering. The issue was never you having money, the issue was always money having you. He taught His followers priority, i.e., to put God before money, and when they did that, God would take care of their needs. Jesus said, "But seek first the kingdom of God and His righteousness, and all these things shall be added to you. Therefore do not worry about tomorrow, for tomorrow will worry about its own things. Sufficient for the day is its own trouble" (Matt. 6:33-34).

HOW DOES GOD WANT US TO GET THINGS?

The Eighth Commandment does not say, "You shall not have things." So, money or STUFF is not wrong to have. As a matter of fact, you need STUFF, because STUFF is an automobile... a pair of shoes... a computer... a watch... or furniture in your house. Having stuff is not wrong.

God says it's alright to get STUFF, "Let him that stole, steal no longer, but rather let him labor, working with his hands... that he may have something good" (Eph. 4:28). Therefore, God wants you to work to get money so you can buy STUFF.

STUFF is the means by which we identify ourselves. A wedding band says we are married, and a suit says that we are executives, just as bib overalls say you are a farmer. A construction worker needs a pickup truck, and a housewife needs pots and pans. STUFF gives us self-identity.

And what about work? Work also gives us our self-identity, it is a means by which we identify ourselves, and earn self-respect from others. When you say, "I am a teacher," that's a means of self-identity. Just like a wife says, "I am a physician," or "I am a receptionist." She gets self-esteem from her work.

Some people don't work for STUFF, they get it by making it with their hands, such as people in many Third World countries or the pioneers who settled our nation. They got STUFF by making it. Some eat the STUFF by growing it, they're farmers. Still others get STUFF because of investments.

Still others get STUFF by inheritance. Their parents or grandparents or rich uncle dies, leaving them to buy STUFF. "That I may cause those who love me to inherit wealth" (Prov. 8:21).

And still others get STUFF through divine provision. When you pray each day, "Give us this day our daily bread," (Matt. 6:11), you are asking the Divine to provide for your daily STUFF. That's how foreign missionaries and people of the cloth live.

Jesus' View of Investing Money

Jesus endorsed investment of money to make a living. Remember the businessman, who delegated different talents to his workers, i.e., one talent, three talents, and five talents. Wasn't that an investment? Notice the results, "So he who had received five talents came and brought five other talents, saying, 'Lord, you delivered to me five talents; look, I have gained five more talents besides them.' His lord said to him, 'Well done, good and faithful servant; you were faithful over a few things, I will make you ruler over many things. Enter into the joy of your lord'" (Matt. 25:20-21).

DIFFERENT WAYS PEOPLE STEAL

There are many ways to steal, not just by breaking into a house to steal fourteen white shirts, and a graduation gown. Notice the following:

Stealing by theft. The word *theft* comes from the Old English word *to crouch*, which describes, "one who takes illegally, by secret or stealthily" (*Webster's Dictionary*). This is a sneak thief or a burglar. They take when no one is watching. One of the reasons we shouldn't steal is because Jesus is always watching, and you don't know how He will punish.

A thief had broken into a house when he heard the voice, "Jesus is watching you." The thief froze, not knowing what to do. Then he heard it again, "Jesus is watching you." Not knowing what to do, the thief shined his flashlight toward the voice, and he saw a talking parrot in a cage. The thief said, "You're nothing but a parrot," and thinking he had nothing to fear, the thief turned to go about his looting. Then the parrot said,

"Jesus is a rotweiler, and He's watching you."

Stealing by robbery or mugging. Thirty years ago I was visiting in the church basement where a large inner city bus ministry was conducted among under-privileged children. I saw one inner-city rascal pinning an obvious "Sunday school boy" against the wall, while a second boy went through his pockets, looking for his Sunday school offering. They were stealing by robbery. Obviously, I stopped the robbery and turned the "robbers" over to the Sunday school superintendent.

Jesus' View of Thief Victims

Jesus describes a man who had his possession stolen by mugging. "A certain man went down from Jerusalem to Jericho, and fell among thieves, who stripped him of his clothing, wounded him, and departed, leaving him half dead" (Luke 10:30). This wasn't a computer thief, or pick-pocket, this was a mugging. It is obvious from the story that Jesus had compassion on the victim and felt that someone should help the hurting man. God has compassion on those who are victims of a thief.

Theft by seizure. When you capture someone else's possession without permission, you have stolen by seizure. I was an advisor to the board for St. Petersburg Press, an inter- denominational Christian publishing company, set up in St. Petersburg, Russia, to print Christian materials to evangelize Russia. The company had approximately $400 thousand in assets, i.e., a printing press, computer and office supplies. One day the Russian Mafia walked in, and took over. At first, they said they would print whatever Christian needs we had, but they never printed anything. They just seized the business, and because of the lack of Russian legal infrastructures, there was nothing the Christians could do.

Theft by deceit. Some people steal without robbery, mugging, or seizure. They gain things deceitfully. This involves stealing and using a credit card number through computer thief. What about the businessman who adds mileage to his expense account or the businessman who makes false advertising claims, or the salesman who sells something to people that they don't need, or those salesmen who make promises they cannot keep? This involves mechanics charging for work not done, or the butcher with a dishonest scale to weigh his meat. What does God say? "Diverse weights are an abomination to the LORD, and dishonest scales are not good" (Prov. 20:23).

Jesus' View of Stealing

Jesus repeated the Eight Commandment to the young ruler, "You shall not steal" (Matt. 19:18). While Jesus did not elaborate on this commandment at this place, the selfish possession of things—perhaps acquired illegally-was this man's problem. The young man's problem was STUFF; he probably didn't steal, but he was guilty of GREED, one of the reasons why people steal. Then Jesus said, "Assuredly, I say to you that it is hard for a rich man to enter the kingdom of heaven. And again I say to you, it is easier for a camel to go through the eye of a needle than for a rich man to enter the kingdom of God" (Matt. 19:23-24).

Theft by defrauds. Webster's Dictionary says to defraud is "to deprive of something by deception; the Old English word meant to cheat." When you withhold something from a person that is rightfully theirs, you have defrauded them, you have stolen

from them. If you don't pay your debt for 120 days, you have not allowed them to use their money, i.e., you have stolen their capital or interest for 120 days. If you are paid for eight hours work, but you "goof off" on the job, or even catch a nap; you have defraud your employer.

WHAT HAVE THEY STOLEN?

When someone has stolen from you, they have stolen your use of your possessions; you no longer get its benefit. They steal your time, so that you have to go back and work more hours to purchase the STUFF they have stolen. Or, they have stolen your talents. I wrote a 20-page outline of how to have a successful Sunday school library and presented the material in a workshop in Toronto, Canada, in 1963. A couple of years later I saw my material printed and distributed with someone else's name on it. When I phoned the person long distance, they immediately recognized what they had done and asked for my forgiveness. But, the damage was done. They had gotten credit for my material. So, I expanded the outline into a book that went through fourteen printings, i.e., *Successful Church Libraries*. (Available on-line free, i.e., http://www.elmertowns.com/. See Books Online on toolbar).

When someone steals from you, they take your reputation, or they take the respect that you have from other people. If one man steals a wife from another, has he not stolen the first man's love and passion?

What Does a Thief Take?

Your dreams and hopes, they steal your future.

Your ability to serve God, they steal your passion.

Your ability to use it to become better and stronger, they steal your growth.

An elder of a church was held up at gunpoint, and his wallet was stolen. Later, he stood up in church to give a testimony. He was not bitter but said, "I am thankful that the thief did not take my life. I have the ability to make more money. I am thankful he didn't take my ability to make more money, he could have shot me and left me an invalid. But most of all, I am thankful I was not the thief. I thank the Lord Jesus Christ for saving me and giving me a passion to be honest before Him, and my fellowmen."

Jesus' View of Financial Security

Jesus taught that you cannot get security in storing up this world's treasures because thieves will many times steal them, or else they waste away, or they will decrease in value. "Do not lay up for yourselves treasures on earth, where moth and rust destroy and where thieves break in and steal; but lay up for yourselves treasures in heaven, where neither moth nor rust destroys and where thieves do not break in and steal" (Matt. 6:19-20).

Don't be like your enemy. Your enemy is the devil, he is the original thief. When Jesus gave a series of stories in John 10, He described the Devil, "The thief does not come except to steal, and to kill, and to destroy" (John 10:10). While Satan comes to steal, Jesus has come "that they may have life, and that they may have it more abundantly" (John 10:10).

The devil also comes to kill, which is breaking the Sixth Commandment, "You shall not murder." Jesus said, "He (the devil) is a murderer from the beginning" (John 8:44).

But not only that, the devil breaks the Ninth Commandment, "Thou shalt not lie." Notice what

Jesus said of the devil, "He (the devil) is a liar, and the father of it" (John 8:44).

WHY STEALING IS A SIN?

Jesus' View on Stealing

Jesus reinforces the Eighth Commandment when He told the rich young ruler, "You know the commandments: 'Do not commit adultery,' 'Do not murder,' 'Do not steal'" (Luke 18:20). Jesus gave the motive behind treating all people equally, "You shall love your neighbor as yourself" (Matt. 22:39). You can't love your neighbor and steal from him.

Every person is made in the image of God (Gen. 1:26, 27). With that image of God, individuals get certain rights, and one of those rights is the right to own property. Therefore, any person who would steal from you, would also steal from God's standard, and those who steal will be judged by God.

God has made you to worship and serve Him. However, when something is stolen from you, you cannot properly carry out your service to God. Stealing suffocates and crushes you.

When your spirit is demolished, you have difficulty worshipping God. So, a thief is not just stealing STUFF, he is stealing a man's spirit.

STUFF is never the issue, whether it's stealing a cow or a million dollars. Stealing harms a person who loses something. The victim becomes discouraged, or he may fly into a rage against the thief, or he may even contemplate murder. A thief makes his victim break the other commandments of God, and when a thief makes his victim sin, isn't he also guilty for that sin?

But, don't just look at what stealing does to the victim; look at what stealing does to the thief. He becomes guilty before God. The person who would steal your money, would also steal from God. "Will a man rob God?" "Yes, but you asked the question, 'Where have I robbed God?'" God's answer, "You robbed me in tithes and offerings" (Mal. 3:8, 9, author's translation).

When you think of thieves, the first person to come to mind is Achan, who stole the spoils taken from the destruction of Jericho. God had said to burn the city completely. The city was to become a burnt offering unto God. But, Achan just couldn't bring himself to burn up bars of silver and perfectly good Babylonian garments. So, he stole, then hid them in a hole in the ground, under his tent. But God, who sees all, knew what was happening; God withheld His blessing from Israel until Achan was dealt with.

Ananias and Sapphira stole from God. They didn't actually take money out of the offering plate, but they were guilty of deception. Barnabas, another church leader, sold a piece of ground and gave all the money to God, receiving the praise and esteem of the church. Ananias and

Sapphira wanted the same esteem, so they sold a piece of ground; but didn't give all the money to God.

They didn't give all their money to God; they just let everyone THINK they were giving all. They deceived the church. Because of their sin, God judged Ananias and he fell down dead. Later, Sapphira came into the church—she was probably out shopping with the money they stole— so she didn't know what was happening to her husband. When Peter asked about the finances of the "deal," she agreed to the lie of her husband. She also was judged of God.

Jesus' View on Stealing Money

Jesus' teaching about the STUFF was contrary to the ideas in His day. He did not approve of stealing. He disapproved of those who stole from the good Samaritan. Jesus wanted His followers to be giving people, not taking people. Jesus said if someone demands your outer garment (cloak), also give him your inner garment (tunic) as well (Luke 6:29). Jesus said life is not measured in possessions or abundance (Luke 12:15, Matt. 6:31, 32). Jesus taught that the spiritual man will not let his money keep him from the Kingdom, nor harm his spiritual life. "It is easier for a camel to go through the eye of a needle than for a rich man to enter the kingdom of God" (Mark 10:25).

Today, we live in a permissive society where preteens may walk through a store and pocket small items, i.e., a candy bar, a phone card, or a ballpoint pen. Kids justify themselves, "They will never miss it." That's not the point! It's what stealing does to the character of the young kid. "If you'll steal a dollar, you'll steal a million," I've always heard.

When I was in the fifth grade, I decided to steal a lead soldier from Fox's Variety Store, a small store across the street from Waters Avenue School, where I attended. My motive was to "Keep up with the Joneses," or in this case, "Keeping up with the Hoffmans who lived next door to us." When I played toy soldiers with Shirley Hoffman, she had more lead soldiers than I did, and better ones. I only had five or six lead soldiers left over from World War I. They had old-fashioned tin helmets and only rifles to fight a battle. Shirley Hoffman had modern World War II soldiers, and a couple of machine guns. One of them was a soldier lying on his stomach with a machine gun. I call him "Bellyacher."

I fixed my lust on "Bellyacher," and determined to have one. Fox's Variety Store had three for sale, and as I conceived a crime, I sat in my classroom. After school I walked into the store, waved to the lady at the cash register at the front who was reading a movie magazine, and casually "shopped" myself to the back of the store where the lead soldiers were located. When she wasn't looking, I slipped it into my jacket pocket and was satisfied that I could do it. I put the lead soldier—by this time I had called him "Bellyacher"—back on the counter. As I left, I waved and said, "Goodbye, see you tomorrow," she grunted. I had cased "the joint" and knew I could get away with the heist.

All the next day in school I thought about the joy of playing with "Bellyacher," alternatively shivering with guilt knowing that stealing was wrong. But, as soon as school was over, I went into Fox's Variety Story, and said, "Hi..." to the clerk, again she didn't look up from her movie magazine. Half way back to the toy department, I pretended to be shopping and picked up a tube of lipstick. Without looking up the clerk said, "Don't touch the merchandise..." she saw me without even looking.

Then two ladies came in and walked straight to the back of the store where I was looking at "Bellyacher." I couldn't do a thing while they were watching, but as soon as they turned their backs; I quickly slipped "Bellyacher" into my pocket. Then walking past the clerk, I again waved and said, "See ya tomorrow..." She grunted.

On the sidewalk I realized I had done it. I stole a lead soldier and got away with it.

However, half way home I saw Sergeant Sullivan—he lived on the next block from me—coming toward me in a police cruiser. It was the old-fashioned type with the big siren on the front fender.

I didn't know what to do; I thought about dropping "Bellyacher" in the grass, but then I had seen movies about police going back to find evidence, so I didn't drop my loot. The police cruiser came straight toward me and as he approached, Sgt. Sullivan threw up a hand to say, "Hello…"

I was so overwhelmed with guilt that I threw both of my hands up in surrender, I thought I was being arrested. Then to cover myself, I meekly waved back with one hand and squeaked out, "Hello."

As I approached the home, I realized I couldn't play with "Bellyacher," Shirley Hoffman would ask me where I got it. She knew we didn't have that kind of money to "waste" on lead soldiers. I was positive that Shirley Hoffman would tell her mother, who in turn would tell my mother; who in turn would give me a beating. So I crawled under the house and hid him among the floor joists. Later in life, as I wrote this story, I realized that my father would come home to hide his liquor under the house, under the floor joists, from my mother. Like father, like son!

I was so eaten up with guilt that I never retrieved "Bellyacher" to play with him, so I didn't enjoy the fruits of my crime. Within a few days, I had completely forgotten about "Bellyacher," and didn't remember this story until I was middle-aged. When I went back, the house had been sold to Habitat for Humanity, and moved five miles away. As far as I am concerned, stealing is not worth it.

PRINCIPLES TO TAKE AWAY

- Stealing is wrong because God gave each person the right to own property.
- You can't "love your neighbor or yourself" if you steal from them.
- Stealing harms the character of the one who steals.
- You should be a giving person, not a taking person.
- A thief takes more than STUFF; they take your dreams, hopes and future.

Chapter Nine

LIVE BY THE STANDARD OF TRUTH

Ninth Commandment

"You shall not bear false witness against your neighbor" (Exodus 20:16).

DURING a series of executive seminars over an eight-year period, James Kouzes and Barry Posner asked over 5,000 managers to identify those characteristics they most admired in a business leader. The results were surprising. Eighty-seven percent of those surveyed said that honesty was the quality they looked for most in a leader. The business community in America is looking for honest leadership.

But not only business community is looking for honesty, it's a value sought by most in our society. Unfortunately, many who value integrity, think they can produce the *fruit* without nurturing the *root*. Telling the truth is not an isolated part of a personal lifestyle. It's not something you decide to do today. Telling the truth is something you are. Truthful people tell the truth. People who struggle in the area of lying are people who lack integrity at the core of their being.

Because integrity is important to God, He said, "You shall not bear false witness against your neighbor" (Exod. 20:16). Those who lie, displease God. Among the seven things God hates, both "a lying tongue" and "a false witness," are listed (Prov. 6:17, 19). Because integrity is important to God, it should also be important to you.

Why didn't God say, "You shall not lie?" Because lying is just what you do.

So God told us, "You shall not bear false witness against your neighbor," because a "false witness" is against another person. And when you hurt your neighbor, you also hurt yourself.

God doesn't have to tell us lying is wrong. You know that lying is wrong, because you can't lie to yourself. You hate it when someone harms you by lying to you. So you hate it when you harm yourself by lying to yourself.

So God says don't bear false witness about your neighbors. Since God is included as our *neighborhood*, we end up lying to God when we bear false witness about them.

Lying can be simple deception. When the phone rings, you say, "Tell them I'm not here." Lying can be exaggeration, "You never do any of the work around here." Lying can be "buttering up a friend, "You have the prettiest baby I've ever seen." Or, "You look younger (or slimmer)." Sometimes lying can include our silence, "Who did this?" You did it, but refused to take responsibility. Or, lying can be taking the credit for a job that someone else has done.

Jesus' View on Lying

Jesus re-affirmed the Ninth Commandment when He told the rich young ruler, "You shall not bear false witness" (Matt 18:19). The young man seemed to think he hadn't broken this Commandment because he said, "All these things I have kept from my youth. What do I still lack?" (Matt. 19:20). The young man who thought he had never lied, was really lying to himself. His deeper problem was self-deception and unwillingness to face reality. At another place, Jesus taught lying came from a person's sinful heart (Matt. 14:17-20).

When Is a Lie, a Lie?

There are at least three ways a lie may be expressed or practiced. The first is an active lie. This is what most people think about when they think about lying. The dictionary describes an *active lie*, "to make an untruthful statement with the intent to deceive."

A second is a *passive lie*. Those who engage in passive lying sometimes attempt to justify themselves, noting they did not meant to "say" anything untrue. As they deny saying an *active lie*, they create a false or misleading impression that they didn't mean to lie, when really they did. When a person attempts to convince someone of an untruth, he or she is engaged in *passive lying*.

The third is an *inner lie*. An *inner lie* involves tolerating internal compromise with what you know is right. When a person obviously believes an untruth about something, and does nothing to convince them otherwise, they are engaged in an *inner lie*. The real danger of an *inner lie* is that we give life to a lie. If this practice continues, we may be successful in deceiving ourselves into believing the lie that another believes.

Jesus' View on Lying

Jesus explained that the Pharisees were outwardly good, and they said good things, but the attitude of their heart determined their words. "How can you, being evil, speak good things?" (Matt. 12:34). If a person has a lying heart, he will tell lies. That's why Jesus explained, "An evil man out of an evil heart will speak evil things and spread evil results" (Matt. 12:35, author's translation).

SEVENTEEN WAYS TO LIE

How many of these lies have you seen in recent weeks? How many of these lies have been expressed by you?

Perhaps the best-known expression of lying is the *white lie*. This lie expresses an untruth that is perceived good for both the liar and the victim of a lie. Two people on a diet convince each other, "We need a banana split."

Another common lie is the *political lie* or flattery. When a person compliments the attractiveness of a garment that they believe is unattractive, he or she is engaged in a political lie.

Gossip is another expression of lying. Gossip takes place when we tell what we know we shouldn't. Scripture describes the gossip or talebearer as one who reveals secrets.

A fourth kind of lie is the *sinister lie*. This involves passing on an untruth for an evil purpose. "An evildoer gives heed to false lips; a liar listens eagerly to a spiteful tongue" (Prov. 17:4).

Perhaps the most commonly accepted form of lying is the *jovial lie*. This involves lying in an obvious way, without malice as a joke. An example of a jovial lie is to tell someone you are much younger than the truth.

A *half lie* involves telling the truth, but not the whole truth. In a half lie, one tells the truth with the intent of deceiving. When Abram went to Egypt with his wife Sarai, he reported Sarai was his sister but failed to identify her as his wife. His half lie was true, but he intended to deceive the Egyptians about their relationship.

Sometimes, an *excuse* may be offered as a lie. When a person uses an excuse, the reason given may or may not be true. Often an excuse is an attempt to misrepresent the truth concerning some failure on our part. "I would have done that job, but I didn't know it was my responsibility."

An eighth expression of lying is *hypocrisy*. The Greek word translated "hypocrite" originally referred to the actors in a play who used masks and costumes to play the roles of others. This term came to be used widely of those who claim to be something they are not. The hypocrite attempts to deceive others into thinking they are someone different than they really are.

Some lies may be described as *justifying lies*. These are lies people tell to justify their actions. Often, the purpose of a *justifying lie* is to convince others they would have adopted a similar behavior under the circumstances. "If my wife wouldn't nag me so much, I wouldn't be so crabby."

A similar kind of lie is the *face-saving lie*. Sometimes people lie to avoid embarrassment. God confronted Sarah with her private laughing in unbelief after she heard the prophecy concerning her pregnancy. Sarah immediately told God, "I didn't laugh." She lied to avoid the embarrassment of the moment.

Sometimes Christians use the expression *evangelistic lying* to describe the practice of stretching the truth to make the work of God look good. A pastor may exaggerate the size of his congregation or the amount received in the offering to make his church appear more prosperous. An evangelist may exaggerate the number of people responding to his invitations to exaggerate his effectiveness. In the early church, Ananias and Sapphira lost their lives when they attempted to stretch the truth about their generosity.

A twelfth expression of lying is the *propaganda lie*. During times of military conflict, it is common to report different results after a battle to confuse the enemy. Each side tells only the facts which best suits their purpose. People also tell propaganda lies when they tell their account to make their position sound more reasonable.

Advertising lies are another common expression of lying in our society. They throw around terms like bigger, better, new, revised, or improved. We wonder if the product really is what is advertised. Advertisers may use words like "virtually" as a legal disclaimer as they attempt to deceive consumers about the merits of their product.

Cheating is another form of lying. When a student cheats on a test, he or she is attempting to deceive the teacher. They present test answers that are not theirs. A common expression of *cheating* occurs each spring as people complete their income tax forms.

Scripture also identifies *demonic lies*. These are dangerous lies that have their source in evil spirits. A society that rejects the light of God will exchange "the truth of God for the lie, and worshipped and served the creature rather than the Creator" (Rom. 1:25). Paul warned the Thessalonians of a time when "God will send them strong delusion, that they should believe the lie" (2 Thess. 2:11).

Sometimes the expression *putting a spin on the truth* is used to describe another form of lying. In this lie, people attempt to interpret the obvious facts of a situation to their favor. This often happens during election campaigns as politicians explain away negative pole results.

A seventeenth expression of lying may be described as the *plausibility of denial*.

Sometimes, people conspire to conceal their involvement by claiming they did not know what was happening around them. If a lie is likely to be believed, an individual or group may release an immediate statement denying knowledge of a situation and avoid being confronted about what they did know.

Jesus' View on the Accountability of Our Words

Jesus taught that people's words reflect their heart. What a person said was reflective of their true nature. Therefore, a person was responsible for every word they spoke. Obviously, this included lying and bearing false witness. But it also involved telling the truth to harm another, deceive another, or mislead another. "But I say to you that for every idle word men may speak, they will give account of it in the day of judgment" (Matt. 12:36).

Four Steps in Making a Lie

The practice of lying involves a process by which lies are produced. This process involves four steps. The first step begins with the liar when a person *determines* to create deceit. Lies, like most sins, exist as attitudes before they exist as expressions. This is one reason why

Jesus addressed the problem of attitudes when He discussed integrity in the Sermon on the Mount (Matt. 5:33-37).

Step two in the process of lying involves *relaying dishonesty*. In this step, the liar expresses an untruth in some manner. Lies may be spoken or written or expressed in some other way. As noted above, a lie may be expressed actively or passively.

Step three in this process is intending to *misrepresent the truth*. Liars know the truth but deliberately attempt to convince others differently.

The fourth step usually involved in lying is an attempt to *avoid moral responsibility*.

This involves covering up the lie. When a person tells a lie, he or she usually has to tell another lie to avoid being caught. One lie quickly becomes a series of lies.

JESUS' VIEW ON THE SOURCE OF LYING

Jesus was not content to deal with the lies of a person's mouth. He dealt with a person's heart (Matt. 15:13) and the sources of lies, i.e., the Devil. "You are of your father the devil, and the desires of your father you want to do. He was a murderer from the beginning, and does not stand in the truth, because there is no truth in him. When he speaks a lie, he speaks from his own resources, for he is a liar and the father of it" (John 8:44). Jesus offered Himself as "truth" (John 14:6) and those who followed Him would walk in truth (John 8:32-36).

HOW TO BE A TRUTHFUL PERSON AND OVERCOME THE HABIT OF LYING

With so many different ways to lie, it is easy to see why so many people practice lying and become enslaved by the habit of lying. One of the biblical descriptions of the devil is "liar," so we should not be surprised when the world system he controls is given over to lying. But one of the descriptions of God is "truth," so Christians should be careful to build integrity into their life. There are ten things we can do to overcome the habit of lying and become a truthful person.

The first thing we need to do is *look to our standard*.

JESUS' VIEW OF THE TRUTH

To understand truth, we must look to the standard, i.e., Jesus. He said, "I am the way, the truth, and the life. No one comes to the Father except through Me" (John 14:6). If we want to become truthful people, we must look to the source of truth, i.e., Jesus. Then, we must look to the example of truth, i.e., Jesus. As we become more like Him, we become more truthful.

Next, learn to *recognize the source of lies*.

JESUS' VIEW OF LIES

Jesus taught that lying began with Satan. He said, "You are of your father the devil, and the desires of your father you want to do. He was a murderer from the beginning, and does not stand in the truth, because there is not truth in him. When he speaks a lie, he speaks from his own resources, for he is a liar and the father of it" (John 8:44). Since God is truth, Satan is the opposite of truth. Jesus taught that those who are controlled by lies, were really influenced by Satan. To learn how to be truthful a person needs to discipline his sinful nature and receive a new nature from God (2 Cor. 5:17).

Third, *admit your human nature is deceitful*.

JESUS' VIEW OF LIES

Jesus taught that we were born with a sin nature, this is the source of lies. Jesus said, "What comes out of man, that defiles a man. For from within, out of the heart of men, proceed evil thoughts, adulteries, fornications, murders, thefts, covetousness, wickedness, deceit, licentiousness, and evil eye, blasphemy, pride, foolishness. All these evil things come from within and defile a man" (Mark 7:20-23).

Fourth, *recognize the ultimate consequence of lying*. "But the cowardly, unbelieving, abominable, murderers, sexually immoral, sorcerers, idolaters, and all liars shall have their part in the lake which burns with fire and brimstone, which is the second death" (Rev. 21:8. emphasis added).

Fifth, if you want to overcome lying you must *adopt the lie-busting strategy* proposed by Paul to the Ephesians. "Therefore, putting away lying, 'Let each one of you speak truth with his neighbor,' for we are members of one another. Therefore, putting away lying, each one speak truth with his neighbor, for we are members of one another" (Eph. 4:25). We will only overcome lying in our life when we fulfill our Christian obligation of telling the truth to others.

Sixth, determine to be a *radical disciple*. This means allowing discipleship to reach down to the root of your being. Jesus described radical discipleship when He said, "If anyone desires to come after Me, let him deny himself, and take up his cross daily, and follow me" (Luke 9:23).

Seventh, learn to *walk in forgiveness* rather than guilt. When Israel was guilty of lying to God, "He, being full of compassion, forgave their iniquity and did not destroy them. Yes, many a time He turned His anger away, and did not stir up all His wrath" (Psa. 78:38). In the New Testament, we are reminded, "If we confess our sins, He is faithful and just to forgive us our sins and to cleanse us from all unrighteousness" (1 John 1:9).

God never intended for us to live the Christian life in our own strength. That is why it is important that the eighth principle is to *ask for strength to overcome lying*. That strength is found in Christ. "I can do all things through Christ who strengthens me" (Phil. 4:13).

Ninth, make *a decision to tell the truth*. There is a power in decision-making that gives added strength to what you want accomplished. When you decide to be truthful and announce that decision to others, you are making yourself accountable to them. Knowing you are accountable to tell the truth will help you to tell the truth.

Finally, resolve to be *a person of character*. The liar compromises his or her character when lying. Eventually, the liar erodes all self-trust and self-worth he or she may have had in himself, or others may have had in them. Religious and financial compromise is also often involved when lying.

The world is looking for men and women of integrity today. Christians above all others ought to practice integrity. May God help each of us to deal with the problem of lying and build integrity into our character.

PRINCIPLES TO TAKE AWAY

- People lie because of an evil heart.
- Because lying is so deceitful, there are many ways to lie.
- Because Satan is a liar, he has put within all people a desire to lie.
- God expects you to always tell the truth.
- Because Jesus is the truth, we must know Him to be a truthful person.
- You must make a commitment to tell the truth to be a truthful person.

Chapter Ten

BE SATISFIED WITH THE "STUFF" YOU HAVE

Tenth Commandment

"You shall not covet your neighbor's house; you shall not covet your neighbor's wife, nor his male servant, nor his female servant, nor his ox, nor his donkey, nor anything that [is] your neighbor's" (Exodus 20:17).

HAVE you seen the new religion in America? It didn't just come about with the dawn of advertising when merchants began advertising their products to the general public. This new religion just didn't grow because merchants became "slicker" in their advertising campaigns.

No! This religion is as old as mankind. It is the religion of consumerism that teaches "Thou shall want something you don't have." The ethics of this new religion is "Thou shalt never be satisfied with the things you have."

The Tenth Commandments teaches us that "you shall not covet..." When you look at the positive side of this Commandment, you hear God saying, "Thou shalt be satisfied with what I give you."

The new religion of consumerism proclaims, "Seek ye first the kingdom of *stuff*, and you will find happiness."

The new religion expressed in the words of the Latin conqueror, proclaims, "I came, I saw, I shopped!"

The new religion of consumerism has theologians; that we call *advertisers*, and it has priests, that we call *sales people*. The new religion has its temples that we call *malls*, and its worshippers are shoppers.

The French philosopher René Descartes searched for the existence of truth, and today, in the new religion, he would proclaim, "I shop, therefore, I am."

Does the new religion fill a need in modern man? What is the need of the heart that fuels this new religion? Greed!

The Roman Catholic church originally combined the First and Second Commandments, and said that we should not have any idols before God, or make any images to God. Then they separated the Tenth Commandment into two commandments, i.e., the Ninth Commandment said, "You shall not covet your neighbor's *stuff*," and the Tenth Commandments said, "You shall not covet your neighbor's wife."

Jesus' View on Coveting

Jesus taught that a person should beware and guard against the first urgings of covetousness. "And He said to them, 'Take heed and beware of covetousness, for one's life does not consist in the abundance of the things he possesses.'" Covetousness is the arousal or passion of the heart for something that you shouldn't have. It is the first shadow that crosses the mind to blind a person to the will of God. When any person gives into his or her covetousness, they enter into a blackness of sin. Eventually, every imagination of the heart is evil (Gen. 15:17-20).

WHAT IS COVETING?

There are two different words for *covet* in Exodus 20:17. The first word for covet is, "sparked by things seen by the eyes," i.e., your neighbor's house. This word deals with the *attraction of stuff*. It's like being attracted by the lights of Broadway. This first word is a desire for something because you saw what the other person has. Perhaps you have desired what happiness he has, or what position he has, or what security he has, or anything that your neighbor has.

The second word for *covet* suggests being driven by deep inward desire, i.e., *lust*. This is what you want, even before you see what your neighbor has. This is what John describes, i.e., "The lust of the flesh, the lust of the eyes, and the pride of life" (1 John 2:15). So when you covet your neighbor's wife, it's because of lust.

These two words for *covet* cover the whole spectrum of coveting. First, you covet because of *outward attraction*, and second, you covet because of *inward lust*.

Therefore, when God gives us the final commandment that says, "You shall not covet," it is more than the last on the list of commandments, it's different from the previous nine commandments. In the first nine commandments, God deals with our *outward behavior*; we must not steal, nor commit adultery, nor must we lie. But the Tenth Commandment deals with *inner motives* for stealing, adultery and lying.

Jesus' View on Inward Sin

Jesus taught His followers to avoid sin in its inward forms, not just avoid outward sins. Jesus taught sin was hatched in the heart (Matt. 15:16, 17) and evil was hostile to them. Satan was their enemy (John 8:44ff). Jesus taught them to act wisely about evil, and ever be on guard against it. Jesus taught His followers they would be tempted to follow false teachers, the worldly crowds, and to let outward things substitute for inner faith. Jesus said true faith was known by its inward fruit and would stand the test of opposition and storms (Matt. 7:1-29; Luke 6:37-49).

Basically, the last of the Ten Commandments is the most important of all. Why?

Because the last commandment deals with the reasons why we break the first nine commandments. Have you ever noticed that a person is motivated to violate the law, long before he actually breaks the law?

What does the Tenth Commandment do? It reveals the dark regions of our hearts. This last commandment is a mirror that makes us look beyond our actions; we look to the motivations of sin deep with our heart.

WE ALL BREAK THE TENTH COMMANDMENT

When babies are very young, they want another's toy. And notice their dissatisfaction when they finally get what they wanted. Usually a baby will cry for another's toy and the moment he gets it, he casts it aside looking for something else.

Notice how teens copy the physical clothes and styles of another teen. It's a herd mentality. They all want to look how they think the others appear. Deep down they covet the acceptance or compliments the others get.

A man working out at a gym wants the physique of his trainer. And when he's not thinking about golden tanned biceps, he wants the SUV of the man in the next locker. Women want the outfit of another woman, or at least they want the slim body that they see on models. And even workers are dissatisfied with their computer because someone at a different workstation has more gadgets and more gigabytes. Even parents are not satisfied with their children, they want their children to compete as well in T-Ball as others or better. Parents want their children to excel in test scores as other, and they want their children to behave as well in church as others.

WHAT COVETING DOES TO US

Isn't it all right to turn the pages of the catalog and dream about what you don't have?

Isn't it all right to shop the malls to see what's available? My wife always tells me that she shops for me, so I will know where to find the bargains. What's wrong with that?

If we're shopping for needs, that's one thing. If our shopping feeds our greed, that's another thing. Coveting is seeing what we don't have, and what our neighbor has, and lusting for it. Coveting puts us in competition with our neighbor. "Keeping up with the Joneses." We've got to have what they have so we can be as happy as we think they are. What's wrong with that? Two things. First, if you're keeping up with the Joneses, we don't see your neighbors as God sees him. If you're coveting what your neighbor has, how can you "love your neighbor as yourself" (Matt. 22:39)? If you look at your neighbor the way God looks at him, then you can't be in competition with him.

Why Are You at the Mall?

Shopping for need

or

Satisfying your greed.

There is a second thing that coveting does to you. If blinds you to the things that God has given you. If God has given you your house, why should you covet what your neighbor has? If God has given your neighbor a bigger house than you, perhaps there's a reason, i.e., God's reason. So when you covet, you do three things:

- You question God.
- You outguess God's reason.
- You are dissatisfied with God's provision.

Coveting takes away your belief in God, and makes you doubt His provision, "No good thing will He withhold from those who walk uprightly" (Psa. 84:11).

When you are dissatisfied with what you have, it destroys your fellowship with God. Doesn't God work all things together for good (Rom. 8:28), but when you covet, you say God has not given me good things? Hasn't God provided for your needs? When you covet, you say God has not provided for your needs. You must remember, "And God is able to make all grace abound toward you, that you, always having all sufficiency in all things, may have an abundance for every good work" (2 Cor. 9:8).

COVETOUSNESS IS SELFISHNESS.

Why is coveting wrong? Most of us think that is all right to want something illegal, as long as we don't act on it. Many men think that it is all right to check out the good looks of another woman, as long as they don't do anything about it. While that may be the thinking of the average male, that violates God's standard. The average American male thinks that it is all right to look, just don't touch.

Most women know *that all men look*. After all, "man looks at the outward appearance, but the LORD looks at the heart" (1 Sam. 16:7). The problem is, people eventually *act out* what they fantasize in their mind. Ted Bundy, a convicted serial murderer gave one interview, and said that reading pornography led him to murder.

Jesus' View of Coveting Sex

Jesus re-affirmed the tenth commandment that said, "You shall not covet your neighbor's wife." Jesus placed the problem of coveting within the heart, "Whoever looks at a woman to lust for her has already committed adultery with her in his heart" (Matt. 5:28).

If you have a covetous heart, it's like a pressure cooker. Our grandmothers cooked with a tremendous amount of steam in a pressure cooker. But grandmothers knew that she had to let off steam, or the whole thing would blow up. So, if you're coveting something that is wrong, eventually you have to "let off steam" by acting out your fantasies, or your whole personality blows up.

Isn't it natural to fantasize about *stuff*? It's all right to shop when you need something, but shopping has become the favorite American pastime. We are told to *shop until you drop*.

But the more we look, does it feed our greed? The man who always hangs around the dealership, looking at the latest pickup trucks, will eventually buy one. And the man who always fantasizes about sex with a neighbor's wife, will eventually commit adultery.

There's another reason why God told us not to covet. God knows that STUFF will never make us happy, and when we get what we lust after, then the evil heart will not be satisfied; it will lust for something else.

Jesus' Says Coveting Doesn't Satisfy

Jesus taught that coveting is never an *end in itself*, and that things never satisfy. Jesus taught that a person must put emphasis on eternal treasure, not earthly stuff to find true happiness.

"And He said to them, 'Take heed and beware of covetousness, for one's life does not consist in the abundance of the things he possesses.'" Then He spoke a parable to them, saying: 'The ground of a certain rich man yielded plentifully.' And he thought within himself, saying, 'What shall I do, since I have no room to store my crops?' So he said, 'I will do this: I will pull down my barns and build greater, and there I will store all my crops and my goods. And I will say to my soul, 'Soul, you have many goods laid up for many years; take your ease; eat, drink, and be merry.' But God said to him, 'Fool! This night your soul will be required of you; then whose will those things be which you have provided?' So is he who lays up treasure for himself, and is not rich toward God" (Luke 12:15-21).

What makes people evil? What makes people steal something from another, or to even covet something that another person has? People don't become evil by their friends, their environment, their circumstances, or even their lack of money. People hatch evil in their hearts, and become evil when they live out their evil dreams. People break the commandments because they hatch what is in their hearts.

Jesus' View of the Consequences of Coveting

Jesus taught that coveting makes you dirty. Jesus taught that evil comes out of our heart and makes us a sinner. "What comes out of a person makes them dirty, for out of the heart comes evil fantasizing, or just to break the law, a desire to do away with others, sexual lust, greed, hatred, desire to sneak, sexual liberties . . . all these evil appetites comes from within to make a person dirty" (Mark 7:20-23, author's translation).

Three Big Lies

Lie 1: *Everyone wants stuff, so it must be all right to want.*

Everyone has a desire to improve, a desire to be better, even a desire to be perfect; that is an inborn desire. But when we get in competition with our neighbor about stuff, then it becomes evil.

Jesus' View of Stuff

While Jesus did not expressly deal with the Ten Commandments when confronting the rich young ruler, possessions seem to be his main problem. Perhaps he had stolen them, perhaps not. In any case, Jesus told him, "If you want to be perfect, go, sell what you have and give to the poor, and you will have treasure in heaven; and come, follow Me" (Matt. 19:21).

Lie 2: *Getting what you want will quench your craving.*

Why is it that the baby who wants someone else's toy thinks it will make him happy?

Usually it doesn't. The baby cries for a toy he doesn't have, and when he gets it, he drops it and goes on to cry for something else. When will we ever learn that getting *stuff* will not make us happy?

We have an appetite called "lust of the flesh, and lust of the eyes" and getting what we want doesn't satisfy that appetite. When we feed our illicit appetite, we create addiction. Giving a covetous person what they want is like giving a thirsty man salt water to drink. His thirst is quenched momentarily, but each time he drinks salty water, the thirst doubles in intensity until it kills him.

Lie 3: *Wanting stuff is just my competitive urge to get ahead of my neighbor.*

Most of us are born competitive; sometimes we are the perfectionist neighbor who is compulsive about competition. We want a car that is faster, a house that is bigger, and food that tastes better. Most of us are convinced that we're not covetous, we think that we're just competitive. However, there is a difference between competitiveness and covetousness. When you're pushing yourself to excel, that's competition. When you're pushing yourself to get what your neighbor has, that is covetousness.

CONTROLLING COVETOUSNESS

When you look at the commandment, "You shall not covet...," it's like looking in the mirror at a convicted felon. All of us have a covetous heart, and human effort cannot correct it. The problem is not with our "wanting," the problem is with our *wanter*. While the word *wanter* is not found in the dictionary, it is a description of the heart. Our heart wants everything it doesn't have. It just so happens that we see our neighbor's *stuff*, and we want it.

The only person who can correct his/her covetousness, is a child of God. Because Christianity doesn't deal with the fruit, but the root, Christianity can change the heart.

1. *God expects me to control my heart.* As you read the Scriptures, God knows that you have an evil heart; but He expects you to do something about it. The Proverbs tell us, "Above all else, guard your heart, for it is the source of your life" (Prov. 4:23, author's translation). What this verse tells us is that we should:

- Be aware that our heart is the source of covetousness.
- Don't be surprised of covetous thoughts.
- Work hard to control your desires.

The Bible is filled with illustrations of God asking us to do something that we can't do, then giving us His help in getting it done. This is one of those occasions. God expects you to control your heart, when He knows you can't control your heart. But God doesn't just leave you frustrated; He will do something about it.

JESUS' VIEW OF THE CONSEQUENCES OF COVETING

Jesus taught that the covetous person will lose his soul if he gets all he wants and doesn't consider God's demands. "For what profit is it to a man if he gains the whole world, and loses his own soul? Or what will a man give in exchange for his soul?" (Matt. 16:26; cp. Mark 8:36-37).

2. *God will help you control your heart.* The heart is the source of your intellect, emotion and will; the heart is the seat of your personality. For out of your heart comes self-direction and self-perception. God knows that the heart believes, but the soul is saved. Because the heart is your moral regulator, God wants you to be concerned about your heart. God knows that only He can control your heart, and He will help you do it. The Lord says, "I will give you a new heart, and I will give you a new spirit; I will take away your evil hard heart, and give you a tender heart" (Ezek. 36:26, author's translation).

3. *Turn the ownership of your heart over to the Lord.* Bill Bright wrote the tract, *The Four Spiritual Laws*, and in one presentation, he asks the question, "Who sits on the throne of your heart?" The tract goes on to indicate that either self or Christ will sit on the throne of your heart. The secret to controlling your covetous heart is to give it to Christ, let Him sit upon the throne of your heart. The secret to controlling your heart is to give it to Christ, let Him sit upon the throne

of your desires. "Accept Christ as Lord of your heart" (1 Peter 3:15, author's translation).

4. *Daily obedience will lead to moral victories over covetousness.* Every time you say "No" to the lust of the flesh, you get strength from that victory to face and conquer a bigger obstacle the following day. The Bible speaks of "from victory to victory" and we take that step by going "from faith to faith."

When you are tempted to get something your neighbor has, you need to say "No!" This is called crucifying the flesh (Gal. 6:14). When we say "No!" to a temptation, we treat that covetousness desire as though it doesn't exist. When you say "No!" you crucify your covetousness to death.

PRINCIPLES TO TAKE AWAY

- People are incurable coveters about *stuff*.
- All the *stuff* in the world won't satisfy you.
- Coveting comes from your evil heart.
- God expects you to control your heart and will judge you if you don't.
- You must turn the ownership of your heart over to God.

EPILOGUE

IF God were to rewrite the Ten Commandments today, He wouldn't change any of them. He'd say, "Make Me first in your life." For the Second Commandment God would say, "Don't allow anything to get between Me and you." Third, "Show reverence for Me by the way you use My name." Fourth, "Worship Me on the Lord's Day." Fifth, "Learn to respect authority by honoring your parents." God would still tell us in the sixth law, "Respect the life of others." Seventh, "Make your body My sanctuary and keep your sex life pure." Eighth, "Respect the *stuff* of others," and Ninth, "Always tell the truth." The Tenth and last commandment for modern day would be the toughest to apply, "Be satisfied with what you have, no matter what your neighbor has." If you keep these updated commandments, you'll do what God's children have done for ages, i.e., you'll love and follow God.

APPENDIX A

The Ten Commandments According to the Devil

TEN LIES THE DEVIL TELLS:

1. If you sincerely believe, that's all you have to do.
2. You need room for other gods in your life.
3. Shouldn't you be able to say anything you feel?
4. You need your rest and relaxation on Sunday.
5. Your parents don't understand you.
6. You have to look out for yourself.
7. Sex is all right if you truly love your partner.
8. They will never miss it.
9. People don't want to hear the truth.
10. You'll be happy when you get all you want.

APPENDIX B

Principles to Apply the Ten Commandments

THESE Ten Commandments cover a wide variety of your life to help you make ethical decisions. So, apply these commandments to the different situations in which you find yourself. To help you do this, there are eight biblical guidelines to provide a general rule for making ethical decisions.

The first principles may be described as *obeying light*. This means you must be ready to obey truth that has been clearly revealed. The Bible teaches, "The secret things belong to the Lord our God, but those things which are revealed belong to us and to our children forever, that we may do all the words of this law" (Deut. 29:29). This means in grey areas of taking God's name in vain, only say what is obviously correct and don't say anything that is doubtful. God says, "You shall not take the name of the Lord your God in vain, for the Lord will not hold him guiltless who takes His name in vain" (Exod. 20:7). Therefore, don't trivialize God's name and surely don't use it as a curse word. God expects you to obey the clear light He has given you.

A second biblical principle is *follow rules*. This is what Joshua was told to do, "Observe to do according to all that is written in it" (i.e., the law) (Josh. 1:8). Joshua was directed to obey the rules he learned through meditating on the Scripture. A specific illustration of this principle is apparent in Paul's advice to the Corinthians concerning sexual immorality. He asked, "Do you not know that your body is the temple of the Holy Spirit, who is in you, whom you have from God, and you are not your own? For you were bought at a price; therefore glorify God in your body and in your spirit, which are God's" (1 Cor. 6:20). Because our body is the temple of the Holy Spirit, do not engage in activities that are harmful to the body.

A third is the principle of the *thought seed*. This principle recognizes that sin may be expressed in your mind or attitude long before it is expressed as an action (Jas. 1:14, 15). This principle of *clear thinking* is at the heart of the Tenth Commandment. "You shall not covet your neighbor's house; you shall not cover your neighbor's wife, nor his manservant, nor his maidservant, nor his ox, nor his donkey, nor anything that is your neighbor's" (Exod. 20:17).

Jesus suggested the principle of *thought seed* throughout His Sermon on the Mount when He said murder began with anger (Matt. 5:21, 22), and adultery began with lust (Matt. 5:27, 28).

A fourth biblical principle is *respecting others*. This principle is suggested in the first question ever asked of God. "Am I my brother's keeper?" (Gen. 4:9). The teaching of Scripture is a resounding, "Yes!" This principle of *respecting* others is kept by not killing, committing adultery, stealing and lying.

Throughout the New Testament, the principle of *respecting others* is emphasized in the various responsibilities we have to other believers. Paul applied this principle when he counseled the Corinthians to be careful about eating meat offered to idols. Even though Christians might have liberty to do so, Paul cautioned, "But beware lest somehow this liberty of yours becomes a stumbling block to those who are weak" (1 Cor. 8:9). He reminded them, "But when you thus sin against the brethren, and wound their weak conscience, you sin against Christ" (1 Cor. 8:12).

A fifth principle to help you make ethical decisions is *following Christ's example*. Peter stated this principle in his advice to Christians about suffering. "For to this you were called, because Christ also suffered for us, leaving us an example, that you should follow His steps" (1 Pet. 2:21). In his classic book, *In His Steps*, Charles Sheldon tells the story of a church and community that was transformed by asking the question, "What would Jesus do?" Although Sheldon's story was a fictional account, adopting this principle in real life makes good sense.

How would you answer the question, "What would Jesus do?" The obvious answer...

He would obey the Ten Commandments.

A sixth principle is *following your conscience*. God has given us a conscience to help us discern right from wrong. Paul used this principle when he explained why the heathens who do not know God are condemned by God, "For down in their hearts they know right from wrong.

God's laws are written within them; their own conscience accuses them, or sometimes excuses them" (Rom. 2:15, LB). Sometimes this principle is expressed in the popular statement, "If in doubt, don't!"

Closely related to this is the seventh principle of *internal integrity*. If you think an activity is wrong and you do it, that activity is wrong for you whether it is wrong for others or not. Paul also expressed this principle in his Epistle to the Romans. "But anyone who believes that something he wants to do is wrong, shouldn't do it. He sins if he does, for he thinks it is wrong, and so for him it is wrong. Anything that is done apart from what he feels is right is sin (Rom. 14:23, author's translation).

The eighth principle is *physical integrity*. Our commitment to Christ involves yielding our bodies to God (Rom. 12:1). Therefore, activities which are harmful to our bodies are wrong. Paul used this principle in urging Christians to avoid sexual immorality. "That is why I say to run from sexual sin. No other sin affects the body as this one does. When you sin this sin, it is against your own body" (1 Cor. 6:18, author's translation).

The Christian who is committed to glorifying God in every area of his or her life must be careful to make ethical decisions to help him or her live consistently. Various Christians may disagree over specific behavioral issues, but it is of utmost importance that each of us has a standard by which we live our life. As you seek to obey the Ten Commandments in your life, be careful to apply these and other biblical principles to the issues you face.

APPENDIX C

27 Foundational Principles of Holiness

THE following 27 foundational laws or principles summarize the teachings of this book. These biblical principles are useful in helping you make ethical decisions about the rightness or wrongness of our involvement in a wide variety of activities. Not every principle will be applicable in every situation, but some principles in this list are applicable to each situation you are likely to encounter. The list is provided at the conclusion of this book to help you determine "what is right" in situations you encounter in life which are not specifically covered in the previous 10 chapters.

1. The Principle of Addiction

    The *principle of addiction* states that a Christian should avoid any and all activity which might place him or her in bondage (1 Cor. 6:12).

2. The Principle of Appearances

    The *principle of appearances* states that a Christian should avoid the appearance of evil (1 Thess. 5:22).

3. The Principle of Association

    The *principle of association* states that a Christian should not associate closely to that which is incompatible to living the Christian life (1 Cor. 6:14).

4. The Principle of Barbecue Chicken

    The *principle of barbecued chicken* states that a Christian should have good and balanced taste in artistic matters (1 Cor. 12:31).

5. The Principle of Clear Thoughts

    The *principle of clear thoughts* states that a Christian should have pure thoughts in his or her relationships with others (Matt. 5:28).

6. The Principle of Community Morals

    The *principle of community morals* states that a Christian should live by and above the commonly accepted moral standards in his or her community (1 Cor. 5:1).

7. The Principle of Consequences

    The *principle of consequences* states that a Christian should avoid evil actions that produce harmful consequences (1 Cor. 15:33).

8. The Principle of Cultural Expectations

    The *principle of cultural expectations* states that our Christian life should be expressed within our cultural world view (Rom. 2:14).

9. The Principle of Influence

    The *principle of influence* states that Christians should consider the effect of an action upon them before engaging tin that activity (Gal. 6:7).

10. The Principle of Financial Stewardship

    The *principle of financial stewardship* reminds Christians that they are stewards of God's resources entrusted to them (Psa. 24:1).

11. The Principle of Following Christ's Example

    The *principle of following Christ's example* states that Christians should pattern their lives after that of Christ (1 Pet. 2:21).

12. The Principle of Following Your Conscience

    The *principle of following your conscience* states that a Christian should never violate his or her conscience (Rom. 2:15).

13. The Principle of Following Rules

    The *principle of following rules* states that a Christian should always obey the clear teaching of Scripture (Deut. 29:29).

14. The Principle of Incompatibility

    The *principle of incompatibility* states that a Christian is radically different from the world and, therefore, should avoid engaging in a partnership with another who does not share his or her values (2 Cor. 6:14-16).

15. The Principle of Intent

    The *principle of intent* states that a Christian should examine his or her motives in participating in a questionable activity (Jas. 1:14, 15).

16. The Principle of Public Image

    The *principle of public image* states that a Christian should be careful to live in such a way that the message or image of his or her life causes others to glorify God (Matt. 5:18).

17. The Principle of Obeying Light

    The *principle of obeying light* states that a Christian should act in accordance to the light he or she has on a matter (Acts 17:30).

18. The Principle of Personal Commitment

    The *principle of personal commitment* states that a Christian will be firm in their ethical decisions when they tell someone else (Ruth 1:16, 17).

19. The Principle of Personal Integrity

    The *principle of personal integrity* states that a Christian should avoid doing what he or she believes may be wrong, whether it is wrong or not (Rom. 14:23). Sometimes this is expressed in the maxim, "If in doubt, don't."

20. The Principle of Physical Integrity

    The *principle of physical integrity* states that a Christian should avoid activities that cause him or her to compromise his or her body (1 Cor. 6:18).

21. The Principle of the Questionable Environment

    The *principle of the questionable environment* states that a Christian should avoid places where he or she is unlikely to bring glory to God (John 17:5).

22. The Principle of Respecting Others

    The *principle of respecting others* states that a Christian has a moral responsibility to be concerned for the welfare of others (1 Cor. 8:9, 12).

23. The Principle of Stewardship of Time

    The *principle of stewardship of time* states that a Christian should make good use of the time available (Eph. 5:16).

24. The Principle of the Stumbling Block

    The *principle of the stumbling block* states that a Christian should avoid any and all activities which might cause a weaker brother or sister to stumble in their Christian life (1 Cor. 8:9).

25. The Principle of Godly Thinking

    The *principle of godly thinking* states that the focus of a Christian's personal thought life should be compatible with the message of the Gospel (Phil. 4:8).

26. The Principle of Ultimate Objective

    The *principle of ultimate objective* states that the chief purpose of the Christian is to bring glory to God in all he or she does (1 Cor. 10:31; Phil. 1:21).

27. The Principle of Value Education

    The *principle of value education* states that Christian parents have a God-given responsibility to teach biblical principles to their children (Deut. 6:7-9).

    May God bless you as you continue in the midst of an evil world, to live for Jesus every day and in every way.

PART TWO

THE TEN COMMANDMENTS ACCORDING TO JESUS

70 Daily Devotions

Day 1

WHAT IS IMPORTANT ABOUT LAW?

"One of them, an expert in religious law, tried to trap him with this question: 'Teacher, which is the most important commandment in the law of Moses?' Jesus replied, 'You must love the Lord your God with all your heart, all your soul, and all your mind.'"

Matthew 22:35-37, NLT

"But now you must be holy in everything you do, just as God who chose you is holy. For the Scriptures say, "You must be holy because I am holy."

1 Peter 1:15-16, NLT

WHY does God want us to keep law, i.e. The Ten Commandments? Because the nature of God is both positive and negative. Remember, God is love (1 John 4:8), and God is holy (1 Peter 1:15). First, look at the negative reason why you want to keep God's law. Because God is holy, He punishes all sinful people. You don't want God's rejection and punishment, so attempt to do what He teaches, both inwardly and outwardly. Remember, God wants you to be holy because He is holy.

Lord, forgive me when I don't keep Your law. Because I love You, I want to please You, I come to deal with my sin. Forgive me by the blood of Christ and cleanse me from sin (1 John 1:9). Now I want to fellowship in Your love and worship You as my Lord. Amen.

When you fellowship with God you show your positive love for Him. Remember, love is defined as giving yourself completely to the one you love. So, because you love God, you want to be with Him, and be like Him, and give yourself to Him.

Lord, I have a sinful nature that tempts me to reject holiness. Come live in my heart to keep me strong and motivated to live a holy life. Let Your holy life flow through me as a testimony to others to live for You. Let Your love flow through me to attract them to give their hearts to You. Amen

READ:

Isaiah 6:1-13;

1 Peter 1:13-20

REFLECTION

Day 2

LIFE IS CHOICE

"I gave these commandments to Moses saying, "I am the Lord your God, and have brought you from bondage in Egypt. 'You shall not have any of the world's gods before me.'"

Exodus 20:1-3, BBJ

CHOICE is important, for without your honest response of worship, God would not be worshipped, nor would He be number one in your life or anyone's life. Because God made you in His likeness and image, He gave to you and all humans the marvelous power of choice. You can live the way you choose; you can do what you choose, and you can become the type of person you want to become. Have you chosen to believe in God, and follow Him, and be like Him? If you have made that choice, the next choice is easy, "You shall not have any other God but Him" (Exodus 20:3, ELT).

Lord, I have chosen to believe in You. I have accepted Jesus as my Savior, and I have decided to follow Him in my inner and outer life. I have made that choice, give me strength to make it happen in my life. Amen.

Because life is choice, purpose not to acknowledge any other god – whether man made idols, or those false gods created in the minds of evil men. Choose Jesus for salvation from sin, and choose to turn from sin. Choose Jesus to guide your life and reject suggestions from those who have chosen to believe in false gods and live in sin. Life is choice, you will become who you choose to be, and live accordingly to the way you choose.

Lord, I choose to say "yes" to Your salvation and You commandments. I choose to reject the lust of the flesh, the world and pride of life. I choose to obey You and live a holy life. (1 John 2:15-17). Amen.

READ:

1 John 2:1-29

REFLECTION

Day 3

HIS HOLINESS

"You must not have any other god but me."

Exodus 20:3, NLT

"Pray like this: Our Father in heaven, may your name be kept holy."

Matthew 6:9, NLT

WHEN you begin praying The Lord's Prayer, you acknowledge the holiness of God that is the foundation for The Ten Commandments. When you pray, "Our Father... may Your name be kept holy," you are asking for The Ten Commandments to influence your life with the holiness of God as a testimony to others. So, whether you repeat The Ten Commandments or pray The Lord's Prayer, you are acknowledging His holiness in your life. So, pray both to influence your testimony to others.

Lord, I have chosen to believe in You. I have accepted Jesus as my Savior, and I have decided to follow Him in my inner and outer life. I have made that choice, give me strength to make it happen in my life. Amen.

Because life is choice, you can purpose to reject any and all other false gods – whether man made idols, or those false gods created in the minds of evil men. You can choose Jesus for salvation from sin, and you choose to turn from sin. You can choose Jesus to guide your life and reject suggestion from those who have chosen to believe in false gods and live in sin. Life is choice, you will become who you choose to be, and live accordingly to the way you choose.

Lord, I choose to say "yes" to Your salvation and You commandments. I choose to reject the lust of the flesh, the world and pride of life. (1 John 2:15-17). Amen.

READ:

1 John 2:1-29

REFLECTION

Day 4

OTHER GODS

"You must not have any other god but me."

Exodus 20:3, NLT

WHERE do the other gods come from? There are false gods of Greek Mythology, and there are idol gods created by heathen tribes, and false gods of other world religions. The Lord God (v. 2), didn't make them. Man is made in the image of God (Genesis 2:7), but the world, the flesh and the devil attempt to draw people from God, using false gods to pull all people away from the true God. People are born with a sin nature that pulls them from God. People cerate false gods in the image of themselves and to fulfill their human instinct and lust. So, to be a follower of the true God, begin by rejecting the existence of all other gods and anything you want from them.

Lord, I believe You are the eternal God who existed before time began. You are the Almighty One, the Creator who created the trillions of galaxies, representing the billions of powerful burning stars with more light that mere mortal can imagine. Yes, I believe in the Trinity, composed of my heavenly Father who watches over me, and Jesus who saved me from sin and indwells my life, and the Holy Spirit also guides me and keeps me safe. Amen.

False gods are made by humans, to satisfy the needs of humans, and at the same time these false gods give permission to humans to do evil and commit the sins they want to do. Because humans are idol-makers, they create false gods to justify their actions and give them false standards of life.

Father protect me from the false gods of others. Jesus forgive me of my sins, and the Holy Spirit live in my heart to make me holy in my heart, and spiritual in my life. I will not be an idol-maker who creates false gods to justify myself before You. Amen.

READ:

Romans 1:1-32

REFLECTION

Day 5

WHAT DOES "HAVE" MEAN?

"You must not have any other god but Me."

Exodus 20:3, NLT

WHAT did God mean when He said, *"You must not have any other god but Me"* (v. 3). Does the word *have* mean possess, as someone holding an idol or their stuff? Does it mean *own*, such as someone else owns an idol but you worship it, but you didn't buy it and it is not in your possession? Does *have* mean you couldn't make idols as a workman would carve it from stone? So, you buy one! Some look for loopholes to get around God's standards. Some stretch the truth to worship false gods belonging to others, but they never have owned one. No! The word *have* means put it in your heart, or to worship one, or even allow it to influence your home or life.

> *Lord, I want to be a 100 percent follower of Jesus Christ. I don't want a false God anywhere in my life. I want to worship my heavenly Father and be indwelt by Jesus Christ and be empowered by the Holy Spirit to live a holy life. Amen.*

The First Commandment does not say "do not worship false gods," but what does *do not* mean? When God said do not have any gods in your life, this is an all-inclusive starting point for your Christian life. No means no, and that is all it means. Make God the only focus of living. There is no one other than God.

> *Lord, I want to have You only as the Lord of my life. I will not have any false gods anywhere in my thinking and actions. Come sit on the throne of my heart and direct my life. Amen.*

READ:

Acts 17:16-34; Acts 14:8-22

REFLECTION

Day 6

WHAT IS IN GOD'S FACE?

"Thou shalt have no other gods before me."'
Exodus 20:3, KJV

WHAT does it mean when the Scripture teaches us to not have any gods "before Me"? The King James' phrase "before Me" suggests God would see it. The Apologetic Study Bible translates it "beside Me" suggesting you are elevating false gods to the level of the LORD God. The Living Bible translates it, "you may worship no other God but Me," suggesting when you put any idol in God's face you are putting down the almighty God, and elevating some false gods the human worshipper. This verse means God is number one, no other gods exist. God is first, there are no gods in second place.

> *Lord, I want to see You with the eyes of my heart. I want to worship You with the voice of my heart. I want to bow before You with my outward body and my inner person. I will not have any gods before You. Amen.*

Some have wrongly interpreted this phrase "before Me" to mean don't bring false gods into God's presence. It means that and more. Some have wrongly thought it to mean, "don't give idols any of your time, before you give God His time." It means give God all your time, talent and treasure and none to false gods. Again, some have wrongly interpreted it to mean, "don't let false gods attract the eternal God's attention." The phrase "before Me" is all inclusive. Put the Lord God first... at all time... in all ways.

> *Lord, teach me to focus only on You when I worship. Forgive me for any distractions or daydreaming when I should be praying. I surrender all. Amen.*

READ:

Deuteronomy 4:15-23, 5:6-33

REFLECTION

Day 7

LORDSHIP IS A CHOICE

"You must not have any other god but Me.'"

Exodus 20:3, NLT

"So now I am giving you a new commandment: Love each other. Just as I have loved you, you should love each other. Your love for one another will prove to the world that you are my disciples."

John 13:34-35, NLT

SALVATION is a choice when you decide to have no other gods in your life before the Lord. It is a *love-choice*, because God wants us to love Him with all our hearts. Then it is an *obedient – choice*. People are not born as little babies following God, even if they were born in a church family. Then it is a *faith-choice* when you choose by faith to put God first and exclude all other gods or religions, or distractions. Next, it is a *Lordship-choice*. That means the Lord God of the Bible will direct all the decisions of your life, and all your decisions of what you want to become, and all the everyday choices of what you will do and become. "Faith makes things certain, even when you can't see" (Hebrews 11:2, *BBJ*).

Lord, I choose to follow You because I found truth in the Scriptures. I choose to obey Your commands, because it please You. Guide my worship and my daily life. I give You priority in all things. Amen.

Your relationship with your Lord is based on the foundation of The Ten Commandments. It is not about obeying because of rules. It is not about being punished when you disobey. It is about a love-relationship. When you love the Lord your God with all your heart, you will obey Him.

Lord, I love The Ten Commandments because I love You. I keep them because of our relationship. I am not always perfect, sometimes I slip, or I am ignorant of what I should do. Forgive me, accept me, and use me in Your service. Amen.

READ:

John 13:31-14:29

REFLECTION

Day 8

AN IDOL IS NOT LIKE GOD YOUR FATHER

"You shall not make for yourself a carved image—any likeness of anything that is in heaven above, or that is in the earth beneath, or that is in the water under the earth; ⁵ you shall not bow down to them nor serve them. For I, the Lord your God, am a jealous God, visiting the iniquity of the fathers upon the children to the third and fourth generations of those who hate Me."

Exodus 20:4-5, KJV

THE Second Commandment says you must not worship a bird, or animal, or fish. Don't let anything represent God, because nothing represents God. Jesus said, "God is Spirit" (John 4:23), so you must offer Him spiritual worship. That is worship motivated by the Holy Spirit, and flows from the Holy Spirit who indwells your heart (John 14:17). Those who think they need a *picture* or *carved* idol to focus their worship on *God* are not really focusing on the Lord God of heaven. A thing cannot represent God because a *thing* is not God and it can never represent Him. Remember Jesus said, God is Spirit."

Lord, I close my eyes to see You in my heart when I pray. I don't need anything to represent You. I need Your Spirit to fill me, Your power to answer my prayers, and Jesus hear my prayers and answer them. Amen.

First, Jesus told the woman at the well a necessary focus, "God is Spirit." That means an idol is nothing like God the Father. Second, Jesus told her, "True worshipers shall worship the Father in spirit and in truth" (John 4:23-24). God is not like a carved animal, He is like a Father... your heavenly Father who loves you, hears your prayers and guides and protects you.

Father, I come worshiping You because You love me and listen to me when I pray. Since I was made in Your image (Genesis 2:7), I yield myself to You. Fill me with wisdom to serve You today. Amen.

READ:

Genesis 1:26 -2:7

REFLECTION

Day 9

WORSHIP IS RELATIONSHIP

"You shall not make for yourself a carved image—any likeness of anything that is in heaven above, or that is in the earth beneath, or that is in the water under the earth; ⁵ you shall not bow down to them nor serve them. For I, the Lord your God, am a jealous God, visiting the iniquity of the fathers upon the children to the third and fourth generations of those who hate Me."

Exodus 20:4-5, KJV

"True worshipers will worship the Father in spirit and truth; for the Father is seeking such to worship Him."

John 4:23, KJV

WHEN talking to the woman at the well (John 4:6-29, *KJV*), Jesus gave the correct focus of worship, i.e., the Father in heaven. Idol worshippers focus on birds, animals, and fish. But God the Father is not like them, and He says He is jealous when anyone substitutes an idol-god for Him. Twice in today's passages Jesus gives God a personal name, i.e., *Father*. Worship is a relationship, it is you praising the heavenly Father for all He is, and for all He has done for you. God is a Father who receives worship. Humans – including you – were created to be a worshiper.

Father, I blow to worship You with all my heart. First, because You invited me to worship You. Second, because I need to worship You, because I am empty. But third, I worship You because You desire all my praise, adorations and thanksgiving. Amen.

Make sure you don't worship the wrong thing by focusing on a carved idol. Nothing can replace God the Father. But also make sure you don't worship wrongly by the way you do it, or the reasons you do it. Those who worship an idol-god, do it to get something. You must worship the Father because of all He is and His holiness, love, goodness and what He has done for you, i.e., saved you, indwelt you, given you purpose, and joy.

Father, I pray for idol worshipers that they may be saved and worship You. Thank You for saving me, and indwelling me, and giving me a purpose in life to serve You and worship You. Amen.

READ:

John 4:4-42

REFLECTION

Day 10

WORSHIP GOD YOUR FATHER

*"True worshipers will worship the Father in spirit and truth;
for the Father is seeking such to worship Him."*

John 4:23, KJV

ONE of the main temptations for Old Testament Israel was idol worship. It was because of the idol-worshipping nations around them. Abraham, their spiritual father was called from an idol worshiping generation. But Jesus introduced a new argument against idol-worship. He called God the heavenly Father. This was a new title for God, He was not given the name Father in the Old Testament although God was likened to a father by metaphors. God's three primary titles in the Old Testament were God (Elohim, Creator), LORD (Jehovah the personal I am that I am), and Lord (Adonai, or Master). In the New Testament, God is your heavenly Father... personal... intimate... and He responds in a relationship to you.

Father, I come worshipping You as Creator, Jehovah, and Master. I know You as a Person and I pray to You as the eternal God. Thank You for Your love and care for me. Amen.

Just as a human father has children on earth, so all *believers* are called children of God (Romans 8:16). Because of this Paul said, "We call Him our Daddy, or Father" (Romans 8:15, *ELT*). This makes Christianity a relationship. This is infinitely superior to idol-worshippers whose god is represented as a bird, animal or fish.

Father, thank You for You for a living relationship with You through prayer and obedience Jesus thank You for an intimate relationship with You through the indwelling Holy Spirit. Thank You for personal guidance and protection. Amen.

READ:

Romans 8:1-17;
Galatians 4:4-9

REFLECTION

Day 11

WHY PUT GOD FIRST?

"You did not see the Lord's form on the day He spoke to you from the heart of the fire at Mount Sinai. So do not corrupt yourselves by making an idol in any form—whether of a man or a woman, an animal, a bird, a small animal or a fish. And when you look up into the sky and see the sun, moon, and stars – all the forces of heaven – don't be seduced into worshiping them. Remember that the Lord rescued you to make you His very own people and His special possession."

Deuteronomy 4:15-20, NLT

GOD is telling you not to worship carved idols that represent wildlife, nor worship heavenly bodies. Why? Because God wants worship. God is perfect and doesn't need anything. Since we are created in the image and likeness of God, we should worship Him. What a pathetic sight, a human made in the image of God becoming a "god-maker" creating an idol and worshiping it. This Second Commandment, which is against idol-making tells you to put God first, i.e., worshipping Him *only* for who He is and what He does.

Father, I see the wonders of the heavens and the earth – and worship You as Creator. I look at human beings and marvel at Your intricate design of life; and I bow and worship You as our Creator and Savior. Amen.

The Father doesn't force you to worship Him. He invites worship and rewards those who worship Him (Hebrews 11:6). But the Father has warned you not to worship anything else besides Him. In today's verse the Father warns you *"not corrupt yourselves"* (v. 16). But also, God offers you a social reward when you worship only Him. God will make you *"His very own people and His special possession"* (v. 20).

Father, that is what I want most of all – to be Your very own people and to be Your possession. I want a deeper relationship with You... to know You... to follow You... to serve You... and fellowship with You. Amen.

READ:

Deuteronomy 4:1-20

REFLECTION

Day 12

GOD DOESN'T HAVE A BODY

"Thou shalt not make unto thee any graven image."
Exodus 20:4, KJV

"Do not carve any idols... nor bow down to them."
Exodus 20:4, ELT

LOOK carefully at the phrase, *"Thou shalt not make."* In one sense it doesn't say carve, but it means that. Most idols were carved from wood or stone. The word "make" could mean "to create" as using hands to sculpt from clay or mud. It could be an artist creating a picture of an idol with sketching, or with painting. It could be a writer creating an image of God in an essay or composition. In essence God said make no physical substance or representation of Me. Why? Because "God is Spirit" (John 4:23-24) and the human eye cannot see a spirit. Moses reminded Israel, "You saw no form when the LORD spoke to you."

Lord, I will not make any physical replica of You, but when I close my eyes in prayer or mediation, I see You in my heart. Thank You for Your closeness and intimacy. I will talk to You in prayer, and listen for Your inner communication to me. Amen.

A father was driving his young son home from Sunday school, when the boy asked, "Dad... why can't I draw a picture of God with my crayons?" The father answered, "Because there is nothing to see." By that he meant, God is Spirit. His eternal nature doesn't have a physical body and is invisible.

That is a refence to the Father and Holy Spirit, but of course in the fullness of time Jesus was born in the flesh.

Lord, I bow to You at anytime and anywhere for any reasons. You are Spirit and You are eternal, You are always near to me. You are omnipresent, not bound by space, but everywhere present. I worship You. Amen.

READ:

Psalm 106:19-23;

1 John 5:21

REFLECTION

Day 13

GRAVEN IMAGE

"Thou shalt not make unto thee any graven image."

Exodus 20:4, KJV

WHY did the people of Israel make idols, or even choose another god than the LORD God of heaven? They were doing it for selfish reasons, not to honor or worship the LORD God. Were they carving a beautiful idol because it brought glory to them as craftsmen? Were they bosting of their rational ability to think and create a replica of what they thought of God? Or where they making an idol to justify their pleasure and selfish desires? That meant they wanted their idea of a god rather than admitting the LORD God had a real existence and demanded their worship.

Lord, I repudiate all false ideas of other gods, or anyone's thinking that there is another god than You. I believe You are the true God... the only God... the Creator God... and You are the saving God who has redeemed me from sin. I yield my life to you. Amen.

When you please any type of false god, you are not doing it because the false god ask for your recognition or worship. Absolutely not! You are doing it for your own selfish reasons. The LORD God understands the motives of humans. That is why He said, "Don't make for yourselves." Humans wanted to make a god like themselves... or according to their thinking... or representing their craftsmanship. Don't be deceived, people don't make an idol to please the substitute god. No! They do it for themselves.

Lord, forgive me for any occasion when I put anything else in Your place. Whether it was money, stuff, people or ambitions. I confess my sins, forgive me and cleanse me (1 John 1:9). Amen.

READ:

1 Corinthians 8:1-7;

1 Thessalonians 1:9;

1 John 5:21

REFLECTION

Day 14

MAKE FOR YOURSELVES

"You shall not make for yourself a carved image—any likeness of anything that is in heaven above, or that is in the earth beneath, or that is in the water under the earth; ⁵ you shall not bow down to them nor serve them. For I, the Lord your God, am a jealous God, visiting the iniquity of the fathers upon the children to the third and fourth generations of those who hate Me."

Exodus 20:4-5

THE original *King James* uses the word "graven image." *The New King James* says, "carved image." Why does God say not to make anything in His image? Because people were originally made in God's image, i.e., God was the divine sculptor, you are made in His image. But humans want to take God's place and so they make an idol in their image. Humans are doing the opposite of what God did. Those who reject the true God try to bring God down to their size. They want to be god-makers.

Lord, I pause to think how terrible idols are and how blasphemous their existence. You are our Lord, and You created all things. I believe it, I tell it to others, and I will live as one created in Your image. Amen.

How terrible is idol making? God says idol making is hating Him. Look at the rest of the Second Commandment. "I the LORD God, I am a jealous God, visiting the iniquity... of them that hate Me." (Exodus 20:5, *KJV*). The word "iniquity" means "to be bent" or "to be controlled." Those who worship an idol are controlled by the evil spirit in that idol. Therefore, those who think they are worshiping the carved image, are really worshipping a demon spirit.

Lord, You have told us to avoid idol worship and demon worship. I will worship You my LORD and Creator – Commandment One. I will never worship an idol, or anything man makes – Commandment Two. Amen.

READ:

Joshua 24:1-28

REFLECTION

Day 15

NO VAIN WORDS

*"Thou shalt not take the name of the Lord thy God in vain;
for the Lord will not hold him guiltless that taketh his name in vain."*

Exodus 20:7, KJV

WHAT is the meaning of in vain? The word *vain* found in the old King James meant using His name wrongly. You use it wrongly when you swear with God's name; whether cussing or showing anger at God, or blasphemy or profanity. But is also means don't use God's name lightly or irreverently. Therefore, don't use it with filthy speech. Don't take in vain the church... heaven or hell... or the Bible and its promises. Because God's name represents Him and His person, you are not reverencing God when you wrongly use His name. God wants you to hallow His name (Matthew 6:9), as when you pray the Lord's Prayer. Don't degrade or insult God or His name.

Lord, I come praying Hallowed be Thy name ... in my speech ...in my thoughts and in all I do. I want my speech to honor You. Forgive me for anytime my speech has dishonored You. Help me speak on earth as I will speak in heaven in the presence of You and the angels. Amen.

Not using God's name in vain should be important to you, because God listed it number three in His prohibitions. Use God's name lightly in prayer, worship, praise, teaching, preaching, prophecy, communion, and singing to God in heaven. Your speech should be positive, reflecting your love for God... your inner thoughts... your testimony to Christians and the unsaved.

Lord, I speak Your name cautiously and with awe. I want my outward word to reflect my inner thoughts, both about You and people and things. I yield my mind to You. May the

*words of my heart and the thoughts of my heart be acceptable to You (Psalm 19:14, ELT).
Amen.*

READ:

James 3:1-18

REFLECTION

Day 16

DO NOT TRIVIALIZE GOD'S NAME

"You shall not take the name of the Lord your God in vain, for the Lord will not hold him guiltless who takes His name in vain."

Exodus 20:7

THERE are many questionable ways to use God's name in vain. Where some would never curse or swear with God's name, they speak lightly of Him, or make jokes about Him or Christian things. Some may say, "God cannot do miracles today," or question His ability to answer prayer, pulling God down to their level of thinking. Some laugh at Christian standards about adultery, drunkenness, gambling or tithing. Still others take God's name in vain when they trivialize worship, church ministry, faith promises, or gospel invitations they don't like. Some filling pledge do it by cards, knowing they don't plan to give the money.

Lord, give me spiritual eyes to see my heart, especially to see times I disobey and take Your name in vain. Help me be a positive testimony to those in the church and those on the outside. Amen.

There is an old saying," mean what you say, and say what you mean." Hymn singing is another challenge. Many sing "I forsake all" when they don't. Some claim "I surrender all" when they have a dark cave in their heart that Christ does not control. When Christians sing Christmas carols to worship the Baby King, but they think more of Santa Clause than Jesus. Remember using God's name in vain means irreverently using it lightly.

Lord, I love Your names and what they mean. I worship You Creator God (Elohim) for Your power. I bow in worship to you LORD (Jehovah) for Your love and kindness to me. I submit to You Adonai (Master), I will worship and serve You. Amen.

READ:

Matthew 15:1-20

REFLECTION

Day 17

BE CAREFUL WHAT YOU SAY

"But those things which proceed out of the mouth come from the heart, and they defile a man. For out of the heart proceed evil thoughts, murders, adulteries, fornications, thefts, false witness, blasphemies. These are the things which defile a man, but to eat with unwashed hands does not defile a man."

Matthew 15:18-20, KJV

JESUS interpreted taking "the name of God in vain" much narrower than the religious leaders of His day, or of many professing Christians today. Jesus would condemn attacking or breaking the standards of purity of sex, purity of a curse or blasphemy to God's name. Filthy speech leads to filthy thoughts acts and filthy lives. What does both God the Father and Jesus want? They want to be the center of your life and conversations both in everyday talk, and religious talk in church.

Lord, I have a sinful nature (old man) that tempts me to get angry and say things I should not say. Forgive me for any and all past sins with my mouth. Forgive even those words or phrases I think are all right...You know the truth. See my heart and cleanse me. Amen.

Believers must be people of the Word (John 1:1, 17:18), meaning they live by the Bible. But they also must be people of their word, meaning they will live and act according to their speech. They should live by the old saying, "mean what you say, and say what you mean." When someone curses or uses filthy words, they tell observers their conversation reflects the evil or filth of their heart. Christians don't lower your speech to the level of the world, lift it to God's standard.

Lord, teach me to watch my speech. I want to be a good testimony for You. May the words of my mouth and the thoughts of my heart glorify You. Amen.

READ:

Matthew 15:1-20

REFLECTION

Day 18

GUILTLESS

"Even so the tongue is a little member, and boasteth great things. Behold, how great a matter a little fire kindleth! And the tongue is a fire, a world of iniquity: so is the tongue among our members, that it defileth the whole body, and setteth on fire the course of nature; and it is set on fire of hell."

James 3:5-6, KJV

JAMES tells us the tongue can be dangerous "world of iniquity" (James 3:6), even responsible for some in hell. So, James begins his letter telling you "Be slow to speak" (James 1:19). Then he tells you to "bridle" (James 3:2) the tongue. A bridle is used to restrain or guide a horse. That is what our tongue needs, i.e., discipline against wrong or evil words, restraint against anger, or guiding our life for God.

Lord, use my tongue to glorify You in all I think or say. Then give me strength and discipline to think positive thoughts and "bridle" my tongue by guiding me by the Holy Spirit. Amen.

God says He will not let you go unpunished if you miss use His name (Exodus 20:7, NLT). Hell will be filled with people who have cursed, or blasphemed and broken this Third Commandment (Revelation 21:8). But there is good news! Jesus died for the thief who broke this Commandment (Matthew 27:44). All sin was nailed to the cross. Jesus "canceled the record of charges, against us and took it away by nailing it to the cross"(Colossians 2:14, NLT). That means God will forgive the sin of cursing and taking His name in vain by the blood of Christ.

Lord, thank You for the blood of Christ that cleanses from all sin – including cussing – thank You for forgiveness. Now, I will praise You with my mouth for all Christ has done for me. Amen.

READ:

James 3:1-18

REFLECTION

Day 19

WORDS ARE POWERFUL

"How forcible are right words!"

Job 6:25, KJV

WORDS are powerful because they reflect what is in your heart. The words "I love you" gives emotional connection to the relationship between a man and woman. The words, "Our Father, hallowed by Thy name" gives a prayer relationship between God and you. On the other side of the coin James said, "The tongue... is an unruly evil" (James 3:8). The evil words of your tongue can destroy you. But it is not the words, but it is what comes from the heart, your mouth speaks, and reflects the evil heart. So, God wants you to reverence Him, so He said it, "Don't take the name of the Lord in vain." Why did He say that? Because God knows what is in our hearts, better than we do.

> *Lord, forgive my words when I hurt others and forgive my heart that didn't praise and worship You. Forgive the sins of my heart and give me a new clean heart (Ezekiel 36:26). Amen.*

Our hearts should remember what Christ has done for us and our words should thank Him for forgiveness and cleansing (1 John 1:9). Then we remember how the Father called us to salvation, then we must worship and praise Him for His eternal goodness. Then we should praise Him what the Holy Spirit has done in regenerating us, determine to live daily in the power of His indwelling. The words of your prayers are right words and forceful words, and they give you power with God.

Lord, I come to You for acceptance and intimacy. Help me know You. I also come for guidance and growth, help me walk and talk as Your child. I come for power and discipline, help me use my speech to glorify You and bring unsaved people to Christ. Amen.

READ:

Psalm 119:169-176

REFLECTION

Day 20

SPEAK YOUR HEART

*"For God is Spirit, so those who worship him
must worship in spirit and in truth."*

John 4:24, NLT

JESUS taught us we cannot worship God with just our thoughts, we must express it in truthful words and Spirit filled words. So, try to always speak right words in worship and everyday life. Avoid using the language of the world that is not acceptable for Christians. Avoid using language that interferes with your Christian growth and testimony. Let your speech always reflect your Christian character. Separate yourself from those who curse (Ephesians 4:32). Then Paul tells us, "let your speech always be with grace, seasoned with salt that you may be able to answer everyone"(Colossians 4:6).

Lord, I will give attention to every word I use, and I will carefully guard my speech. Forgive me where I have failed and give me strength to be a strong positive witness for You. Amen.

In light of biblical expectation, it is imperative to use proper language and refrain from vulgar and filthy curse words. When you control your outward speech, you begin to control your inward person. Character is habitually knowing and saying the right thing, in the right way, at the right time, for the right purpose.

Lord, I want to be like Jesus who always said the right thing. Then I want to be like Him when He knew not to speak, He "opened not His mouth." Thank you for my ability to speak, help me to use it for Your glory. Amen.

READ:

John 4:14-30;

Psalm 100:1-5

REFLECTION

Day 21

TRUTHFUL WORDS

"Again, ye have heard that it hath been said by them of old time, thou shalt not forswear thyself, but shalt perform unto the Lord thine oaths: But I say unto you, swear not at all; neither by heaven; for it is God's throne: nor by the earth; for it is his footstool: neither by Jerusalem; for it is the city of the great King."

Matthew 5:33-35, KJV

JESUS elevated the Third Commandment to a higher and positive level. He wanted you to be responsible for every word from your mouth and every inner thought. Why? Because your words – whether spoken or thought – expresses who you are. Your words are you, i.e., your personality, including your emotions, your mind and your power of decision making. There is an old saying, "what's in the well, comes up in the bucket." So, whatever is in your heart comes out of your mouth. Do you take God's name in vain by laughing at God or His name... or making fun of God or the church? The bottom line, reverence God's name and respect Him with words of praise or worship.

Lord, forgive me for every curse word I have said before my conversion, and for every wrongly spoken word about Your name spoken after I was saved. I want my speech to honor You and point others also to honor You. Amen.

Jesus wants you to be in the habit of telling the truth. So, "don't swear at all." He meant any more that simply telling the truth "cometh evil" (v. 37). When you have to add an oath or you have to swear, you admit your normal conversation is not trusted or truthful. It doesn't mean it is wrong to swear in a court of law to tell the truth, it means Christians should be truthful with themselves and with God, and outwardly with people and institution.

Lord, I want to be a truthful person. Give me discipline when I need it and give me mercy and grace until I gain full victory (1 Corinthians 10:13). Help me be a good testimony for You with my words and actions. Amen.

READ:

Matthew 5:1-20, 33-37

REFLECTION

Day 22

A POSITIVE COMMAND TO REST

"Remember to observe the Sabbath day by keeping it holy... For in six days the Lord made the heavens, the earth, the sea, and everything in them; but on the seventh day he rested. That is why the Lord blessed the Sabbath day and set it apart as holy."

Exodus 20:8, 11, NLT

THE Fourth Commandment begins with a positive admonition. The first three were negative telling you what not to do. Why? Because God wanted this Fourth Commandment to be a positive benefit to His people, so they could rest, and worship Him. That is why this Commandment is blessed and hallowed by the Lord your God. Israel was to stop working an spend the whole day with God. They could spend six days doing what the had to do, or what they wanted to do... but this was God's day.

Lord, thank You for saving me and calling me to service You. I dedicate Sunday to worship You in a special way. I will make it Your day and serve You, and bring my offerings to You, and worship. Amen.

You and your family – including children – should celebrate the Sabbath as did our Savior. "So, He (Jesus) came to Nazareth, where He had been brought up. And as His custom was, He went into the synagogue on the Sabbath day, and stood up to read" (Luke 4:16). The key phrase "as His custom." Do you have a custom of going to church on Sunday, do your children? I, Elmer Towns the writer of this devotion began Sunday school the week I entered the first grade, and I did not miss a Sunday for

12 years after graduation from high school. It was not me, but a godly Sunday school teacher and the persistence of my mother.

Lord, I will rest on the Sabbath as Jesus did both as a boy and an adult. I will worship You and put You first on Sunday, and every other day. I will take my children (if I have them) to church on Sunday. Amen.

READ:

Luke 4:1-21

REFLECTION

Day 23

REMEMBER

"So, the creation of the heavens and the earth and everything in them was completed. On the seventh day God had finished his work of creation, so he rested from all his work. And God blessed the seventh day and declared it holy, because it was the day when he rested from all his work of creation."

Genesis 2:1-3, NLT

THE Fourth Commandment begins with a command – *remember*. We need to remember what God did on the seventh day of creation; it will tell us how to celebrate Sunday. He celebrated by taking off from work, we should follow His example. We should work diligently when we work, and when the task is finished – *rest*. "In six days, the LORD made the heavens and the earth" (Exodus 20:11). Therefore, before you think about less work, plan to follow God's example of putting work first. Notice the "six day limit," God planned His work so should you. Then God didn't quit early, no; He completed the task. Finally, "He rested," God knew when to stop and rest.

Lord, thank You for giving me a positive example of work. Give me a desire to work, and give me intelligence to do a good job. Then give me strength to finish my work. And when I finish, give me rest, to go do it again. Amen.

You should remember how God worked? Because some work compulsively – work smart. Some work only for money – work six days to please God. Some work for promotion (i.e., the boss) – work for God. Some are lazy, God says "Do all your work" (Exodus 20:9). Some cut corners! Follow God's example, He finished" (Genesis 2:1).

Lord, give me the right motivation about my secular job. Give me the right attitude toward money. Give me a passion to do all my work to please You. Amen.

READ:

Genesis 1:1-2:3

REFLECTION

Day 24

THE SEVENTH DAY

"You have six days each week for your ordinary work, but the seventh day is a Sabbath day of rest dedicated to the Lord your God."

Exodus 20:9-10, NLT

THE Lord's Day is more than catching up on sleep. Remember, Christianity is a relationship with God (more than keeping rules, etc.). So, for six days you work as God worked six days, and you rest one day as God did. First, it is restoration rest, you give your body a chance to get back its strength and vitality. Second, rest gets you away from stress, deadlines and a fussy boss and cantankerous follow workers. Third, rest is enjoying victory. When Jesus said, "Take My yoke and learn from Me... you will find rest (Matthew 11:29). Finish work for the day... for the week... or just completing a task, and you are victorious. Fourth, it's a picture of eternal rest. "Blessed are they who die in Me... they rest" (Revelation 14:13).

Lord, thank You for inner spiritual rest, preparing me to serve You again. Thank You for physical rest, preparing me to work again. I look forward to rest in heaven with You. Thank You for being my rest. Amen.

Rest is beneficial, it prepares you for the future. Also, rest will make you obedient to follow God's example on the seventh day. Resting on the Lord's Day is an opportunity to worship God. One of the meanings of the word worship is serving God with praise. So, rather than serving your earthly boss, or serving your financial needs, Sunday is the day to serve God.

Lord, I look forward to Sunday. I will go to Your house, and worship You with hymns, offerings and Christian service. Thank You for giving us a day of rest and worship. I will follow Your example in all ways. Amen.

READ:

Hebrews 4:1-16

REFLECTION

Day 25

JESUS' VIEW OF THE SABBATH

"One Sabbath day as Jesus was walking through some grainfields, His disciples broke off heads of grain, rubbed off the husks in their hands, and ate the grain. But some Pharisees said, 'Why are You breaking the law by harvesting grain on the Sabbath?'... And Jesus added, 'The Son of Man is Lord, even over the Sabbath.'"

Luke 6:1-2, 5, NLT

THERE will always be the legalist who will complain what believers do on Sunday. Jesus had the same opposition. His disciples picked grain and ate it because they were hungry (Matthew 12:1). Legalistic Pharisees complained to Jesus. Jesus used the example of David eating the shewbread in the Tabernacle that was unlawful. If David – their spiritual hero – they could do it. Then Jesus said. "The Son of Man is Lord of the Sabbath." Here Jesus the Lawgiver is claiming control over the Sabbath.

Lord, may I look beyond the law to You who is the Lawgiver. Teach me to please You before everything I do. Amen.

"On another Sabbath day, a man with a deformed right hand was in the synagogue while Jesus was teaching. The teachers of religious law and the Pharisees watched Jesus closely. If he healed the man's hand, they planned to accuse him of working on the Sabbath. But Jesus knew their thoughts. He said to the man with the deformed hand, 'Come and stand in front of everyone.' So, the man came forward. Then Jesus said to his critics, 'I have a question for you. Does the law permit good deeds on the Sabbath, or is it a day for doing evil? Is this a day to save life or to destroy it?' He looked around at them one by one and then said to the man, 'Hold out your hand.' *So*, the man held out his hand, and it was restored!" (Luke 6:6-10 NLT).

Lord, keep me from being a legalist who is more interested in keeping the law. I surrender to Jesus and will do what He tells me to do. Help me look to Jesus in all I do. Amen.

READ:

Luke 6:1-11

REFLECTION

Day 26

SABBATH A SHADOW OF CHRIST

*"So, don't let anyone condemn you for what you eat or drink,
or for not celebrating certain holy days or new moon ceremonies or Sabbaths.
For these rules are only shadows of the reality yet to come.
And Christ himself is that reality."*

Colossians 2:16-17, NLT

JESUS taught the original meaning of the Sabbath, or Lord's Day. Jesus said, "The Sabbath was made for man, and not man for the Sabbath" (Mark 2:27). The purpose was for man to worship God. Legalist come along and change the meaning of Sabbath. To them the Sabbath and its law was everything. But God gave the Sabbath to bless His people. They could sing hymns of praise to God, give offerings, and worship Him. Nothing is better than worship. So, Sabbath is God's gift to His people. It is not about stopping work, it's about beginning worship. It is not about words written on paper; it is about Jesus the eternal Word.

Jesus, I look forward to worshiping You on the Lord's Day. I will join with Your people to worship and praise You. Thank You for a day to set aside work, and put my emphases on my relationship with You. Amen.

Paul said, "Let no man enslave you" (Colossians 2:16, *ELT*). He is telling believers Christianity is not about rituals, rites, ceremonies, or legalism (Colossians 2:16). Those rules are a shadow of the reality to come – Jesus Christ (Colossians 2:17). The difference between a shadow and the object that causes the shadow are evident. Those rules in the Old Testament were to announce the coming of Christ. So, spend your Sundays in worshiping and serving Jesus Christ.

Jesus, thank You for all Your pictures and predictions in the Old Testament of Your coming. I love them and study them, because they tell me about You. But I love even more talking to You, and listening to You as You speak through Scriptures. Amen.

READ:

Colossians 2:1-7;

Hebrews 7:1-14

REFLECTION

Day 27

FINISH YOUR WORK

"You have six days each week for your ordinary work, but the seventh day is a Sabbath day of rest dedicated to the Lord your God. On that day no one in your household may do any work. This includes you, your sons and daughters, your male and female servants, your livestock, and any foreigners living among you."

Exodus 20:9-10, NLT

WHEN you study the Fourth Commandment, don't spend all your energy studying the cessation of work. Remember, God ordained work. The command was to work for six days. It began when God commanded Adam to tend the Garden of Eden (Genesis 2:15 ff). Proverbs teaches you to work to harvest food (Proverbs 6:6-11). Jesus commended five wise virgins who worked diligent, and condemned the lazy or foolish virgins (Matthew 25:1-13). We are to obey our employers and work diligently (Colossians 3:22-25). Paul also warns about a man who would not work (1 Timothy 5:8).

Lord, thank You for giving me a job to work, and the ability to do it so, and a desire to please You with my faithful secular work. I will also please You with my faithful ministry in my church, and neighborhood. Amen.

The primary giving of the Fourth Commandment was worship on the Lord's Day. But there is a necessary truth that backs it up, i.e., God's people are commanded to work faithfully for six days. (1) Working diligently (Exodus 20:4), (2) work energetically on all you are to do (Exodus 20:11), (3) finishing what you began or were assigned (Genesis 2:1), (d) then rest (Exodus 20:11).

Lord, help me to work to please You, whether in secular or church ministry. Help me do a good job, and help me do all that is required of me. Help me finish on time and complete the job. Then I will rest. Amen.

READ:

Colossians 3:1-4:6

REFLECTION

_____
_____
_____
_____
_____
_____
_____
_____
_____

Day 28

TO HONOR IS TO OBEY

"Honor thy father and thy mother: that thy days may be long upon the land which the Lord thy God giveth thee."

Exodus 20:12, KJV

"For Moses said, honor thy father and thy mother; and, whoso curseth father or mother, let him die the death."

Mark 7:10, KJV

WHAT does *honor* mean? It means as much as honoring your country's flag and President – and more. We salute our flag and stand for our President, but honoring your parents means much more. The word honor means "heavy," i.e. it is a heavy weight of obligation. When you pick up some lumber, it is heavy on your shoulders – you know it is there. So, it's not always easy to honor your parents – its heavy – but it is worth doing. Honor means... obey them... respect them... put them first. When children honor their parents, they are learning the lesson of putting themselves second. The apostle Paul remembers this higher meaning, "Obey your parents" (Ephesians 6:1).

Lord, thank You for my parent., I couldn't praise You for anything if it were not for them. Forgive me when I didn't honor them or obey them. Help me be a faithful parent so I can teach my children to honor and obey You. Amen.

Paul added "obey" to this command, "for this is right" (Ephesians 6:1). Then quickly Paul adds "Honor thy father and mother... thou mayest live long on the earth" (Ephesians 6:3). He adds "live long" because an obedient child will obey their boss at work, and obey their government, and all others with authority over them. This commandment is about authority. Those who are obedient to all human authority can become obedient to God.

Lord, help me to learn obedience so well I can teach it to my children. I will be obedient to You, and then reflect that obedience by obeying those over me at work and in the government. Amen.

READ:

Deuteronomy 6:1-18;
Ephesians 6:1-9

REFLECTION

Day 29

OBEDIENCE BRINGS LONG LIFE

"Honor your father and mother. Then you will live a long, full life in the land the Lord your God is giving you."

Exodus 20:12, NLT

"Children, always obey your parents, for this pleases the Lord."

Colossians 3:20, NLT

OBEYING you parents is wonderful, but honoring them is even greater. Obedience is your outward behavior, but honoring comes from the inward attitude and self-perception. Honoring is more than making a speech or giving compliments. Honoring is obeying to please your parents and living the way they live – it is becoming like them. If children honor their parents when growing up, and treat their children the same way, their children will honor them. It is all about building a relationship of love. Thus, a relationship of love is foundation for the child to have a relationship with Jesus Christ and when the child is grown, they can have a love-relationship within their marriage and seek a love-relationship with Christ and His church.

Lord, I will honor You first in all things. Then honor my parents. When I get married, I will teach my children to honor You and for them to honor me as their parent. Amen.

Obeying and honoring is all about relationship. But deeper than that, it is all about authority. We honor God because He has authority over us, and we form a relationship of salvation with Jesus

Christ and obey Him. Then as parents we have the responsibility to raise our children according to Scriptures, the child must learn to obey their parents as a reflection of their obedience to God. The best picture of all obedience is when children and parents walk in relationship to their God.

Lord, thank You for saving me and allowing me to walk in a love-relationship with You. Help me to pattern that love-relationship to my children. I will pray for them... teach them... guide them... and give them an example of walking in obedience to You and living in relationship with You. Amen.

READ:

Colossians 3:12-25

REFLECTION

Day 30

EXAMPLE OF JESUS

*"Didn't you know that I must be in my Father's house?...
Then he returned to Nazareth with them and was obedient to them.
And his mother stored all these things in her heart."*

Luke 2:49, 51, NLT

"Jesus replied...God says, 'Honor your father and mother.'"

Luke 18:20, NLT

JESUS repeated the Fourth Commandment, "honor your father and mother," but He added an explicit way to do it – obey. He could tell us to obey because He did it. When Jesus was 12 years old, He went with His parents in the Temple. They started home with Him, and He was separated from them. After three days they found Him. He was not disobedient, but He told them, "I must be about My Father's business" (Luke 2:49, KJV). Then they returned home as the Bible adds, "He was obedient to them" (Luke 2:51, NLT). What a great example for all children today – especially those who think they know better than their parents – Jesus is an example in all things even in His boyhood obedience to His earthly parents.

Lord, I thank You for the example of Jesus' obedience to His parents. Forgive me when I was disobedient to my parents. Help me love and teach my children so they will be obedient to me and to You. Amen.

Jesus was not only obedient to His earthly parents in His boyhood, He also was obedient to His heavenly Father during His ministry on earth. When He was challenged by unbelievers, Jesus replied, "I do nothing on My own, but only what the Father taught me" (John 8:28, *NLT*). Then to amplify His obedience to the Father, Jesus said, "I always do what pleases Him" (John 8:29, *NLT*). Jesus lived out the meaning of the Fourth Commandment, thus giving Him the authority to tell us to do it.

Lord Jesus, because You believed in the Fourth Commandment and preached it, I will obey it until I am married. Then I will teach it to my children. Amen.

READ:

Luke 18:18-29;
John 8:39-52

REFLECTION

Day 31

FAMILY

"Honor your father and mother. Then you will live a long, full life in the land the Lord your God is giving you."

Exodus 20:12, NLT

NOTICE the Fifth Commandment is not aimed at parents to love their children, or respect them. Because the Lord gave parents a natural love for their children. When God created Adam and Eve, He instructed them to "reproduce themselves," and gave them the ability to do so. But also, God gave parents a love for their children to provide for them and protect them. God also knew the family's natural environment would be where parents as role models could influence them. The home is where positive lessons are both *caught* and *taught*. Note also, God did not tell parents to obey or honor their children, but He reversed the order. God built the natural relationship within the family, because He created the family.

Lord, thank You for giving parents love for their children, and thank You for the provision and protection I receive from my parents. May I show my appreciation by looking and caring for my children. Amen.

Because God told children to honor their parents, that suggests He wanted fathers and mothers to be honor-worthy. They must do more than try to be godly examples, they must sacrificially do and give their children all the godly advantages to make them like God. Then the *rebellious* child would see all the reasons why they should obey and honor their parents. Remember the parents are under the authority of God, and their children are under the authority of *Mom* and *Dad*.

Lord give me eyes to see beyond myself and my selfish desires. Help me see all the sacrifice my mother and father made for me. I honor them now. In the future, I will love and sacrifice for my children to help them honor You and me. Amen.

READ:

Proverbs 4:1; 13:24; 20:7; 22:6; 23:22

REFLECTION

Day 32

PROMISE OF LONG LIFE

"Honor your father and mother. Then you will live a long, full life in the land the Lord your God is giving you."

Exodus 20:12, NLT

"If you honor your father and mother, 'things will go well for you, and you will have a long life on the earth.'"

Ephesians 6:3, NLT

THIS is called the First Commandment with *promise*. God promises you will live a long life if you honor your parents. "Things will go well with you, and you will have a long life. There are many reasons for a long life. The key is authority, when youth fight authority (of parents and others), their rebellious attitude towards life will get them in trouble at school, work, the neighborhood, and with the government. Maybe social retaliation will shorten their life... maybe ulcers or other health problems related to stress... maybe lack of good social relationships. Maybe spiritual reasons, like God doesn't' put a hedge around their life to protect them from the evil one.

Lord, if I could grow up again, I would be more honoring of my parents. Now I will seek a spiritual relationship with my children, so they may have a long life. Amen.

It seems Paul also explained the additional promise. "Things will go well with you" (Ephesians 6:3). That means your present life will be better when you honor and obey your parents. Yes, you are promised a long life, but also, an enjoyable life. That phrase could be a comparative example. If you honor and obey your parents, your life will be better than expected, considering the problems in your environment or in your physical body.

Lord I look to You to live as long as You intend. But I also look for a productive life and I look for a faithful life of ministry. Bless me, use me. I honor and obey my parents. Amen.

READ:

1 Kings 3:5-15;

Deuteronomy 6:12;

Psalm 91:1-16 (emphasis on verse 16).

REFLECTION

Day 33

WHY HONOR?

"Children obey your parents because you belong to the Lord, for this is the right thing to do. Honor your father and mother. This is the first commandment with a promise: If you honor your father and mother, things will go well for you, and you will have a long life on the earth. Fathers do not provoke your children to anger by the way you treat them. Rather, bring them up with the discipline and instruction that comes from the Lord."

Ephesians 6:1-4, NLT

YOU should honor your parents because they made a decision to give your physical life. You received everything from your parents at birth. When you examine a young child, it is difficult to determine from which parent they got their personality. Then think of the first necessities of life – shelter, clothing, and food – you would not have lived without these, if it was not for your parents. Beyond that they protected you, gave you direction. And let's not forget correction, every child needs to learn lessons from mistakes, telling lies, and rebellion. But don't forget correction with love and support from parents. The greatest need of every child is love, and its only natural for a mother and father to love each child.

Lord, I thank You for my mother and father... what they sacrificed for me... did for me... taught me and loved me. I honor them. Help me to do as much for my children and more. Amen.

When you honor your parents it is about them, and not yourself. This First Commandment with promise guarantees you will have a better life. That may mean happier and productive, not necessarily richer. You will also, live longer, and that means longer than expected when you were born. So, when you go against your selfish desire, you make it possible for God to do something for you that would not have happen if you remain in your old selfish ways. Supposed you get ten percent longer to life because you obeyed and honored your parents – isn't this reason enough to do it?

Lord keep me from being selfish. I respect my parents... honor them... obey them...and thank You for them. Help me be a parent worthy of honor. Amen.

READ:

Matthew 15:3-9

REFLECTION

Day 34

OBEY YOUR PARENTS

*"Children obey your parents in the Lord: for this is right.
Honor thy father and mother; which is the first commandment with promise;
That it may be well with thee, and thou mayest live long on the earth."*

Ephesians 6:1-3, KJV

WHAT does Paul mean when he said, "Obey your parents in the Lord?" Does it mean if your parents are not saved, you don't have to obey them? Does it mean if children turn against God, they don't need to obey their parents? Some say the Ten Commandments don't apply to unsaved parents. But obedience is not about faith, it is about authority. God expects respect, protection and order in all realms of life – government, church, business and the home. God wants everyone to honor their parents for all they do and have done for the child. A child's obedience will determine if they become a good citizen or even a good Christian, and eventually good church members. But it comes back to authority. The child is not just obeying parents, they are being prepared to live in a society of law and order. But ultimately it comes back to learning obedience and honor of God.

Lord, thank You for all those who have taught me obedience. Thank You for parents, teachers, and others. Forgive me for my lawless thoughts. Teach me obedience to Your authority. Amen.

Remember the two promises for obedience. First, "things will go well with you" (Ephesians 6:3). Examine the reasons that makes you miserable and those that make you happy. Does it have to do with obedience and honoring God? Then second, you will live longer. How long? That is between you and God.

Lord teach me obedience, first and foremost to You. Then to my boss, my government and finally to myself. Give me a desire to obey You and give me strength to complete that desire. Amen.

READ:

Psalm 128:1-6

REFLECTION

Day 35

MURDER

*"I will require the blood of anyone who takes another person's life...
anyone who murders a fellow human must die... For God made
human beings in his own image."*

Genesis 9:5-6, NLT

"You must not murder."

Exodus 20:13, NLT

LONG before God gave the Sixth Commandment against murder, He had said the same thing to Noah. After the flood, God established a law against murder, i.e., if someone murdered another, the one killing must be put to death. The principle is sanctity of human life. Life is precious because humans were created in the image of God. Therefore, the positive application, "treat other humans the way you would treat God."

*Lord, murder is terrible. I look forward to living in heaven with You where there will be
no hatred... or killing. Now on this earth, keep me trusting You and keep me safe. Amen.*

The first half of the Ten Commandments (1-5), emphasizes your respect for God and obeying Him. The second half of The Ten Commandments (6-10) emphasizes your relationship to others. It begins by respecting their right to live the life God intended for them. Jesus applied this commandment even to hating a person so much you wanted to kill them. "You have heard that our ancestors were told, 'you must not murder"... but I say, if you are even angry..." (Matthew 5:21-22, NLT). Therefore, apply Jesus' interpretation, "Don't even be angry enough to plan to kill them."

Lord deal with the core of my heart. I confess to being angry in the past. Don't let me lose my temper. May I pray for each person I meet, and may I desire to help each person find Your love for them. To do this, I will love them... for You. Amen.

READ:

Genesis 9:1-28;

Matthew 5:1-26

REFLECTION

Day 36

A SIN TO MURDER

"You must not murder."

Exodus 20:13, NLT

"Thou shalt not kill."

Exodus 20:13, KJV

IN high school I got into a big argument with a friend because I went deer hunting. I was accused of breaking the Sixth Commandment because I killed a deer. No matter how much I talked, we were not reconciled. But the Hebrew word is murder, not killing an animal. Think of all the animals killed for a sacrificial offering to God in the Old Testament. God loves every person born (John 3:16), Christ died for all (1 John 2:2), and He wants all to live with an opportunity to receive Christ as Savior.

> *Lord, I know it is wrong to murder, or even have anger. Forgive me every time I have sinned with my anger. Give me a heart for people to love them, pray for them, and may I try to get them saved. Amen.*

Cain killed his brother Abel (Genesis 4:8), and God confronted him. It was wrong then, and it is still wrong today in God's sight. Also, murder is wrong according to the law of the United States. But look at God's other side. He forgives murderers who repent, and their sins are covered by Jesus' blood (1 John 1:7). Saul of Tarsus was a religious zealot who "went house to house, dragging out both men and women to throw them into prison" (Acts 8:3). He also "breathing threats and murder" (Acts 9:1, RSV). Paul called himself "the chief of sinners" (1 Timothy 1:15), yet God used him in a great way, greater than any thing he expected.

Lord, I confess my past times of anger. Forgive me. Thank You for the blood of Christ that cleanses all sin – including all of mine. Amen.

READ:

Acts 8:1-3, 9:1-31

REFLECTION

Day 37

YOU MUST NOT MURDER

"You must not murder."

Exodus 20:13, NLT

"You have heard that our ancestors were told, 'You must not murder. If you commit murder, you are subject to judgment.' But I say, if you are even angry with someone, you are subject to judgment! If you call someone an idiot, you are in danger of being brought before the court. And if you curse someone, you are in danger of the fires of hell."

Matthew 5:21-22, NLT

THERE are many reasons why murder is wrong. First, because everyone has the image and likeness of God, murder is a sin against God. So, capital punishment was not something government thought up. No, it came from God. A second reason is murder is a crime against society. If a person murders someone, you might be next. So, people vote to punish those who murder to protect all people in that society and themselves. Originally, America made murder a violation of God's moral code, but today America and most other civilized nations make it a violation of constitutional law.

Lord, thank You for life and that no one has taken my life from me, and I freely serve You. I pray for a safe nation to live and work and worship. Use preachers, law enforcement officers and the judicial system to make my nation safe for me and for all others. Amen.

The Sixth Commandment prohibits anything or anyone who shortens or snuffing out the life of another. When someone unintentionally kills another, that is called manslaughter, usually a lessor degree of punishment. During Bible times if you unintentionally committed a crime (murder), you could run to a city of refuge for safety and protection (Joshua 21:1-4). Remember, Jesus said murderers could be forgiven (Matthew 12:31, Mark 3:28) when the guilty one repents and asks to be cleanses by the blood of Jesus.

Lord, I believe life is precious because it comes from You. Protect my life, and the life of all my family. I pray mercy for those guilty of manslaughter. I pray all murders will turn to You for salvation, because Jesus who was murdered on a cross died for them. Amen.

READ:

Matthew 5:21-22;

Romans 13:9;

Genesis 9:1-7

REFLECTION

Day 38

SEEKING WORSHIP

"You must not murder."

Exodus 20:13, NLT

"The Father is looking for those who will worship Him... for God is Spirit, so those who worship him must worship in spirit and in truth."

John 4:23-24, NLT

To understand why it is wrong to kill a person, look at the purpose why God created people. The Lord God made man in His likeness and image, with the power of intellect, emotion, will, self-perception and self-direction (Genesis 2:7). More than offerings, holy living or anything else, God wants worship from every person. "The Father seeks worship" (John 4:23). When a person is killed, they are no longer able to obey God and worship Him. Murder destroys the whole reason God placed people on this earth. How does God feel when someone is taken away by murder? They cannot worship Him any longer. That is why God said, "Murderers, sexually immoral... shall all have their part in the lake that burns with fire and brimstone" (Revelation 21:8).

Lord, I come giving all worship to You. I pray that all on earth would worship You before they maybe killed on earth. Thank You for the invitation to worship You. Amen.

Since God hates murder, it is only natural Jesus would tell us the source of murder, "The devil...he was a murderer from the beginning" (John 8:44). Since you are a mirror that reflects God's image, it is only natural that satan would try to hurt you and all people. He wants to destroy God, so he wants to destroy all people made in God's image. Satan wants to take away the opportunity of every person to worship the Father. Satan is against everything the Father stands for.

Lord, thank You for creating me after Your image and likeness. I pray against all murderers and against the work of satan. I pray for as many as possible to be saved and worship You. I pray against murderers, but I want them to eventually be saved as You saved the apostle Paul and other murderers who have turned to You. Amen.

READ:

John 4:4-26, 8:34-47

REFLECTION

Day 39

MURDER IN GOD'S SIGHT

"You must not murder."

Exodus 20:13, NLT

"The Lord accepted Abel and his gift, but he (God) did not accept Cain and his gift. This made Cain very angry... Cain suggested to his brother, 'Let's go out into the fields'...Cain attacked his brother Abel and killed him."

Genesis 4:4-5 8, NLT

FIRST degree murder is when someone intentionally plans to kill another person. Other acts of murder, <u>suicide</u> is a form of murder, but not killing another, but intentionally taking your own life. <u>Genocide</u> is targeting and eliminating a group of people. <u>Euthanasia</u> is taking the life of an elderly or terminally ill person by giving a lethal injection of medicine. Anytime you have pushed aside God's decision on a persons' life is wrong. Remember each person is an image and likeness of God. The real reason why murder is wrong always comes back to God and His plan for each person. When God says, "I have a plan for you" (Jeremiah 29:11), it doesn't mean to shorten your life.

Lord, I come thanking You for life and the God who created life, and the Lord in whose image I was made. I praise Jesus who died for me that I might live. Give me a deeper respect for the life of others and I will pray for their salvation. Amen.

There are unintentional acts that shorten life, things we never intended to lead to an earlier death. Cigarettes can take approximately 6 years off your life, so can excessive alcohol addiction. What about those who drive dangerously or contract HIV? Anorexia, or overeating resulting in obesity?

Lord, my life is a treasured gift from You. I may not have a perfect body, but I believe it is Your temple and You live in me. May my body be a testimony to You and Your goodness to people. Amen.

READ:

Genesis 4:1-12;

Jeremiah 29:11-13

REFLECTION

Day 40

LOVE YOUR NEIGHBOR

"Jesus replied, 'You must love the Lord your God with all your heart, all your soul, and all your mind.' This is the first and greatest commandment. A second is equally important: 'Love your neighbor as yourself.'"

Matthew 22:37-39, NLT

OBVIOUSLY, the Lord want you to love Him with all your heart, soul, mind and your physical body. But look at the bottom line, "love God as your love yourself." Two truths you must love, God with all your material and immaterial life. So, the last devotional we asked the question, "when you practice habits or actions, or diet, that shortens your life, is this a form of self murder? So, step one says, love God and give your self to Him unconditionally. But look at that second condition, "love others" Obviously this rules out murderer. Anyone who murders another is committing a double crime. First, they murder another, then they violate the second half of the greatest commandment, they don't love their brother, they murdered him.

Lord, I love You more today that yesterday or any day in the past. Forgive me for any faults or sins. Give me strength to love You even more tomorrow. And Lord, I pray for my neighbors that they will be motivated to love You with all their hearts. Amen.

Loving your neighbor is a basic foundation for a Christian testimony to others. Loving your neighbor means praying for them and doing good deeds. While the Ten Commandments is negative telling you not to murder your neighbor, the greatest commandment is positive. It tells you to love them! How much love? Enough to get them to follow Christ... enough to motivate them to grow in Christ and serve Christ... enough to change their life and yours. And won't your life be changed if you love all your neighbors that way?

Lord, teach me to love as You love me and gave Yourself for me. I want to love my neighbors and motivate them to get saved and serve You. Transform my prayer life so I can do more for You. Teach me to believe for greater things in the future. Amen.

READ:

Luke 10:25-37

REFLECTION

Day 41

KILLING AND MURDER, IS THERE A DIFFERENCE?

"What? know ye not that your body is the temple of the Holy Ghost, which is in you, which ye have of God, and ye are not your own?"

1 Corinthians 6:19, KJV

THE greatest truth about Christianity is not just doctrine taught in the Bible. Yes, doctrine is great, but the transforming truth is Christ lives in you (Colossians 1:27). Because He lives in you, and controls your life, you should never get angry enough to murder anyone. Christ should control your temper, and everything else. Someone asked, "Can a Christian be a soldier and kill the enemy?" There is a world of difference between a solider *killing* in defense of his nature and the word *murder*, which is intentionally planning to kill another. A Christian can be soldiers who defends their country against an enemy and the evil anger aims of one who hates so much they murder.

Lord, help me clearly understand the difference between murder and killing. Keep me from ever taking another's life. I will follow You and serve You. Amen.

You should never kill another person, for that one may be a Christian. You have destroyed their usefulness and continued ministry for Christ. You have destroyed one though whom Christ may work. But also, if the one you murdered is not a Christian, then that person will go to hell and after death there is no second chance. As we live in a society that seems to be less and less godly, we will often face the truth of murder and what to do. But hopefully you will not experience it.

Lord, thank You for including the Sixth Commandment in the Bible. I believe it and will live according to its expectations. Protect me, yet not my will but thine be done. Amen.

READ:

Colossians 1:9-14, 25-29

REFLECTION

Day 42

TRANSFORMING MURDERS

"He will wipe every tear from their eyes, and there will be no more death or sorrow or crying or pain. All these things are gone forever."

Revelation 21:4, NLT

"But cowards, unbelievers, the corrupt, murderers,... fate is in the fiery lake of burning sulfur. This is the second death."

Revelation 21:8, NLT

THAT is a terrible condemnation – all murderers will go to hell. But look on the better side, God forgives murderers. It begins with the principle. "The blood of Jesus... cleanse from all sin" (1 John 1:7, NLT). The word all means all. Beyond the principle of forgiveness of sins, there is the practice of forgiving murderers. Jesus looked from the cross to the thief crucified beside Him, giving the promise to those who repent. "Today, you will be with Me in paradise" (Luke 23:43). Even those who were crucifying Jesus could be called murderers. He said to them, "Father, forgiven them, for they know not what they do"(Luke 23:34).

Lord, You are a gracious Father to forgive even those who crucified Your Son. Forgive me for the times I have been angry with people. Amen.

There is forgiveness for another murderer who hated. "Saul was uttering threats with every breath and was eager to kill the Lord's followers" (Acts 9:1, NLT). Before the apostle Paul was transformed by Jesus, he was ready to kill God's servants. Since God completely transformed Paul, he can do the same for anyone who calls on the name of Jesus. Therefore, pray for the conversion of murderers, rather than asking God to judge them. How has God transformed you?

Lord thank You for transforming the apostle Paul. Do in my life the supernatural work You did for Paul. I praise You for Your forgiveness...Your mercy...Your power...Your love for all sinners. Amen.

READ:

Revelation 8:1-8;

Acts 8:1-4; 9:1-22

REFLECTION

Day 43

YOUR BODY SHALL BE GOD'S SANCTUARY

"Thou shalt not commit adultery."

Exodus 20:14, KJV

"Run from sexual sin! No other sin so clearly affects the body as this one does. For sexual immorality is a sin against your own body. Don't you realize that your body is the temple of the Holy Spirit, who lives in you and was given to you by God? You do not belong to yourself, for God bought you with a high price. So, you must honor God with your body."

1 Corinthians 6:18-20, NLT

BEFORE we look at the negative side of adultery, look at the positive side of sex and your body. God created Adam into a human body that was able to reproduce itself into another human who could also reproduce. God created the human body for many uses, i.e., to learn... to work... to interact with family, friends and eventually to marry and reproduce. But the ultimate purposed of the human body was to receive God's love and in turn worship Him. God wanted humans to worship and serve Him through their body. But most of all God wanted to live in the human body as His sanctuary. The positive view of the Seventh Commandment is "your body shall be My sanctuary." The concept of sanctuary is among the most beautiful in the Bible, whether it is the human sanctuary, or the Tabernacle in the wilderness, the Temple in Jerusalem, or the church scattered around the world.

Lord, thank You for indwelling my body when I accepted Christ and was saved. Thank You for forgiveness, but even greater; thank You that I can be holy because the Holy Spirit indwells me, and I can be spiritual because the Holy Spirit ministers to and through me. Amen.

Human sex that reproduces a human being is another beautiful thing. But sex outside of a love-relationship in marriage is wrong for many reasons (see next devotions). But the primary reason is the human body is God's sanctuary. He brings glory to Himself through your body. But adultery turns the beautiful function of the body into an ugly thing.

Lord, I again surrender my body to You. Once again cleanse me... fill me with Your presence and power. Prepare me for ministry... lead me...use me. Amen.

READ:

1 Corinthians 6:12-20

REFLECTION

Day 44

AVOID ADULTERY

"You must not commit adultery."

Exodus 20:14, NLT

"You shall not have sex with anyone who is not your spouse."

Exodus 20:14, BBJ

THE Seventh Commandment is not just against the negative sin of adultery, it is about personal wholeness and wellness. Jesus reinforced it, "you shall not commit adultery" (Matthew 19:17-18). Avoid adultery because it may produce a human without a "whole" family to give him/her love, clothes, food, education. Also, because the baby conceived in sin, may grow up with that stigma, plus it may lack spiritual role models to guide in proper social growth.

Lord, thank You for the beauty of sex. I will always embrace it according to Your commandments, and I will recognize Your purpose for reproduction of life. I will and I have preserved the beauty of sex for marriage and will glorify You through it. Amen.

God has limited sex to marriage because of what sex outside marriage does to both parties. When one breaks God's commandment, they harden their heart against God, but also against civil law (if it exists), or against human/social expectations. Adultery hardens the human mind to spiritual things. But also, spoils one's emotions to the purity of love. Then, the human will is weakened so that it must give into other sins or break other (civic) or human laws. Finally, their conscience accuses them or is hardened (Romans 2:15; Hebrews 3:13).

Lord, I give my body to You again and promise to have a healthy and holy sex life. I want You to be glorified in all I do. Keep Your protective love on me in this area. Amen.

READ:

Proverbs 4:1-17; 18-5:25

REFLECTION

Day 45

WIDER VIEW OF ADULTERY

"But because there is so much sexual immorality, each man should have his own wife, and each woman should have her own husband. The husband should fulfill his wife's sexual needs, and the wife should fulfill her husband's needs."

1 Corinthians 7:2-3, NLT

"You have heard the commandment that says, 'You must not commit adultery.' But I say, anyone who even looks at a woman with lust has already committed adultery with her in his heart."

Matthew 5:28, NLT

JESUS had a much wider view of the Seventh Commandment than the Jews of His day. While the legalist focused on the physical aspect, Jesus taught that adultery was more than a physical act. He said adultery begins in the mind and human heart before it becomes a physical act. He understood the enemy of spiritual faith – satan – can work on the emotions to break down a person's spiritual resistance to adultery. Then the enemy will entice and tempt a person (man or woman) to engage in adultery. With every commandment, God warned of the consequences.

Lord, forgive my every immoral thought or desire. Forgive me and cleanse me to be Your servant. Keep my thoughts pure and wholesome. Teach me how to keep my thoughts on You and do what You command. Amen.

Also, God offers a responsible remedy for each Commandment. In the Seventh Commandment, it is marriage. Even through Jesus wasn't married, He supported it by attending a wedding and approving of it (John 2:1-17). Thus, Jesus continued the Old Testament endorsement. God brought the man and woman together in the Garden of Eden for the first marriage ceremony. "The Lord God brought her to the man... therefore shall a man leave his father and his mother, and shall cleave unto his wife, and they shall be one flesh" (Genesis 2:23-24).

Lord, thank You for the gift of love between a man and woman that leads to marriage. In this negative commandment I see the positive ministry and hope of love. Keep my eyes on love and obedience. Amen.

READ:

Matthew 5:27-30;

Genesis 2:7-25

REFLECTION

Day 46

BEAUTIFUL

"Haven't you read the Scriptures?" Jesus replied. 'They record that from the beginning God made them male and female.' And he said, 'This explains why a man leaves his father and mother and is joined to his wife, and the two are united into one.' Since they are no longer two but one, let no one split apart what God has joined together."

Matthew 19:4-6, NLT

GOD created a beautiful relationship in a marriage of a man and a woman. It is two becoming one flesh. Each marriage is a work in progress, as each becomes more mature and fulfilling. Adultery violates the purpose God intends for each marriage. First, Adam needed a "helpmeet," one to share dreams successes, burden, and failures. Marriage overcome the pain of loneliness. But, second, marriage provided a family setting, when they not only share the pleasures of life, they share the burdens and challenges of raising children. God's promise to Adam and Eve they would be "one flesh" (Genesis 2:2). This meant two things. First, they would be one in spirit and heart, but secondly meant one in flesh, they would produce a child.

Lord, thank You for the gift of marriage with all it's blessings and contributions. Thank You for my father and mother and all they taught me. Help me to pass on to my children all I have learned from my parents, plus all the other positive lessons needed by children. Amen.

Sexual bonding in marriage is not accidental, nor is it incidental. God planned for a safe place for the expression of love and sexuality. God approved of the sexual experience "honoring the sanctity of the marriage vows because the marriage bed should be kept pure. I will punish adulterers and sexually immoral people" (Hebrews 13:4, *BBJ*). So, God speaks on both sides of the issue of sex. It is wrong outside of marriage, but has His blessings inside the wedding vows.

Lord, give me spiritual eyes to see Your Scriptures on marriage and sex. Help me never to abuse it, nor violate it. But Lord, help me to honor You in all I do. Amen.

READ:

Song of Solomon 1:1-2: 17

REFLECTION

Day 47

CLEAN IN MIND AND BODY

"Don't you realize that your bodies are actually parts of Christ? Should a man take his body, which is part of Christ, and join it to a prostitute? Never! And don't you realize that if a man joins himself to a prostitute, he becomes one body with her? For the Scriptures say, "The two are united into one." But the person who is joined to the Lord is one spirit with him."

1 Corinthians 6:15-17, NLT

THERE is an old saying, "cleanliness is next go godliness," and it has a much deeper meaning in relationship to sex. The Corinthians thought they could do anything, epically related to sex but Paul answering them said, "Not everything is good for you" (1 Corinthians 6:12, *NLT*). Then Paul reminded them "you cannot say that your bodies were made for sexual immorality... don't you realize your bodies are actually parts of Christ" (1 Corinthians 6:13-15, NLT). He reminded them their bodies were sanctuaries for God. Therefore "keep your body holy," and we can add, "keep them clean." Being sexually clean within its boundaries actually express your godliness, bringing praise to God, and a positive testimony to everyone.

Lord, thank You for creating my body. I will keep it a clean temple for Your glory, and as a testimony to others. Use me as a positive testimony, and use me in ministry. Amen.

Sex outside of marriage could lead to a sexually transmitted diseases, that will infect your body and your spouse's body as well. It may also infect the new life that is conceived in the sexual act. These diseases may cause more serious complications with all types of neurological problems, congenital abnormalities, etc. It will create family disorder, and community problems. Adultery is direct disobedience to the Word of God.

Lord, keep my family safe from all the physical psychological and financial problems that comes from adultery. I will live a holy, clean life and I will give testimony to Your goodness and keeping power. Amen.

READ:

1 Corinthians 6:9 -7:4

REFLECTION

Day 48

REMEDY NOW (PART 1)

"Walk in the Spirit, and you shall not fulfill the lust of the flesh."

Galatians 5:16

RECOGNIZE that your body is a sanctuary where God dwells. Make a commitment that it will be a healthy body and physically clean. *First*, let the Holy Spirit help you control your physical appetites. We live in a culture that believes "If it feels good, do it!" God wants you to be holy, so let the Holy Spirit control your life. *Second*, avail yourself of God's power by practical habits. (a) pray to be clean and holy, (b) read God's Word, (c) let spiritual people mentor you, (d) choose faith based activities, (3) fill your mind with God's thoughts and spiritual activities. *Third*, recognize how vulnerable you are. James said, "Blessed *is the man who endures temptation; for when he has been approved, he will receive the crown of life*" (James 1:12). Just as you would practice and train for an athletic event, develop a winning attitude so your body is prepared and filled with the Holy Spirit.

Lord, I am committed to living a clean, holy life separated from sexual sins. Guide my thoughts and actions to think like Christ and claim His victory. I will guard myself in sexual matters. Amen.

The fourth reminds you to resist your spiritual enemy – the devil. "by purity... by the Holy Spirit ... by the word of truth... by the power of God... by the armor of righteousness" (2 Corinthians 6:6-7). How should you resist... with you attitude... with your activities... and with your affiliations? When you make those four choices you are on the right path to making your body a sanctuary for God.

Lord, I commit myself to do those four remedies to stay clean and spirit filled for Your glory. Give me strength as my day demands (Deuteronomy 33:25). Amen.

READ:

2 Corinthians 5:11-17; 6:1-17

REFLECTION

Day 49

REMEDY NOW (PART 2)

(Continuation from day 48)

"And what union can there be between God's temple and idols? For we are the temple of the living God. As God said: 'I will live in them and walk among them. I will be their God, and they will be my people.'"

2 Corinthians 6:16, NLT

THE fifth remedy is to guard your heritage. Your family needs more from you than money, shelter and *stuff*. They need your integrity. It comes from focused faith, spiritual choices, godly practices and a tenacious commitment to a godly marriage. So, plan to give your family and children the influences of your spiritual and moral character. Remember, character is habitually doing the right thing in the right way, for the right purpose, at the right time. The sixth remedy is developing a purpose-driven lifestyle. Paul gave us a good start, "For me to live is Christ." (Philippians 1:27). Therefore, live every day for Christ so everyone knows "Christ lives in you and you live in Christ" (John 14:20, *ELT*).

Lord, I want to leave a Christian heritage when I die, or You come for me in the rapture. I pray my spouse and children will live as I have lived, and hopefully do more for You in their life and ministry. Amen.

The sixth remedy is to commit your self to your marriage relationship and then commit your marriage to God. Follow these important steps: (a) confide in your spouse, (b) avoid intimate relationships with the opposite sex, (c) express your sexuality only with in your marriage, (d) put your spouse first, (e) practice random expression of love in many ways. Maybe you have broken the Seventh Commandment in one way or another. Remember, God forgives, those who confess and repents. Begin living the positive purpose in the Seventh Commandment.

Lord, I recommit my marriage to You. Again, I yield myself completely to You to be filled with the Holy Spirit to be guided by a godly attitude. Daily I will practice a clean life. Amen.

READ:

Proverbs 7:1-27

REFLECTION

Day 50

REASONS NOT TO STEAL

"You must not steal."

Exodus 20:15, NLT

"Respect the stuff of others."

Exodus 20:15, ELT

THE traditional *King James Bible* reads, "you shall not," suggesting it was the wrong thing to do. But a closer reading of the text makes it an absolute command, "you must not." Yes, this command recognizes the property rights of others, but there are other factors that intensifies this prohibition. First, the thief became an identified sinner with God. Second, the thief has potentially become an outlaw, breaking local ordinances. Third, the victim who had their "stuff" stolen is suffering loss. Some lives or business have been destroyed when something valuable was stolen from them. Finally, the thief's character has been further harmed, or perhaps destroyed.

Jesus, I know You forgive and can transform thieves because You forgave the thief on the cross beside You who asked for forgiveness. I will see him in Heaven because You promised, "Today, you shall be with Me in paradise." Amen.

Those who have lost "stuff" to a thief are usually angry because they lost a possession. Next, they _____ because they cannot use the stolen item any longer. Third, they usually feel powerless because they cannot get it back. And finally, they lose face or prestige among those who know about the lost them. What can you do when something is stolen from you? Pray Jesus' response, "Father forgive them.'" Then pray for their salvation. "To be with (you) in paradise."

Lord, thank You for all the possession You have allowed me to have. I yield everything to You. Help me use all my possession for Your ministry and glory. Thank You that I am not a thief! Help me stay honest in all things. Amen.

READ:

Matthew 6:19-21,

Luke 23:39-49

REFLECTION

Day 51

WORK NOT STEAL

"So, don't worry about these things, saying, 'What will we eat? What will we drink? What will we wear?' These things dominate the thoughts of unbelievers, but your heavenly Father already knows all your needs. Seek the Kingdom of God above all else, and live righteously, and he will give you everything you need."

Matthew 6:31-33, NLT

JESUS was not against ownership of property and things, nor was He against working extra hard to earn extra money. He commended two diligent workers who doubted their wages by hard work (Matthew 25:14-30). But Jesus did rebuke the lazy worker who had little ambition and little results. It was not how little money; it was the lazy workers attitude that Jesus rejected. In another parable, Jesus commended the laborers working for money (Matthew 20:1-16). But in another occasion, Jesus criticized those giving lots of money to God, but commended the woman who quietly gave very little. Jesus constantly taught priority with money. It is not a matter of having money, the issue is always money having you. Jesus taught His followers to put God first in living for Him.

Lord, sometimes I have been possessed with making money, and I have worried over lack of money to pay my bills. I yield my money management to You. Show me what I have done wrong. I repent. Show me how to properly use my money for Your will for my life. Amen.

Jesus taught His followers to handle their money the way the Father wanted them to spend it, and He would take care of them. They were to seek first God's Kingdom and "all those things will be added to you." (Matthew 6:33). The principle is to yield all you money to God. Then you must tithe first

(Malachi 3:10) and He will show you the bills to pay and where the rest of your money should go. God doesn't want all your money, pay your tithe first, then live on the rest for His glory.

Lord, it is so easy to get in money troubles Forgive me when I have spent my money foolishly, for the wrong things. Teach me biblical stewardship and guide me to honor You with my money. Amen.

READ:

Matthew 6:19-34;

Matthew 25:14-30

REFLECTION

Day 52

WHAT HAVE THEY STOLEN?

"Don't store up treasures here on earth, where moths eat them and rust destroys them, and where thieves break in and steal. Store your treasures in heaven, where moths and rust cannot destroy, and thieves do not break in and steal."

Matthew 6:19-20, NLT

WHEN someone steals your possessions, they take more than items they steal part of your life. An elder of a church was held up at gun point while his wallet was stolen. Later he stood before the church to testify. "I am thankful the thief did not take my life. I can make more money. I am glad he didn't shoot me and leave me an invalid. But most of all, I am trunkful I am not the thief. I have a free conscience before God and free from guilt. Then again, I am free from fear that the police are looking for me as a criminal. Today, you should thank God that you are free from the penalty of sin, because Christ paid the price for your sin.

Lord, I agree with the elder described above. Thank You for saving me from sin. If I have stolen anything ignorantly or intentionally, I will repay. Forgive me. Thank You for a free conscience and for Your mercy and grace. Amen.

When someone steals, they take more than money or things, they steal your reputation, because people might criticize you for not being careful with your money or possessions. They steal your dreams – future, because you cannot use what has been taken. They steal your purpose in life because you cannot use your possessions. Maybe you will get too discouraged to work hard to replace it. Finally, they steal your future because you cannot use it to work, or grow, or become better and stronger.

Lord, I give all my possessions to You. I will use them as You lead me. When someone steals from me, they steal from You. So, everything I am or possess belongs to You, and I will serve You with it all. Amen.

READ:

John 10:6-18;

Ephesians 4:28;

Romans 2:21; 13:9

REFLECTION

Day 53

STEALING FROM GOD

"Now a certain ruler asked Him, saying, 'Good Teacher, what shall I do to inherit eternal life?' 'You know the commandments: 'Do not commit adultery,' 'Do not murder,' 'Do not steal,' 'Do not bear false witness,' 'Honor your father and your mother.'"

Luke 18:18, 20

JESUS reinforced the Ten Commandments. Here He lists five. They are based on a high regard for people, their rights, their property, and their responsibility to God. Jesus teaches you to love others – your neighbors. "You shall love your neighbor as yourself" (Matthew 23:39). You cannot love or respect your neighbors and steal from them. Every person is made in the image of God (Genesis 1:26-27; 2:7). Their image of God gave them certain "rights" because all people are God's subjects, and eventually will answer to Him. Can we say a person who would steal from you will also steal from God? Eventually, they will be punished by God if they don't repent and take Christ as Savior from sin.

Lord, thank You for giving me the privilege of owning money, property and things. I yield them all to You and will use them for Your ministry and glory. Help me love all people as You required, and I will pray for them. Amen.

You should yield all your money to God, giving Him 10% tithe, then use all the rest as God leads and blesses you. Actually, your gift to God is an act of worship. So, when someone steals from you, you cannot carry out your service to God. So, is the thief stealing from God when he steals from you?

God will hold him responsible because the thief is personally guilty for his sin, but the thief also has violated your time of worship and service to God. He has also stolen your privilege and responsivity.

Lord, help me look at possession through Your eyes. Help me use each and every possession to worship You as I use every possession for Your glory. Amen.

READ:

Luke 18:18-34

REFLECTION

Day 54

STEALING MANY WAYS

"You must not steal."

Exodus 20:15, NLT

THERE are many ways to steal, not just a *sneak thief* who breaks into a home and walks off with your possessions. The word *thief* comes from the Old English word "to crouch," which describes "taking illegally, by secret or stealth." (Webster). The sneak thief or burglar takes when no one is watching. But remember Jesus sees everything. The second is stealing by mugging or robbing which means taking violently from the victim. The parable of the Good Samaritan describes the condition of the victim (Luke 10:30-37).

Lord, all stealing is wrong, whether by fraud or by mugging. Help me if and when I face such a situation. Protect me and use me to be a testimony to all. I pray for all my friends who have been robbed. Amen.

Third, *thief by seizure,* is taking someone's possession using authority or force, either from you or those protecting your money or assets. The next is *thief by deceit*. This is stealing using your credit card, or another assess code of yours. Deceit could be selling something that is advertised by fraud or deception (Proverbs 20:23). Finally, *thief by defrauding*. Webster's says, "to defraud is to deprive someone by deception." This is an Old English word that means "to cheat." Defraud is a student who cheats on an exam, or someone who cheats filling out an application, or by making a promise that you know will not happen.

Lord, guard my old nature so I don't cheat. I want to be honest, so I confess my past conversations that promised things that were not true, or would not happen. Forgive me. I will walk daily in the light so the blood of Christ will forgive and cleanse me (1 John 1:9). Amen.

READ:

Acts 5:1-11;
Luke 18:18-30

REFLECTION

Day 55

GOOD STEWARDS OF MONEY

"Will a man rob God? Yet you have robbed Me!
But you say, 'In what way have we robbed You?'
In tithes and offerings. You are cursed
with a curse, for you have robbed Me."

Malachi 3:8-9

THIS is not a lesson asking you to give a tithe, but an examination of those people who are not obedient with their money. Ananias and Sapphira stole from God. They didn't actually take money out of the offering plate, but were guilty of deception. When Barnabas sold property and gave it to the church, he was praised and esteemed. Ananias wanted the accolades and praise that Barnabas got. So, he sold his property, and only gave part to the church – his sin was also lying. He claimed he gave all the money to God. God struck him dead in front of the church leaders. Pride and greed are terrible sins, especially when tied to deceptive use of money.

Lord, I confess any and all exaggerations I have made about money or property. Forgive me and accept me back into Your fellowship. I don't just promise to repay, I give all to You. I am your servant. I give the tithe and ask You to show me how to spend the rest of my money. Amen.

Can a person who has been deceitful with money ever be used of God? Absolutely! Look at Matthew, one of the 12 disciples. When Jesus saw him setting at the tax table said, "follow Me." Matthew left all to follow Jesus. The legalist complained about Matthew and his friends, calling them "disreputable sinners" and "scum" (Mark 2:15-16). Tax collectors added their high commission to the taxes they collected. Just as Jesus forgave Matthew and accepted him, so He will receive all people who have lied about money and stole to get rich.

Lord, thank You for illustrations in Scriptures of Matthew's transformation of his attitude toward money. Do the same in my heart. I want to be trustworthy in all financial matters. I yield my life, my money, my service and future to You. Amen.

READ:

Acts 4:32 – 5:11;

Mark 2:13-17

REFLECTION

Day 56

WHO CONTROLS YOUR MONEY?

"And he said unto them, take heed, and beware of covetousness: for a man's life consisteth not in the abundance of the things which he possesseth." (v. 15)
"For where your treasure is, there will your heart be also." (v. 34)

Luke 12:15, 34, KJV

WHEN you think of those in the Old Testament who stole money, Achan usually comes to mind. God promised His people they would capture the first and largest city in the Promised Land – it was Jericho. They capture it by faith and obedience. They walked around the time one day for 7 days, and 7 times on the 7th day. God commanded the people to not receive the victor's spoil or anything at all, i.e., money, or possession. It was to be "consecrated to the Lord" (Joshua 6:19). Any guilty person who lusted or kept anything would be "cursed... before the Lord" (Joshua 6:26). Achan and his family took "a Babylonian's garment, and two shekels of silver, and a wedge of gold" (Joshua 7:21). Through a series of circumstance, God revealed to Joshua that Achan was guilty. It wasn't a small crime. It was huge because it was against God. Achan and his family were stoned to death.

Lord, teach me to be honest in big things and little matters. I want Your blessing on my life and my family. I want to be an honest person that is respected by my church and community. Amen.

When it comes to money, you cannot hide it in a "hole under your tent" like Achan. Nor can you hide it in your investment stock or bank account as Ananias and Sapphira. God sees everything, and

He knows all things. Be honest with your money because God will bless you, and meet all your needs. Be a giving person; give to God, give to the church, and give to others. Don't be a stingy taking person. Remember, the picture of two hands clutching money as opposed to the two hands giving money. You can't out give God.

Lord, it is hard to yield all my possessions and money to You. But I surrender all. I want Your presence in my life, and I want Your blessing on my work. I want Your protection on my family, and I want Your guidance throughout life. Amen.

READ:

Joshua 6:10-21 7:1-26

REFLECTION

_____
_____
_____
_____
_____
_____
_____
_____
_____
_____

Day 57

BEARING FALSE WITNESS

"Thou shalt not bear false witness."

Exodus 20:16

WHAT is the worst thing about bearing false witness against your neighbor, or rather; lying to your neighbor, or anyone? First, you hurt your neighbor, or anyone to whom you tell a lie. A lie about money could hurt them financially. A lie about their work habits could get them fired, and potentially a family goes hungry. A lie about some element of danger could harm them physically, or even death. But in a second place, lying hurts those who lie in more than ways than one. They could plan their life on their lie and suffer damage or server losses. It could lead to physical harm, or emotional instability. It could lead to eternal judgment (Revelations 21:8). But don't forget a lie hurts God who is truth. When His children lie, it hurts God's reputation. Also, a lie may hurt some good thing God planned for that person that can no longer be done.

Lord, open my eyes to see Your truth in all situations. Then give me strength to speak the truth I see. Finally, send the Holy Spirit to convict me of sin or lying when I do it. Amen.

A rich young leader in the Jewish community asked Jesus what he had to do to inherit eternal life. Jesus told him not to break the commandments, among them, "thou shalt not bear false witness" (Exodus 20:16). The young man claimed to have kept all the commandments, meaning he was self-deceived about his false goodness and he was blinded by his lie that had not broken any law. Jesus told him, "Sell all... give to the poor... follower Me." The self-deceived young man went away because he had "many possessions" (Matthew 19:22).

Lord, give me spiritual eyes to see and understand truth. Give me spiritual ears to hear and understand any lie that I hear. Give me a gracious heart to deal with the issue Give me the spirit of truth to always tell the truth. Amen

READ:

Matthew 19:16-30

REFLECTION

Day 58

MANY WAYS TO LIE

*"For whatever is in your heart determines what you say.
A good person produces good things."*

Matthew 12:34-35, NLT

THERE are many ways to lie. One of the acceptable ways telling a *white lie*. You tell an untruth that is both good and acceptable to speakers and listeners. The next is *flattery*, sometimes called *political lie*. You tell someone they look healthy when they may actually be suffering an illness. A *sinister lie* is telling an untruth or lie for an evil purpose (Proverbs 17:4). Then a *half lie* is not telling the whole truth, but the intent is to deceive. Sometimes an excuse is a lie, by giving the wrong reasons for either doing or not doing something. In a real sense *hypocrisy* is a lie because the person is misleading others by claiming to be something or someone they are not.

Lord, give me sensitive discernment to realize when others are not telling me the truth. Give me an honest heart to always be who I am, and act the way I should. Keep me from hypocrisy. Amen.

Some people will tell a falsehood to justify themselves, i.e., *justifying lies* usually to protect themselves, trying to make themselves look good in the eyes of another. That is the same thing as a *saving face lie*. Sometime pure propaganda is a lie to confuses an enemy. An *advertising lie* describes a product as newer, better, revised or improved. But the product is not what it advertises. Cheating on an exam, or any way is stealing answers that are not their own. Also, plagiarism is committing the same lie, claiming you wrote a document, when actually someone else did. *Putting a spin* on something misinterpreting a negative situation, to make you look good.

Lord, because lying is so deceitful and can be done in so many ways, keep my heart from doing it and from believing it when others do it to me. Amen.

READ:

Proverbs 12:22;

Leviticus 19:11-12, 35;

Deuteronomy 19:14;

Psalm 101:7

REFLECTION

Day 59

TRUTH TELLERS

"Jesus asked... the words you speak come from the heart—that's what defiles you. For from the heart come evil thoughts, murder... lying, and slander."

Matthew 15:16, 18-19, NLT

WE can learn to be "truth tellers." Jesus said that lies come from the heart. But Jesus is the truth, so we must learn from Him and release His power in our life. Because telling the truth is something we must learn to do. Having an honest character is something we can become and a life we can achieve. Telling the truth is not a convenient reaction you can practice when we need it. Telling the truth is something you are, because truthful people tell the truth. Those who struggle with telling the truth lack integrity and have a weak character. An honest character consistently tells the truth, at all times, in all places, for all reasons... to the glory of God.

Father, my goal in life is to be an honest person who is believed and respected by family, friends and everyone else. Forgive me for each falsehood I have said. I confess my weak self-will and lack of discipline that keeps me from developing integrity. Make me truthful. Amen.

Because God is integrity and truth, it was important for Him to expect, "You shall not bear false witness." The Eighth Commandment stated, "against your neighbor (Exodus 20;16). But primarily your lies are against God because He knows all things. He knows the truth. Those who lie, displease God. Among the seven things God hates, "a lying tongue and a false witness" (Proverbs 6:16-17, 19). Because integrity is paramount with God, let it become imperative to you.

Father, I see Your perfect standards and confess my faults and "stretching the truth." Forgive me again, I have already confessed my problem of not telling the truth in the past. Help me live an honest life that I want for myself. Amen.

READ:

Matthew 15:1-20

REFLECTION

Day 60

LYING

"You must not testify falsely against your neighbor."

Exodus 20:16, NLT

"Always speak truthfully."

Exodus 20:16, ELT

TELLING a lie is not an isolated thing. Jesus included lying as one of the evils of the sinful nature we were born with. "From the heart comes evil thoughts... theft, lying and slander" (Matthew 15:19, NLT). It is only natural for an unsaved person to lie. Lying comes from satan who told a "veiled lie" to Eve in the Garden of Eden to get her to sin (Genesis 3:1-5). Jesus identified satan as the source of lying, "You are the children of your father the devil... there is no truth in him. When he lies, it is consistent with his character; for he is a liar and the father of lies" (John 8:44). Since you were born with a sinful nature with a bent to lying, then "telling the truth" is something you must learn to do.

Father, I confess that I have told lies in the past, but I want to change. When I met Jesus Christ as Savior I repented of my sins and asked Him to live in my heart and transform me. Thank you for a desire to be honest and tell the truth. Amen.

We don't have to quote Scriptures to prove to people we are born with a sinful nature and naturally lie. Look at a little child you know. There were two chocolate cookies on the table, and one is missing.

Ask a little girl if she took one. "No," she emphatically answers. Yet there are crumbs on her hands and chocolate on her mouth. Truthfulness is hard to learn; we know we are not telling the truth. We need to learn truth from Jesus who said, "I am the truth" (John 14:6).

Jesus, I have told many lies, and I know it. Help me live honestly and learn to always tell the truth. Forgive me for every exaggeration and lie I have told. Make me a truth teller. I want to live the truth as You did, and I want You to live in my heart and empower me to always be honest. Amen.

READ:

John 8:30-59

REFLECTION

Day 61

HOW TO BE A TRUTHFUL PERSON

"Stop telling lies. Let us tell our neighbor the truth, for we are all part of the same body... let everything you say be good and helpful, so that your words will be an encouragement to those who hear them."

Ephesians 4:25, 29, NLT

WITH so many different ways to lie, let us commit ourselves to truth-telling. *First*, look to our standard, i.e., Jesus Christ who said, "I am the way the truth and the life" (John 14:6). When He controls our speech, we will speak the truth. *Second*, recognize satan is the sources of lies and Jesus called him "the father of lies" (John 8:44). Third, admit your human nature is deceitful (Romans 3:23), but God can give you a new nature to serve Him and speak for Him. Fourth, let the consequences of lying scare you to tell the truth (Revelations 21:8). Fifth, adapt the strategy Paul gave in today's Scripture by putting away lying and determine to tell the truth... always.

Lord, I admit to lying in the past. Forgive me, but more importantly, make me a truth-teller. Deliver me from being a poor example of my faith. Make me a positive example of You. Amen.

The *sixth* step is to commit yourself to radical discipleship. Follow Jesus who said, "If any of you wants to be my follower, you must give up your own way, take up your cross daily, and follow me" (Luke 9:23, NLT). *Seventh*, walk in forgiveness. When you confess and turn from lying, He will forgive and cleanse you (1 John 1:9). *Eighth*, claim the strength of Jesus Christ who lives in you, to keep you from sin (Philippians 4:13). *Finally*, commit to always telling the truth, to all people at all times.

Lord, help me commit these nine practical steps to my memory and better still, help me keep them as my commitment to You. Give me strength to do what You want me to do, and I know I must do. Amen.

READ:

Ephesians 4:17-32

REFLECTION

Day 62

FOUR STEPS TO LYING

"An evil man with of an evil heart will speak evil things and spread evil results."
Matthew 12:35, ELT

SOMEONE had said there are four steps in telling a lie. First, look at the heart where the lie is produced. A lying heart gives occasion to a lying mouth, meaning a liar intends to lie; perhaps even before a lie pops in his mind or comes out of his mouth. Jesus said, "what comes from inside that defiles you" (Mark 7:20, NLT). So, realize it is possible for anyone to lie in one of the many ways discussed in these devotions on *ways to live*. Those who proudly announce, "I will never tell a lie" may have just proven themselves wrong.

Lord, I want to be honest with You and honest with myself. Give me a passion to always tell the truth and give me the strength to keep that commitment. Keep me from being naive but make me strong in the truth of the gospel in Christ and the Word of God (John 14:6, 17:17). Amen

Step two is to see dishonesty in the heart. In this step an untruth is expressed in your words or deeds. You may tell a lie or sometimes by your silence you may led people to believe a lie, or your silence may communicate a lie. The third step is to misrepresent the truth. Liars know the truth but lead people to believe a lie by their miss representation. The fourth is the liar's attempt to avoid responsibility. They may deny a lie sometimes to hide a lie with another lie. Those who go through these four steps need Jesus in their heart, then they need Jesus to instruct them in truth-telling. Finally, they need Jesus to forgive them, cleanse them, and heal them and let His power make them truth tellers.

Jesus, it is so easy to follow my nature Open my spiritual eyes so I can see my sin. Give me strength to repent and follow Your example. Make me a truth teller. Amen.

READ:

Matthew 12:22-45

REFLECTION

Day 63

LIVE AND SPEAK TRUTH

*"I am the way, the truth and the life, no one comes
to the Father, except through Me."*

John 14:6

THE opposite of lying is telling the truth. A dictionary defines, "truth is that which is consistent with itself, i.e., what it represents, and truth corresponds to reality." Jesus had said He was the truth (John 14:6). When being tried Jesus told Pilate, "To this end I was born... that I shall bear witness to truth, everyone that is of the truth hears My voice" (John 19:37, KJV). Notice those who respond to Jesus are "of the truth." When truth appears with an article "the" it refers to Jesus or the gospel, i.e., the good news. Truth is derived from the character of God; it is what He is and does." It is impossible for God to lie" (Hebrews 6:18), or to deny Himself (2 Timothy 2:13).

Lord, I confess You are the truth, and You know every time I have exaggerate or denied the truth. Forgive me. Give me passion to speak the truth and be a good witness to You. Amen.

Moses realized he could not handle all the problems of the vast number of Ishmaelites coming out of Egypt. He was counseled to delegate some task. He was told to get "men of truth" who could make decisions in his place. What are "man of truth"? Integrity of character, adherence to Israel's values and rules, they had to behave on the outside what they believed on the inside. Why don't you promise to be a "person of truth."

Lord, I will be a person of truth. I believe the truth of the gospel of Jesus who saves those that call on Him. Hallelujah, He has saved me. I believe the teaching and commands of Scriptures and will live by them. Amen.

READ:

John 18:33-40;

Exodus 18:14-27

REFLECTION

Day 64

THE LAST IS THE WORST

"Take heed and beware of covetousness: for a man's life consisteth not in the abundance of the things which he possesseth."

Luke 12:15, KJV

COVETING in knowing what you don't have, then seeing someone else with it and lusting for it; i.e., wanting it so bad you will do anything to get it. These are two words in the original language for coveting. The first definition is "sparked by things seen with your eyes." It deals with the *stuff* that attracts you. The second word deals with your inner desire, i.e., lust. This is what you want and *must have* even before you see your neighbor's possessions (1 John 2:15). These two meanings cover the whole spectrum of The Ten Commandments. The first nine Commandments cover your outward behavior – that disobeys God. This Tenth Commandment deals with inward drives and motivation that makes someone lie... steal... commit adultery... satisfy themselves instead of obeying God.

Lord, I have a sinful heart that pulls me away from You and Your Commandments. Forgive me when I break a Commandment in my thoughts. Give me discipline to obey outwardly Your Commandments. I want to follow You. Amen.

This last Commandment is mostly about *stuff*. You want the things of life that will make you happy. This Tenth Commandment also includes lusting for positions, or relationships and activities that are prohibited. The word *covets* deals with the force within your personality that makes you break the first 9 Commandments. Aren't we motivated to break a law long before we actually do it?

Lord, I have a sinful nature. I confess my weakness to sin. Forgiven me each time I break Your Commandments. I want to live victoriously for You and glorify You with my life. Amen.

READ:

James 3:15-16;

Psalm 73:1-4;

Galatians 5:19-26;

Titus 3:2-3

REFLECTION

Day 65

WHAT COVETING DOES TO YOU

*"Jesus said,... 'Guard against every kind of greed.
Life is not measured by how much you own.'"*

Luke 12:15, NLT

"Thou shalt not covet stuff."

Exodus 20:17, ELT

SHOPPING for your needs is one thing. Shopping just to see what there is, is different. If you don't guard yourself, you will *spy* some stuff and buy it just because you saw it, but you never needed it, and now you don't need it. Be careful because seeing stuff can be a slippery slope to covetousness. Then, coveting blinds you to the things God has given you. If God has given you a house, why do you want a bigger house like the Jones? Coveting does three things, (1) makes you question God's provision, (2) makes doubt God's reasons when He said "No", (3) makes you dissatisfied with God's praise.

Lord, forgive me every time I covet things and I know it. Forgive me when I ignorantly let my greed control me. Thank You for my health...my family... and those who love me. Thank You for a home... food...possessions to live... to work... and a desire to continue living for You. Amen.

Coveting eats away at your trust in God, and surely steals your thankfulness for what God has given you. When you are dissatisfied with what you have, it destroys your trust in God and fellowship with Him. The Bible says, "all things work together for good to them who love Him." But your covering takes away your trust in God. Remember, God may have a reason why you don't have the *stuff* your neighbor has.

Lord, when I am not grateful, make me thankful for what You have supplied. When I begin to covet, rebuke me and convict me. When I actually try to get stuff, I don't need, stop me. Forgive me for every time in the past I have coveted stuff. Amen.

READ:

Luke 12:13-34

REFLECTION

Day 66

SPIRITUAL EYES NEEDED

"For what profit is it if you gain the whole world but lose your soul."
Mark 8:36, ELT

THERE are three lies that people hear and believe. First, everyone wants stuff and does everything to get it, so it must be alright. We have inborn desires to improve our lives, and be better at what we do, and we even have a decision to be perfect. But it is wrong when you get in self competition with your neighbor, or *lust* after the stuff of your neighbor. The second is that getting all the *stuff* you want will quench your craving and make you happy. But people are controlled by their inner heart that is sinful (Jeremiah 17:9), and the inner motive is *lust* that is condemned by God (1 John 2:15-18).

Lord, I need to grow as a believer and get closer to You. Open my spiritual eyes and let me see the possession of my life as You see them. Forgive me when I covet after the wrong things for the wrong reasons. Help me live for You. Amen.

The third lie we all believe in wanting stuff is just my competitive edge to live. Most people think wanting things is just their competitive nature. But there is a difference between competitiveness and covetousness. Pushing yourself to excel and do your best is natural. Be the best you can be. But pushing to get what your neighbor has is wrong. Your competition is not your neighbor. Live according to His standards for you.

Lord, teach me to look at things through Your eyes, and may my possessions please You. May all I strive to do please You. May my standard in life be about You, and not others or their possessions. Amen.

READ:

Mark 7:20-23, 8:34-38

REFLECTION

Day 67

CONTROLLING COVETOUSNESS

"Jesus told him, 'If you want to be perfect, go and sell all your possessions and give the money to the poor, and you will have treasure in heaven. Then come, follow me.'"

Matthew 19:21, NLT

WHEN you look at the Tenth Commandment, it is like looking in the mirror – you see yourself. All have a covetous heart and your human effort cannot correct it. The problem is not with what you want, the problem is your *wanter*. While the word *wanter* is not found in the dictionary, it is a description of your heart. Your heart wants and it just happens to see what your neighbor has. And then there are magazines... television ads... radio ads... and what our family and friends talk about. It is *stuff*. So, what can help? First, only you can guard your heart, "above all else, guard your heart, for it is the source of your life" (Proverbs 4:23). Second, Only God can change your heart. He promises, "I will give you a new heart... and take away your evil heart" (Ezekiel 36:26, ELT).

Lord, when I look at my heart though Your eyes, I see my covetousness. Forgive me for lusting. Cleanse my desires. Teach me discipline. Guards my thoughts and desires. May I glorify You with what I possess, and wear, and drive, and where I live. Amen.

Bill Bright founder of Campus Crusade for Christ asked in his writings, "Who sits on the throne of your heart?" He goes on to explain, "Either yourself or Jesus Christ will sit on the throne of your heart." The secret of controlling the covetousness desires of your heart is to give your heart to Jesus Christ. He has the power to control your desires and covetousness.

Jesus, I (now) invite You into my heart to be saved. Thank You for forgiving all my sins, including my wrongful desires for things. Clean me. Now sit on the throne of my heart, I give all of myself to You. Amen.

READ:

Ephesians 2:1-22

REFLECTION

Day 68

CONTROLLING COVETOUSNESS (PART 2)

"But sanctify the Lord God in your heart.'"

1 Peter 3:15, KJV

"I can do all things through Christ who strengthens me."

Philippians 4:13

WHEN you look at the Tenth Commandment "you shall not covet…" it is hard to obey in the flesh. First, we know it is natural to need things… want things… and desire the best. Some have a hard time knowing when they are wanting things naturally or is it lust. But then the old sinful nature is always with us. So, are you feeding your illicit lust, or your planning to meet the needs of your life. The first secret is to pray and ask for spiritual eyes to understand God's goal and perfect will for your life. Then ask God to show you the right things you need, and the right thing to do, and to keep you from covetousness. Once God shows you, then ask Jesus Christ to give you strength to resist covetousness and power to plan right… pray right… desire right and make Christ the love of your life.

Jesus, I confess I have a heart that deceives me about good things and wrong things. Give me eyes to see the difference. Then give me eyes to plan how I can use the good. Finally, give me spiritual strength to recognize the wrong and strength to resist it. Amen.

The secret for controlling your heart is Jesus Christ. In the last lesson you prayed for Jesus Christ to sit on the throne of your heart. Now let Him guide you into right choices. Then determine to let Him live through you. Paul's motto, "For me to live is Christ" (Philippians 1:21). So, surrender to Him now!

Jesus, I have asked You to sit on the throne of my heart. Now I want You to rule all of my life... my thinking... my attitudes... my reactions to others... my habits and daily actions. I again yield to You and ask for Your strength to give me victory. Amen.

READ:

Ephesians 1:15-23;
Philippians 4:1-20

REFLECTION

Day 69

CONTROLLING COVETOUSNESS (PART 3)

"You must not covet.'"

Exodus 20:17, NLT

"The temptations in your life are no different from what others experience. And God is faithful. He will not allow the temptation to be more than you can stand. When you are tempted, he will show you a way out so that you can endure."

1 Corinthians 10:13, NLT

EVERYONE breaks the Ten Commandments in acts, desires and through hidden ways. A small child will cry for the toy of another. Teens want to be like other teens, but it is deeper, more than wanting the clothes another is wearing. They want acceptance by their peers. The secret to spiritual victory is learning daily obedience. Ask for strength from Jesus who indwells your heart (Philippians 4:13). Then the Bible promises, "Thank God! He gives us victory" (1 Corinthians 15:57, NLT). When you are tempted to want *stuff* that others have you must learn to say "No!" Getting strength, you to go from *victory to victory*. What is this step? It is not your self-determination, but the Bible describes going "from faith to faith" (Romans 1:16-17). You stand on your *saving faith* then step to *living by faith*. Then you have, "the faith of victory over lust, and the temptation of the devil" (1 John 2:15-18).

Jesus, I confess I have not always lived in victory over sin. Forgive me and cleanse me (1 John 1:9). Now give me strength of determination, I claim faith in You power of victory. Give me victory and determination. Amen.

When you are tempted by the things of your neighbors – or by television ads – you need to look within to see God's warning. Then listen to God's "no." Fully claim God's victory. Paul said, "My interest in this world has been crucified, and the world's interest in me has also died" (Galatians 6:14, NLT). Crucifying is treating your lust as dead.

Jesus, I want to live for You. Give me strength of vision. Then give me spiritual power to say "no" to wrong things, and spiritual determination to say "yes" to the right things. Amen.

READ:

1 John 5:1-5;

Galatians 6:11-16

REFLECTION

Day 70

KEEPING ALL OF THEM

"If ye love me, keep my commandments."

John 14:15, KJV

*"He that hath my commandments, and keepeth them, he it is that
loveth me: and he that loveth me shall be loved of my Father,
and I will love him, and will manifest myself to him."*

John 14:21, KJV

IF Jesus would re-write the Ten Commandments for today – He would not change their meaning, but He might express them positively. He would begin "Make Me first in your life" (Matthew 22:37). The Second Commandment He would say, "Don't allow anything to get between Me and you" (Philippians 1:21). The Third Commandment would be, "Show reverence for Me by the way you use My name" (Matthew 5:34-35). The next, "Worship Me on the Lord's Day" (Luke 4:16). the Fifth Commandment would be "Learn to respect and honor your parents as a foundation to a prosperous life" (Matthew 15:4).

Lord, I want to keep all of these Commandments. You know my weaknesses and strengths. Help me overcome my faults, and weaknesses. Strengthen my determination to worship and serve You. Amen.

He would say the Sixth Commandment is to respect the life of others in every way (Matthew 5:21-22). Next, He would tell you your body is His sanctuary, keep it clean (Matthew 5:27-30). Next, respect the rights and property of others, never steal or take anything from them. The Ninth Commandment always tell the truth (Matthew 12:36). Finally, be satisfied with what you have no matter what your neighbor has (Luke 12:15).

Lord, I will do what You want me to do. I will follow You by obeying Your Word. May I give glory to You by all I say and do. Amen.

READ:

Matthew 9:1-17

REFLECTION

PART THREE

THE TEN COMMANDMENTS ACCORDING TO JESUS

Lessons

Introduction:

ANSWER KEY

THE TEN COMANDMENTS BY JESUS

A. THE COMMANMENTS/LAWS ARE ME

1. A commandment/law is the **extension of My existence** and is the **power or energy** by which I operate/manage all life in the universe.

    a. I am life and My life gives energy to everything.

    b. Atoms (protons, neutrons, and electrons).

    c. **Cells**, the building block of organisms

    d. Law of gravity.

    e. Even the law (power) of the **theory of evolution**.

2. A commandment/law is extension of My nature.

    a. I **love** all humans, and I am love. To love is **give**.

    b. I am **holy**, and all worship Me saying, holy, holy, holy. The opposite is separation of **judgement**.

3. My commands/laws operate by My _____.

    a. **Omnipresence**, I am everywhere present, equally, at the same time. Therefore, My commandments/laws operate everywhere.

    b. **Omniscience**, I know all things actual and possible. Therefore, I am present to knowingly operate My commands/laws.

    c. **Omnipotence**, I can do all things doable, therefore, I have the ability to administer the successful operations of My commands/law, and I must punish those breaking My commands/laws.

B. WHAT I SAID ABOUT MY COMMANDMENTS/LAWS

1. I come to earth to **perfectly** live by the commands. "I didn't come to do away with the teachings of the Old Testament, but to fulfill them" (Matthew 5:17).

2. The commandments were written **by Me and for Me**. "To fulfill the teachings about Me" (Matthew 5:17).

3. My commandments were expressed in My words, and these words **can't be changed**. The Sadducees who denied the resurrection debated Me about a woman married 7 times. "Whose wife shall she be." I said you are wrong because you do not understand the scriptures" (Matthew 22:29). Abraham had been dead 400 years, but I told the Sadducees that I hid Moses, "I am the God of Abraham... I am the God of the dead" (Matthew 22:32).

4. My commandments are expressed in letters that make up words that can't be changed. "Not one dot, or tittle can be changed in the law" (Matthew 5:18).

5. The commandments are about **Me, a Person**, not just about rules. "The law of the Old Testament... fulfilled by Me" (Matthew 5:17).

6. I obeyed the command in **letter and spirit**. "These Old Testament rules were only a shadow of coming things because they pointed you to Me, who fulfilled these rules" (Col. 2:17).

C. WHAT I DID ABOUT THE COMMANDMENTS

1. Every broken law had to be punished. "The Father punishes everyone for their sins" (Rom. 2:6).

2. I died in your place and took **your punishment** for the law you broke.

3. I became **your sin**. "The Father made Me—who never sinned—become your sin" (2 Cor. 5:21).

4. You can become as perfect as Me. "That you might become My righteousness before the Father" (2 Cor. 5:21).

5. I nailed the 10 Commandments to the cross. "I wiped your record clean of all charges against you, forgetting them; by nailing them to My cross" (Col. 2:14).

D. WHAT ABOUT THE COMMANDMENTS NOW?

1. Accept Me and follow Me. "My gift is eternal life" (Rom. 6:23). "But as many as received Me will become the children of the Father" (John 1:12).

2. My commandments are a guide to **living**.

3. You can follow My commandments as you **follow Me**. "You can do all things through Me when I strengthen you" (Phil. 4:130.

4. I am your example. "As many as receive Me, walk into My presence" (Col. 2:6).

5. The way I obeyed the 10 commandments is your **example**. "I left you an example that you should follow My steps. I did not commit one sin, nor was I ever deceitful in anything I said" (1 Peter 1:21-22).

Introduction:

QUESTIONS

THE TEN COMANDMENTS BY JESUS

A. THE COMMANMENTS/LAWS ARE ME

1. A commandment/law is the _____ and is the _____ by which I operate/manage all life in the universe.

   a. I am life and My life gives energy to everything.

   b. Atoms (protons, neutrons, and electrons).

   c. _____ , the building block of organisms

   d. Law of gravity.

   e. Even the law (power) of the _____ .

2. A commandment/law is extension of My nature.

   a. I _____ all humans, and I am love. To love is _____ .

   b. I am _____ , and all worship Me saying, holy, holy, holy. The opposite is separation of _____ .

3. My commands/laws operate by My _____ .

   a. _____ , I am everywhere present, equally, at the same time. Therefore, My commandments/laws operate everywhere.

   b. _____ , I know all things actual and possible. Therefore, I am present to knowingly operate My commands/laws.

   c. _____ , I can do all things doable, therefore, I have the ability to administer the successful operations of My commands/law, and I must punish those breaking My commands/laws.

B. WHAT I SAID ABOUT MY COMMANDMENTS/LAWS

1. I come to earth to _____ live by the commands. "I didn't come to do away with the teachings of the Old Testament, but to fulfill them" (Matthew 5:17).

2. The commandments were written _____ . "To fulfill the teachings about Me" (Matthew 5:17).

3. My commandments were expressed in My words, and these words _____ . The Sadducees who denied the resurrection debated Me about a woman married 7 times. "Whose wife shall she be." I said you are wrong because you do not understand the scriptures" (Matthew 22:29). Abraham had been dead 400 years, but I told the Sadducees that I hid Moses, "I am the God of Abraham... I am the God of the dead" (Matthew 22:32).

4. My commandments are expressed in letters that make up words that can't be changed. "Not one dot, or tittle can be changed in the law" (Matthew 5:18).

5. The commandments are about _____ , not just about rules. "The law of the Old Testament... fulfilled by Me" (Matthew 5:17).

6. I obeyed the command in _____ . "These Old Testament rules were only a shadow of coming things because they pointed you to Me, who fulfilled these rules" (Col. 2:17).

C. WHAT I DID ABOUT THE COMMANDMENTS

1. Every broken law had to be punished. "The Father punishes everyone for their sins" (Rom. 2:6).

2. I died in your place and took _____ for the law you broke.

3. I became _____ . "The Father made Me—who never sinned—become your sin" (2 Cor. 5:21).

4. You can become as perfect as Me. "That you might become My righteousness before the Father" (2 Cor. 5:21).

5. I nailed the 10 Commandments to the cross. "I wiped your record clean of all charges against you, forgetting them; by nailing them to My cross" (Col. 2:14).

D. WHAT ABOUT THE COMMANDMENTS NOW?

1. Accept Me and follow Me. "My gift is eternal life" (Rom. 6:23). "But as many as received Me will become the children of the Father" (John 1:12).

2. My commandments are a guide to _____ .

3. You can follow My commandments as you _____ . "You can do all things through Me when I strengthen you" (Phil. 4:130.

4. I am your example. "As many as receive Me, walk into My presence" (Col. 2:6).

5. The way I obeyed the 10 commandments is your _____ . "I left you an example that you should follow My steps. I did not commit one sin, nor was I ever deceitful in anything I said" (1 Peter 1:21-22).

Lesson 1:

ANSWER KEY

THE FIRST COMMANDMENTS

A. INTRODUCTION

A line is drawn through the ages; it extends from Heaven to man and reaches around the earth. The line crosses the deserts of North Africa, and is drawn on the sand at the foot of Mount Sinai. On one side is God and the blessings of Heaven. On the other side is Satan with all the false religions and idols of Hell. That line is the Ten Commandments. Which side of the line will you choose?

First of 10 Commandments

Thou shalt have no other gods before Me. (Exodus 20:3).

Jesus Greates Commandment

JESUS GREATEST COMMANDMENT

Teacher, what commandment is the greatest in the law? And I answered, "You must love the Lord your God with all your heart, and all your soul, and all your mind... the second is like it, you must love your neighbor as yourself" (Matthew 22:36-39).

B. WHY 10 COMMANDMENTS?

1. To <u>reveal God</u>. "I am the Lord God." Reveals My self-existing nature.

2. To <u>separate us from the world</u>. "I am the Lord God, which have brought you out of the land of Egypt, out of the house of bondage" (20:2).

3. To **help us live right**. "Showing mercy... unto them that love Me and keep My commandments" (20:6).

4. To keep from **being punished**. "Visiting the iniquity... of them that hate Me" (20:5).

5. To **prosper**. "That your days may be long" (20:12).

6. To **test us**. "For I am come to prove you" (20:20).

7. To **seek forgiveness**. "An altar of earth you shalt make unto Me, and shall sacrifice" (20:24).

8. For **worship**. "I will come to you, and I will bless you" (20:24).

C. WHAT DOES EACH PHRASE MEAN?

1. Thou shalt -
   - Why didn't the Father force you to worship only Him? You are given a **free choice**.
   - Why does the Father give you the opportunity to worship other gods? So you can **demonstrate** your choice to love Him.
   - The Father has given you the free will to obey His commandments; what does it mean? You are **accountable to Him**.

2. Have -
   - Why didn't the Father say own? **Borrow**.
   - Why didn't the Father say make? **Buy**.
   - Why didn't the Father say worship? Not even have **another god in our possession**.

3. No -
   - What does the word "no" mean? **Never, none, not any.**
   - How much time does this mean? **Not 50-50, but all**.
   - What does "no" imply? **I want all of you.**

Thou shall love the Lord thy God with all thy heart, with all thy soul, and with all thy mind (Matthew 23:37, KJV).

4. Other gods -
   - Why didn't the Father say, "no other thing"? **Because a god elicits passion**.
   - Why didn't the Father say *idol*? The idol only represents the **false god**.
   - What is a demon idol? **To the spirit(s)**.
   - What is a Christian idol? **Worship God with world's means**.

Why Do I Recognize Other Gods?

Because I recognized **man's rebellion**.

Because **satan has a false religion**.

Because I created you as a **worshipper**.

5. Before -
   - Does "before" mean in front of the Father's space? **No, I am everywhere**.
   - Does "before" mean in priority of time? **No time with Me**.
   - Does "before" mean in My attention? **No, I know all**.
   - What does "before" mean to you? Don't bring a false god into **any place** of your life, at **any time**, for **any reason**.

6. Me -
   - How do I feel about other gods? **Abomination**.
   - What's left? **You and Me**.

D. WHAT DOES THE FIRST COMMANDMENT TELL YOU TO DO?

1. You are **free** to worship other gods, but **accountable** to Me, your Creator, the Lord God.

2. You must **make a choice** to worship Me your Creator.

3. You must come in **My presence**. Just as I don't want false gods in My presence. I don't want you in their presence. I want you in My presence.

4. You must realize your **weakness and self-deception**. Man is an incurable "idol-maker."

5. To realize you have an **obligation to please Me**. All law is an extension of My nature. To violate My law is to disobey Me.

6. You must seek **forgiveness when you break My law**. "The law was your schoolmaster to bring you unto Me, that you might be justified by faith" (Gal. 3:24).

7. You must be **grateful** for forgiveness. The First Commandment teaches you to come into the My presence with thanksgiving.

Lesson 1:

QUESTIONS

THE FIRST COMMANDMENTS

A. INTRODUCTION

A line is drawn through the ages; it extends from Heaven to man and reaches around the earth. The line crosses the deserts of North Africa, and is drawn on the sand at the foot of Mount Sinai. On one side is God and the blessings of Heaven. On the other side is Satan with all the false religions and idols of Hell. That line is the Ten Commandments. Which side of the line will you choose?

First of 10 Commandments

Thou shalt have no other gods before Me. (Exodus 20:3).

Jesus Greates Commandment

JESUS GREATEST COMMANDMENT

Teacher, what commandment is the greatest in the law? And I answered, "You must love the Lord your God with all your heart, and all your soul, and all your mind... the second is like it, you must love your neighbor as yourself" (Matthew 22:36-39).

B. WHY 10 COMMANDMENTS?

1. To _____ . "I am the Lord God." Reveals My self-existing nature.

2. To _____ . "I am the Lord God, which have brought you out of the land of Egypt, out of the house of bondage" (20:2).

3. To _____ . "Showing mercy... unto them that love Me and keep My commandments" (20:6).

4. To keep from _____ . "Visiting the iniquity... of them that hate Me" (20:5).

5. To _____ . "That your days may be long" (20:12).

6. To _____ . "For I am come to prove you" (20:20).

7. To _____ . "An altar of earth you shalt make unto Me, and shall sacrifice" (20:24).

8. For _____ . "I will come to you, and I will bless you" (20:24).

C. WHAT DOES EACH PHRASE MEAN?

1. Thou shalt -
   - Why didn't the Father force you to worship only Him? You are given a _____ .
   - Why does the Father give you the opportunity to worship other gods? So you can _____ your choice to love Him.
   - The Father has given you the free will to obey His commandments; what does it mean? You are _____ .

2. Have -
   - Why didn't the Father say own? _____ .
   - Why didn't the Father say make? _____ .
   - Why didn't the Father say worship? Not even have _____ .

3. No -
   - What does the word "no" mean? _____ .
   - How much time does this mean? _____ .
   - What does "no" imply? _____ .

The First Commandments

Thou shall love the Lord thy God with all thy heart, with all thy soul, and with all thy mind (Matthew 23:37, KJV).

4. Other gods -

    - Why didn't the Father say, "no other thing"? _____.
    - Why didn't the Father say *idol*? The idol only represents the _____.
    - What is a demon idol? _____.
    - What is a Christian idol? _____.

Why Do I Recognize Other Gods?

Because I recognized _____.

Because _____.

Because I created you as a _____.

5. Before -

    - Does "before" mean in front of the Father's space? _____.
    - Does "before" mean in priority of time? _____.
    - Does "before" mean in My attention? _____.
    - What does "before" mean to you? Don't bring a false god into _____ of your life, at _____, for _____.

6. Me -

    - How do I feel about other gods? _____.
    - What's left? _____.

D. WHAT DOES THE FIRST COMMANDMENT TELL YOU TO DO?

1. You are _____ to worship other gods, but _____ to Me, your Creator, the Lord God.

2. You must _____ to worship Me your Creator.

3. You must come in _____. Just as I don't want false gods in My presence. I don't want you in their presence. I want you in My presence.

4. You must realize your _____. Man is an incurable "idol-maker."

5. To realize you have an _____. All law is an extension of My nature. To violate My law is to disobey Me.

6. You must seek _____. "The law was your schoolmaster to bring you unto Me, that you might be justified by faith" (Gal. 3:24).

7. You must be _____ for forgiveness. The First Commandment teaches you to come into the My presence with thanksgiving.

Lesson 2:

ANSWER KEY

THE SECOND COMMANDMENT

A. INTRODUCTION

1. **People are worshippers**. What is suggested in the Commandments? "If you will indeed obey My voice and keep My commandments... then you shall be a kingdom of priests and a holy nation" (Ex. 19:5).

2. **Worship reflects God**. How should people worship? "God is spirit, and they that worship Him, must worship Him in spirit and truth" (John 4:24).

3. **An idol rejects the Father**. Why is it wrong to worship the Father with "representatives", i.e., idols? "Them that hate me" (v. 5).

4. **An idol replaces the Father**. People begin using "something" to help them worship, but end up worshipping the "thing."

5. **Worship and bow down before the Father**. What is the positive side of the Second Commandment? "Do not make idols of any kind... you must never worship or bow down to them" (v. 3).

Second Commandment

"You shall not make for yourself a carved image--any likeness of anything that is in heaven above, or that is in the earth beneath, or that is in the water under the earth; you shall not bow down to them nor serve them. For I, the Lord your God, am a jealous God, visiting the iniquity of the fathers upon the children to the third and fourth generations of those who hate Me, but showing mercy to thousands, to those who love Me and keep My commandments" (Exodus 20:4-6).

"But all idol worshippers... will be cast into the fiery lake of burning sulfur. This is the second death" (Revelation 21:8).

B. WHAT DOES EACH WORD/PHRASE MEAN?

1. **Thou shalt not make.**
    a. <u>Create</u> an idol.
    b. <u>Substitute</u> anything in place of Me.

2. **For yourself**, i.e., your <u>initiative or pleasure</u>.

3. **Carved (graven)**, i.e., sculpted, <u>your best</u>.

4. **Image… likeness.** "Let us make man in Our image, after Our likeness" (Gen. 1:26).

5. **Heaven… earth… water.** The Living Bible translates this birds, animals, and fish.

6. **Bow down yourself.** <u>Worship</u> is reserved for God.

7. **Serve them.**
    a. Give <u>money or sacrifice</u> to idols.
    b. <u>Obey or please</u> idols.

8. **I am the Lord your God, a jealous God,** i.e., <u>intolerant of rivalry</u>.

9. **Visiting,** i.e., <u>charging</u>. When you worship an idol, you run up the debt on your children's credit card.

10. **Iniquity,** *Aven* root, "to be bent or controlled, i.e., a tree limb <u>bent out of direction</u>.

11. **Them that hate Me,** i.e., to reject Me is to <u>hate Me</u>.

12. **Showing mercy,** i.e., <u>forgiveness</u>.

13. **Thousands,** i.e., <u>generations</u>.

14. **Love Me and keep My commandments.**
    a. To love Me is to place Me <u>first</u>.
    b. To obey Me is to <u>follow My directions</u>.

C. IDOLATRY DEFIES LOGIC

1. You were created in My image, and then you turn around and create something in My image. You become **god-makers**.

2. You think you are honoring Me, but you are bringing Me down to your level. You are guilty of **god-minimizing**.

3. You think you are worshipping Me, but you are worshipping yourselves. We are a **god-compromisers**.

4. I want you to recognize who I am and what I have done for you. I made you a **worshipper**.

D. OUR IDOLATRY

1. Michelangelo said, "Look within the marble to discover what is there, then sculpt it accordingly."

    a. You look within your heart, and then make a **god of it**.

    b. Your god is money, possessions, hobbies, achievements, etc.

    c. Anything that you make in **My place** is an idol.

2. Look within My nature to discover who I am, then worship Me.

    a. Worship Me for My holiness and justice, i.e., **punishment**.

    b. Me for My mercy, i.e., **forgiveness**.

Lesson 2:

QUESTIONS

THE SECOND COMMANDMENT

A. INTRODUCTION

1. _____ _____ . What is suggested in the Commandments? "If you will indeed obey My voice and keep My commandments... then you shall be a kingdom of priests and a holy nation" (Ex. 19:5).

2. _____ . How should people worship? "God is spirit, and they that worship Him, must worship Him in spirit and truth" (John 4:24).

3. _____ . Why is it wrong to worship the Father with "representatives", i.e., idols? "Them that hate me" (v. 5).

4. _____ . People begin using "something" to help them worship, but end up worshipping the "thing."

5. _____ . What is the positive side of the Second Commandment? "Do not make idols of any kind... you must never worship or bow down to them" (v. 3).

Second Commandment

"You shall not make for yourself a carved image--any likeness of anything that is in heaven above, or that is in the earth beneath, or that is in the water under the earth; you shall not bow down to them nor serve them. For I, the Lord your God, am a jealous God, visiting the iniquity of the fathers upon the children to the third and fourth generations of those who hate Me, but showing mercy to thousands, to those who love Me and keep My commandments" (Exodus 20:4-6).

"But all idol worshippers... will be cast into the fiery lake of burning sulfur. This is the second death" (Revelation 21:8).

B. WHAT DOES EACH WORD/PHRASE MEAN?

1. **Thou shalt not make.**
    a. _____ an idol.
    b. _____ anything in place of Me.

2. **For yourself,** i.e., your _____ .

3. **Carved (graven),** i.e., sculpted, _____ .

4. **Image... likeness.** "Let us make man in Our image, after Our likeness" (Gen. 1:26).

5. **Heaven... earth... water.** The Living Bible translates this birds, animals, and fish.

6. **Bow down yourself.** _____ is reserved for God.

7. **Serve them.**
    a. Give _____ to idols.
    b. _____ idols.

8. **I am the Lord your God, a jealous God,** i.e., _____ .

9. **Visiting,** i.e., _____ . When you worship an idol, you run up the debt on your children's credit card.

10. **Iniquity,** *Aven* root, "to be bent or controlled, i.e., a tree limb _____ .

11. **Them that hate Me,** i.e., to reject Me is to _____ .

12. **Showing mercy,** i.e., _____ .

13. **Thousands,** i.e., _____ .

14. **Love Me and keep My commandments.**
    a. To love Me is to place Me _____ .
    b. To obey Me is to _____ .

C. IDOLATRY DEFIES LOGIC

1. You were created in My image, and then you turn around and create something in My image. You become _____ .

2. You think you are honoring Me, but you are bringing Me down to your level. You are guilty of _____ .

3. You think you are worshipping Me, but you are worshipping yourselves. We are a _____ .

4. I want you to recognize who I am and what I have done for you. I made you a _____ .

D. OUR IDOLATRY

1. Michelangelo said, "Look within the marble to discover what is there, then sculpt it accordingly."

    a. You look within your heart, and then make a _____ .

    b. Your god is money, possessions, hobbies, achievements, etc.

    c. Anything that you make in _____ is an idol.

2. Look within My nature to discover who I am, then worship Me.

    a. Worship Me for My holiness and justice, i.e., _____ .

    b. Me for My mercy, i.e., _____ .

Lesson 3:

ANSWER KEY

THE THIRD COMMANDMENT

A. INTRODUCTION

Third Commanment

"Thou shalt not take the name of the Lord thy God in vain; for the Lord will not hold him guiltless that taketh His name in vain" (Exodus 20:7).

"Then I added, 'Do not swear at all, neither by heaven, or God's throne..." (Matthew 5:34).

"I said through James, 'Swear not at all... let your yes be yes and your no be no" (James 5:12).

1. **Not for salvation**. Could you be saved if you kept the third commandment, and never once cursed, or never used My name in vain? "Whosoever shall keep the whole law, and yet offend in one part, he is guilty of all" (James 2:10).

2. **Already redeemed**. What had I already done for Israel? "I am the Lord their God who has brought you out of the land of Egypt" (Exodus 20:2).

3. **A relationship between My people and Me**. The Ten Commandments were never given as divine laws to earn salvation.

B. WHAT DOES "IN VAIN" MEAN?

1. Why does the Third Commandment mention "name" and not other aspects of God, i.e., My Word, My altar, or My promises? **My name means who I am**.

2. What does "vain" mean? **Degrading or insulting**.

3. How can people take My name in vain?

    a. **Joking** about Me.

    b. Showing **unbelief** in My ability.

    c. **Laughing** at Me.

    d. **Not taking Me seriously**, i.e., to trivialize God.

    e. Making a **vow in My name** but not meaning it or doing it.

    f. Repeating **Christian expressions** without meaning.

    g. Use My name **as a curse**.

    h. **Blaspheming Me**, i.e., directing hatred at Me.

    i. Associating **filth** with Me, i.e., remember, I am pure. "Let no corrupt communication proceed out of your mouth" (Eph. 4:29). "Put off all... filthy communication out of they mouth" (Col. 3:8).

4. What is wrong with cursing?

    a. The curser **doesn't believe** in Me.

    b. Reflects **the anger** in the curser's heart.

    c. Cursing takes **My place** to judge people. Only I can condemn a person to Hell or damnation.

    d. Cursing denies **My control** over people and affairs.

5. How can Christians unknowingly take My name in vain?

    a. **False claims to worship**. "And why do you call Me, Lord, Lord, and do not the things which I say?" (Luke 6:46).

    b. Falsely using My name **in service**. "Many will say to Me in that day, Lord, Lord, have we not prophesied in your name? And in your name cast out devils? And in your name done many wonderful works? And then will I tell them, I never knew you: depart from Me, you are working iniquity" (Matt. 7:22-23).

    c. Falsely **praying** in Jesus' name. "Not everyone that says to Me Lord..." (Matt. 7:21). "The evil spirit answered... Jesus I know, and Paul I know, but who are you?" (Acts 19:15).

C. WILL NOT HOLD HIM GUILTLESS

1. **Without charge or innocent**. What does the word "guiltless" mean? "If any one offend not in word, the same is a perfect person" (John 3:2).

2. Your tongue **represents your heart**. Why are your words important? "The tongue is a little member… is set on fire of hell" (James 3:5-6). "The tongue… is an unruly evil" (James 3:8).

3. **Honesty**. With the tongue, "You bless God, even the Father, with your tongue you curse men" (James 3:9). You worship God (which you should do) and you curse men (which you should not do).

D. THE POWER OF WORDS

1. **Your words reflect your heart.** Why are words powerful? "How forceful are right words" (Job 6:25).

2. **The power of memory**. You should worship Me because you remember what I have done in the past.

3. **The power of thoughts**. You should use your intellect to worship Me. You cannot think without words.

4. **The power of analysis**. You can worship Me when you examine your heart to understand what I am doing in your life.

5. **The power of creativity**. You create new ideas with words. "Let the words of your mouth, and the meditation of your heart, be acceptable in My sight, O LORD, your strength, and redeemer" (Psalm 19:14).

Lesson 3:

QUESTIONS

THE THIRD COMMANDMENT

A. INTRODUCTION

Third Commanment

"Thou shalt not take the name of the Lord thy God in vain; for the Lord will not hold him guiltless that taketh His name in vain" (Exodus 20:7).

"Then I added, 'Do not swear at all, neither by heaven, or God's throne..." (Matthew 5:34).

I said through James, 'Swear not at all... let your yes be yes and your no be no" (James 5:12).

1. _____ . Could you be saved if you kept the third commandment, and never once cursed, or never used My name in vain? "Whosoever shall keep the whole law, and yet offend in one part, he is guilty of all" (James 2:10).

2. _____ . What had I already done for Israel? "I am the Lord their God who has brought you out of the land of Egypt" (Exodus 20:2).

3. _____ . The Ten Commandments were never given as divine laws to earn salvation.

B. WHAT DOES "IN VAIN" MEAN?

1. Why does the Third Commandment mention "name" and not other aspects of God, i.e., My Word, My altar, or My promises?_____ .

2. What does "vain" mean?_____ .

3. How can people take My name in vain?

    a. _____ about Me.

    b. Showing _____ in My ability.

    c. _____ at Me.

    d. _____, i.e., to trivialize God.

    e. Making a _____ but not meaning it or doing it.

    f. Repeating _____ without meaning.

    g. Use My name _____ .

    h. _____, i.e., directing hatred at Me.

    i. Associating <u>filth</u> with Me, i.e., remember, I am pure. "Let no corrupt communication proceed out of your mouth" (Eph. 4:29). "Put off all... filthy communication out of they mouth" (Col. 3:8).

4. What is wrong with cursing?

    a. The curser _____ in Me.

    b. Reflects _____ in the curser's heart.

    c. Cursing takes _____ to judge people. Only I can condemn a person to Hell or damnation.

    d. Cursing denies _____ over people and affairs.

5. How can Christians unknowingly take My name in vain?

    a. _____ . "And why do you call Me, Lord, Lord, and do not the things which I say?" (Luke 6:46).

    b. Falsely using My name _____ . "Many will say to Me in that day, Lord, Lord, have we not prophesied in your name? And in your name cast out devils? And in your name done many wonderful works? And then will I tell them, I never knew you: depart from Me, you are working iniquity" (Matt. 7:22-23).

    c. Falsely _____ in Jesus' name. "Not everyone that says to Me Lord..." (Matt. 7:21). "The evil spirit answered... Jesus I know, and Paul I know, but who are you?" (Acts 19:15).

C. WILL NOT HOLD HIM GUILTLESS

1. _____. What does the word "guiltless" mean? "If any one offend not in word, the same is a perfect person" (John 3:2).

2. Your tongue_____. Why are your words important? "The tongue is a little member... is set on fire of hell" (James 3:5-6). "The tongue... is an unruly evil" (James 3:8).

3. _____. With the tongue, "You bless God, even the Father, with your tongue you curse men" (James 3:9). You worship God (which you should do) and you curse men (which you should not do).

D. THE POWER OF WORDS

1. _____. Why are words powerful? "How forceful are right words" (Job 6:25).

2. _____. You should worship Me because you remember what I have done in the past.

3. _____. You should use your intellect to worship Me. You cannot think without words.

4. _____. You can worship Me when you examine your heart to understand what I am doing in your life.

5. _____. You create new ideas with words. "Let the words of your mouth, and the meditation of your heart, be acceptable in My sight, O LORD, your strength, and redeemer" (Psalm 19:14).

Lesson 4:

ANSWER KEY

THE FOURTH COMMANDMENT

A. INTRODUCTION

Fourth Commandment

"Remember the Sabbath day, to keep it holy. Six days you shall labor and do all your work, but the seventh day is the Sabbath of the Lord your God. In it you shall do no work: you, nor your son, nor your daughter, nor your male servant, nor your female servant, nor your cattle, nor your stranger who is within your gates. For in six days the Lord made the heavens and the earth, the sea, and all that is in them, and rested the seventh day. Therefore, the Lord blessed the Sabbath day and hallowed it" (Exodus 20:8-11).

1. Why doesn't the Fourth Commandment begin with "You shalt not work on the Sabbath/Sunday? Too **legalistically**.

    a. To teach **rest**.

    b. The purpose is not to stop working but to **start worshipping**.

2. What should you remember about the Sabbath? **You need rest to keep going**.

3. Who is our Sabbath example? "For in six days did the Lord make heaven and earth…" (Ex. 20:11). I your Lord, rested on the seventh day.

4. What do you know about My example?

    a. I did **much**.

    b. I did it in **six days**.

    c. I **finished**.

    d. I stopped for the seventh day.

    e. I **rested**. The word *Sabbath* means rest.

5. Why does God tell us to remember the Sabbath? You get caught up in your work or you don't think it is necessary to stop working. **Because you forget**.

B. WHAT ARE THE POSITIVE ASPECTS?

1. Why was a Sabbath necessary? "But the seventh day... you shalt not do any work" (Ex. 20:10). **Because you work**.

2. How should you work?

    a. **Completely**. "You shall labor and do all your work" (Ex. 20:9).

    b. **Finish the job**. "All that in them is" (Ex. 20:11).

    c. **Satisfactory**. "And rested" (Ex. 20:11).

3. What is one of the greatest rewards for work? **Rest**.

4. What else are you to do on the Sabbath? **Worship**.

    The word *Holy* means, "to set aside" or "separate." When you worship God, you separate yourselves from your secular work to do your spiritual work. The word worship is *liteago*, i.e., "to serve Me with praise. You "rest" from secular work to minister to Me, i.e., it is called the worship *service*.

5. What will legalists do with the Sabbath/Sunday?

    a. No **work**.

    b. No **job**.

    c. **Negative**.

    d. **Punishment**.

    e. No **hope** (optimism).

C. WHY WE KEEP SUNDAY INSTEAD OF SATURDAY

1. **Resurrection**. The greatest day in history also sanctified Sunday. "Now on the first day of the week, very early in the morning" (Luke 24:1).

2. **Example**. The early church worshipped on Sunday (Acts 20:7; I Cor. 16:2).

3. **My endorsement**. All of Jesus' post-resurrection appearances occurred on Sunday (John 20:19, 26).

4. **My Day of Promise**. Three of the most important Old Testament feasts ended Sunday for their greatest celebrations: (1) Week of Passover ended on Sunday with the Feast of First Fruits; (2) Pentecost was celebrated on Sunday, 50 days after Passover; (3) Feast of Tabernacles ended on the 8th day, i.e., Sunday.

5. **My last physical appearance**. "I was in the Spirit on the Lord's Day when I heard behind me a great voice" (Rev. 1:10).

6. **Tradition**. The Christian Church has celebrated on Sunday since the early church fathers.

7. **My eternal plan**. The Lord's Day was instituted long before the law (Gen. 2:1-2) and continues long after the law is over.

D. SPIRITUAL MEANING OF REST

1. Two kinds of spiritual rest.
    a. **Death**. Blessed are the dead which die in the Lord… They rest from their labours" (Rev. 14:13).
    b. **Spiritual**. "Come unto Me all that labor and are heavy laden, and I will give you rest (salvation). Take My yoke upon you and learn of Me; for I am meek and lowly in heart; and you shall find rest (victory) for your souls" (Matt. 11:28-29).

2. **Future rest**. What does the present Sabbath/Sunday predict? "There remains a rest for My people" (Heb. 4:9). *Sabbatismos* is "Sabbath rest," i.e., do what I did after six days of work.

3. **You possess My life in you**. Observing the Lord's Day is more than "sleeping." It is yielding to Me and "partnering" with Me. It is getting My rest.

E. WHAT REST DOES FOR YOU

1. **Prepares you for the future**. You take your eyes off today's task to become *future oriented*.

2. Makes you **feel good**. I want you to have some enjoyment in life.

3. **Restores your soul**. "I make you to lie down in green pastures. I lead you beside the still waters. I restore your soul" (Psa. 23:2-3).

4. You **obey My command**. "Rest in Me your Lord, wait patiently for Me" (Psa. 37:7a).

5. You **forget the failures and problems** of the past. "I will wipe away all tears" (Rev. 21:4).

Lesson 4:

QUESTIONS

THE FOURTH COMMANDMENT

A. INTRODUCTION

Fourth Commandment

"Remember the Sabbath day, to keep it holy. Six days you shall labor and do all your work, but the seventh day is the Sabbath of the Lord your God. In it you shall do no work: you, nor your son, nor your daughter, nor your male servant, nor your female servant, nor your cattle, nor your stranger who is within your gates. For in six days the Lord made the heavens and the earth, the sea, and all that is in them, and rested the seventh day. Therefore, the Lord blessed the Sabbath day and hallowed it" (Exodus 20:8-11).

1. Why doesn't the Fourth Commandment begin with "You shalt not work on the Sabbath/Sunday? Too _____ .

    a. To teach _____ .

    b. The purpose is not to stop working but to _____ .

2. What should you remember about the Sabbath? _____ .

3. Who is our Sabbath example? "For in six days did the Lord make heaven and earth..." (Ex. 20:11). I your Lord, rested on the seventh day.

4. What do you know about My example?

    a. I did _____ .

    b. I did it in _____ .

    c. I _____ .

    d. I stopped for the seventh day.

    e. I _____ . The word *Sabbath* means rest.

5. Why does God tell us to remember the Sabbath? You get caught up in your work or you don't think it is necessary to stop working. _____ .

B. WHAT ARE THE POSITIVE ASPECTS?

1. Why was a Sabbath necessary? "But the seventh day... you shalt not do any work" (Ex. 20:10). _____ .

2. How should you work?

    a. _____ . "You shall labor and do all your work" (Ex. 20:9).

    b. _____ . "All that in them is" (Ex. 20:11).

    c. _____ . "And rested" (Ex. 20:11).

3. What is one of the greatest rewards for work? _____ .

4. What else are you to do on the Sabbath? _____ .

    The word *Holy* means, "to set aside" or "separate." When you worship God, you separate yourselves from your secular work to do your spiritual work. The word worship is *liteago*, i.e., "to serve Me with praise. You "rest" from secular work to minister to Me, i.e., it is called the worship *service*.

5. What will legalists do with the Sabbath/Sunday?

    a. No _____ .

    b. No _____ .

    c. _____ .

    d. _____ .

    e. No _____ (optimism).

C. WHY WE KEEP SUNDAY INSTEAD OF SATURDAY

1. _____ . The greatest day in history also sanctified Sunday. "Now on the first day of the week, very early in the morning" (Luke 24:1).

2. _____ . The early church worshipped on Sunday (Acts 20:7; I Cor. 16:2).

3. _____ . All of Jesus' post-resurrection appearances occurred on Sunday (John 20:19, 26).

4. _____ . Three of the most important Old Testament feasts ended Sunday for their greatest celebrations: (1) Week of Passover ended on Sunday with the Feast of First Fruits; (2) Pentecost was celebrated on Sunday, 50 days after Passover; (3) Feast of Tabernacles ended on the 8th day, i.e., Sunday.

5. _____ . "I was in the Spirit on the Lord's Day when I heard behind me a great voice" (Rev. 1:10).

6. _____ . The Christian Church has celebrated on Sunday since the early church fathers.

7. _____ . The Lord's Day was instituted long before the law (Gen. 2:1-2) and continues long after the law is over.

D. SPIRITUAL MEANING OF REST

1. Two kinds of spiritual rest.

    a. _____ . Blessed are the dead which die in the Lord… They rest from their labours" (Rev. 14:13).

    b. _____ . "Come unto Me all that labor and are heavy laden, and I will give you rest (salvation). Take My yoke upon you and learn of Me; for I am meek and lowly in heart; and you shall find rest (victory) for your souls" (Matt. 11:28-29).

2. _____ . What does the present Sabbath/Sunday predict? "There remains a rest for My people" (Heb. 4:9). *Sabbatismos* is "Sabbath rest," i.e., do what I did after six days of work.

3. _____ . Observing the Lord's Day is more than "sleeping." It is yielding to Me and "partnering" with Me. It is getting My rest.

E. WHAT REST DOES FOR YOU

1. _____. You take your eyes off today's task to become *future oriented*.

2. Makes you _____. I want you to have some enjoyment in life.

3. _____. "I make you to lie down in green pastures. I lead you beside the still waters. I restore your soul" (Psa. 23:2-3).

4. You _____. "Rest in Me your Lord, wait patiently for Me" (Psa. 37:7a).

5. You _____ of the past. "I will wipe away all tears" (Rev. 21:4).

Lesson 5:

ANSWER KEY

THE FIFTH COMMANDMENT

A. INTRODUCTION: WHAT IS LEFT OUT?

"Honor your father and your mother, that your days may be long upon the land which the Lord your God is giving you." (Exodus 20:12).

1. Why is there no command for parents to love children or respect them? **Love is natural**.

2. What is the basic foundation of the family? **Love**. It is defined as *giving* yourself to the one you love.

3. Why is there no command to care or provide for your children? **Love is reflected in giving**.

4. Why are only mother and father included? **No diverse family styles in the Bible**.

5. Why is there no warning about disobeying parents? **The family is accepting**.

B. WHY OBEDIENCE BRINGS LONG LIFE?

Suppose you get a **10% longer life**, would that be reason enough to keep this commandment.

1. **You will have good children**. When you honor your parents, it's an example to your children. Then they will honor you. Your children won't give you ulcers.

2. **Stress will shorten your life**. When you rebel against your parents, your rebellious lifestyle will shorten your life.

3. **Caress and secure cage.** American experimental rats live 700 days, but Japanese experimental rats live 900 days. Why?

4. **Talking builds a relationship.** Babies whose mothers talked to them have a larger vocabulary, higher IQ, go farther in education.

5. **Social protection.** Those who get along with parents, get along with others, i.e., not hurt or killed.

6. **Spiritual reasons.** God will keep His promises, so if obedient children don't live longer; then the Bible is not true.

C. WHAT DOES HONOR MEAN?

1. **Recognize.** What does the original word "honor" mean? "To sit heavy." It means to know something is there, i.e., "to feel it."

2. **Authority.** What should you recognize about your parents? They represent God's authority in this world.

Youth's Response to Authority

Don't trust anyone over <u>thirty</u>.

I want to do it my way.

You don't know what being young is like.

3. **Obey.** What does Paul add to the concept of honor?

   "Children, obey your parents in the Lord, for this is right. Honor your father and mother, which is the first commandment with promise: that it may be well with you and you may live long on the earth" (Ephesians 6:1-3).

4. **It works.** Are you to honor/obey parents just to live a long life? The child will both be *right* and do *right*.

5. **Your obedience to Me.** Are you only to obey parents if they are "in the Lord"?

6. **Obey parents as representatives of Me.** Does this commandment apply only to saved children, i.e., "children in the Lord"? **No!**

7. What are the two promises for obedience?

    a. Well with you now. **Success**.

    b. **Live longer than expected**.

8. **Be honor-worthy**. What is the challenge of this command to modern parents?

9. What have parents given to us that deserve our honor?

    a. **Physical life**.

    b. **Shelter, clothing, food** (three basic necessities).

    c. **Education**.

    d. **Protection**.

    e. **Direction**.

    f. **Correction**.

    g. **Love and support**.

D. HOW TO HONOR PARENTS

1. Thanks: Write down one specific thing your mother/father did for you.
   _____

2. Reason: Write why your mother/father is special to you.
   _____

3. Memory: I like it when Mom/Dad:
   _____

4. Focus: My Mom/Dad did many things, but they are best at:
   _____

5. Show appreciation: I commit myself to do for Mom/Dad:
   _____

Lesson 5:

QUESTIONS

THE FIFTH COMMANDMENT

A. INTRODUCTION: WHAT IS LEFT OUT?

"Honor your father and your mother, that your days may be long upon the land which the Lord your God is giving you." (Exodus 20:12).

1. Why is there no command for parents to love children or respect them? _____ .

2. What is the basic foundation of the family? _____ . It is defined as *giving* yourself to the one you love.

3. Why is there no command to care or provide for your children? _____ .

4. Why are only mother and father included? _____ .

5. Why is there no warning about disobeying parents? _____ .

B. WHY OBEDIENCE BRINGS LONG LIFE?

Suppose you get a _____ , would that be reason enough to keep this commandment.

1. _____ . When you honor your parents, it's an example to your children. Then they will honor you. Your children won't give you ulcers.

2. _____ . When you rebel against your parents, your rebellious lifestyle will shorten your life.

3. _____ . American experimental rats live 700 days, but Japanese experimental rats live 900 days. Why?

4. _____ . Babies whose mothers talked to them have a larger vocabulary, higher IQ, go farther in education.

5. _____ . Those who get along with parents, get along with others, i.e., not hurt or killed.

6. _____ . God will keep His promises, so if obedient children don't live longer; then the Bible is not true.

C. WHAT DOES HONOR MEAN?

1. _____ . What does the original word "honor" mean? "To sit heavy." It means to know something is there, i.e., "to feel it."

2. _____ . What should you recognize about your parents? They represent God's authority in this world.

Youth's Response to Authority

Don't trust anyone over <u>thirty</u>.

I want to do it my way.

You don't know what being young is like.

3. _____ . What does Paul add to the concept of honor?

"Children, obey your parents in the Lord, for this is right. Honor your father and mother, which is the first commandment with promise: that it may be well with you and you may live long on the earth" (Ephesians 6:1-3).

4. _____ . Are you to honor/obey parents just to live a long life? The child will both be *right* and do *right*.

5. _____ . Are you only to obey parents if they are "in the Lord"?

6. _____ . Does this commandment apply only to saved children, i.e., "children in the Lord"? _____

290 THE TEN COMMANDMENTS ACCORDING TO JESUS

7. What are the two promises for obedience?

   a. Well with you now. _____ .

   b. _____ .

8. _____ . What is the challenge of this command to modern parents?

9. What have parents given to us that deserve our honor?

   a. _____ .

   b. _____ (three basic necessities).

   c. _____ .

   d. _____ .

   e. _____ .

   f. _____ .

   g. _____ .

D. HOW TO HONOR PARENTS

1. Thanks: Write down one specific thing your mother/father did for you.
   _____

2. Reason: Write why your mother/father is special to you.
   _____

3. Memory: I like it when Mom/Dad:
   _____

4. Focus: My Mom/Dad did many things, but they are best at:
   _____

5. Show appreciation: I commit myself to do for Mom/Dad:
   _____
   _____

Lesson 6:

ANSWER KEY

THE SIXTH COMMANDMENT

Sixth Commandment

"You must not murder" (Exodus 20:13, LB).

You knew it has been said, you must not murderer. If you commit murder, you are subject to judgment. But I say to you, if you are even angry with someone, you are subject to punishment" (Matthew 5:21-22).

A. WHY DID GOD CREATE US?

I created you to worship and praise the Father, the Holy Spirit, and Me. "They that worship Us must worship in spirit and in truth" (John 4:24).

1. With an intellect to **meaningfully** worship.

2. With emotions to **passionately** worship.

3. With your will is **freely autonomous** worship.

B. I SET A MORAL RELATIONSHIP BETWEEN YOU AND ME

1. You must put nothing **before Me**. "You shall have no other gods before Me."

2. You must put nothing **between Me and you**. "You shall not make any carved idols."

3. Your **reverence for Me**. "You shall not take My name in vain."

4. You **focus on worship** to Me. "Remember to keep the Sabbath Day holy."

C. WHAT IF YOU BREAK THAT RELATIONSHIP?

1. You trespass on **holy ground**.

2. Worship is **internal**; you can worship anytime, anywhere, under any circumstance.

3. If they kill you, you can no longer worship Me or do My will. Every murder is **between Me and the killer**.

D. WHY THE SIXTH COMMANDMENT?

1. **Murder cuts off worship**.

2. I give life, how can anyone presume to take My place to make that **moral decision**?

3. Murder destroys **My image in people**. "Whoso sheddeth (murders) man's blood, by man (society) shall his blood be shed, for in My image I, made all people" (Gen. 9:6).

4. Murder is a **crime against society**. Government makes a law, i.e., a *social contract* to protect life.

5. I no longer receive praise, nor can I **use the person** who is murdered.

E. WHAT ELSE DOES THE SIXTH COMMANDMENT PROHIBIT?

1. Any thing that **shortens or snuffs out life** is wrong.

2. Some acts are considered murder. Euthanasia, genocide, terrorist acts, **suicide**.

3. Any are self-destructive acts considered murder/suicide? **Alcohol**, cigarettes, **addictive drugs**, anything that shortens life.

4. What about **unintentional** acts that shorten life? Withhold food, clothing, shelter, dangerous driving, dangerous habits, overeating, dangerous prescription drugs.

F. THE STANDARD FOR LIFE.

"I said unto him, you shall love the Father with all your heart, and with all your soul, and with all your mind. This is the first and great commandment. And the second is like unto it, you shall love your neighbor as yourself" (Matthew 22:37-39).

1. Spiritual and physical life are both precious **treasures** from Me. If you do not have physical life, you cannot exercise your spiritual.

2. No **second chance** with physical life. Joyfully receive it and tenaciously protect life.

3. The ultimate expression of the Sixth Commandment is **love**. If you love someone, you would not ever think of killing them.

4. What did I include when I said, "Love others as you love yourselves?"
    a. Self-love, i.e., **love me**.
    b. Self-protecting, i.e., **protect me**.
    c. Self-exaltation, i.e., **exalt me**.
    d. Self-protection, i.e., **protect me**.
    e. I meant you were to respect others and their obligation to love Me, as you respect yourself and love Me.

5. Your **ultimate** love is to the Father, the Holy Spirit and Me. You should love others with the love you have for Us.

G. REVIEW: WHY IS MURDER WRONG?

1. Because of a person's **relationship** to Me.

2. Murder is more about **Me** than it is about a law or a legal social contract with others.

3. When a nation forgets about Me, all forms of murder become **more prevalent**.

Lesson 6:

QUESTIONS

THE SIXTH COMMANDMENT

Sixth Commandment

"You must not murder" (Exodus 20:13, LB).

You knew it has been said, you must not murderer. If you commit murder, you are subject to judgment. But I say to you, if you are even angry with someone, you are subject to punishment" (Matthew 5:21-22).

A. WHY DID GOD CREATE US?

I created you to worship and praise the Father, the Holy Spirit, and Me. "They that worship Us must worship in spirit and in truth" (John 4:24).

1. With an intellect to _____ worship.

2. With emotions to _____ worship.

3. With your will is _____ worship.

B. I SET A MORAL RELATIONSHIP BETWEEN YOU AND ME

1. You must put nothing _____ . "You shall have no other gods before Me."

2. You must put nothing _____ . "You shall not make any carved idols."

3. Your _____ . "You shall not take My name in vain."

4. You _____ to Me. "Remember to keep the Sabbath Day holy."

C. WHAT IF YOU BREAK THAT RELATIONSHIP?

1. You trespass on _____ .

2. Worship is _____ ; you can worship anytime, anywhere, under any circumstance.

3. If they kill you, you can no longer worship Me or do My will. Every murder is _____ .

D. WHY THE SIXTH COMMANDMENT?

1. _____ .

2. I give life, how can anyone presume to take My place to make that _____ ?

3. Murder destroys _____ . "Whoso sheddeth (murders) man's blood, by man (society) shall his blood be shed, for in My image I, made all people" (Gen. 9:6).

4. Murder is a _____ . Government makes a law, i.e., a *social contract* to protect life.

5. I no longer receive praise, nor can I _____ who is murdered.

E. WHAT ELSE DOES THE SIXTH COMMANDMENT PROHIBIT?

1. Any thing that _____ is wrong.

2. Some acts are considered murder. Euthanasia, genocide, terrorist acts, _____ .

3. Any are self-destructive acts considered murder/suicide? _____ , cigarettes, _____ , anything that shortens life.

4. What about _____ acts that shorten life? Withhold food, clothing, shelter, dangerous driving, dangerous habits, overeating, dangerous prescription drugs.

F. THE STANDARD FOR LIFE.

"I said unto him, you shall love the Father with all your heart, and with all your soul, and with all your mind. This is the first and great commandment. And the second is like unto it, you shall love your neighbor as yourself" (Matthew 22:37-39).

1. Spiritual and physical life are both precious _____ from Me. If you do not have physical life, you cannot exercise your spiritual.

2. No _____ with physical life. Joyfully receive it and tenaciously protect life.

3. The ultimate expression of the Sixth Commandment is _____ . If you love someone, you would not ever think of killing them.

4. What did I include when I said, "Love others as you love yourselves?"
    a. Self-love, i.e., _____ .
    b. Self-protecting, i.e., _____ .
    c. Self-exaltation, i.e., _____ .
    d. Self-protection, i.e., _____ .
    e. I meant you were to respect others and their obligation to love Me, as you respect yourself and love Me.

5. Your _____ love is to the Father, the Holy Spirit and Me. You should love others with the love you have for Us.

G. REVIEW: WHY IS MURDER WRONG?

1. Because of a person's _____ to Me.

2. Murder is more about _____ than it is about a law or a legal social contract with others.

3. When a nation forgets about Me, all forms of murder become _____ .

The Sixth Commandment

Lesson 7:

ANSWER KEY

THE SEVENTH COMMANDMENT

Seventh Commandment

"You shall not commit adultery" (Exodus 20:14).

I do not have a Commandment about worshipping Me in a temple or sanctuary. I plan to live in your body. I want to be glorified in your body and carry out My ministry through you. "You have heard it said, 'You must not commit adultery. I say don't even have impure intentions, less you commit adultery in your heart'" (Matthew 5:27-28).

A. WHAT I SAY ABOUT YOUR BODY

"What, don't you know your body is the temple of the Holy Ghost? He lives in you. He is a gift to you from the Heavenly Father. Your body does not belong to you. You are bought with the price of My blood, therefore, glorify Me in your physical body, and in your inner spirit" (1 Corinthians 6:19-20).

1. You invite Me **in your life** at salvation. "But as many as received Me, to that person I gave the right to become the children of the Heavenly Father" (John 1:12). "I in you, the hope of glory" (Col. 1:27).

2. Your body becomes My **sanctuary**. "You are My temple, and the Holy Spirit dwells in you" (1 Cor. 3:16).

3. You must keep your body/temple **holy**. "If you defile your physical temple the Father will destroy you. For My temple is holy, you are My temple" (1 Cor. 3:17).

4. You do not have the right **to do what you want** with your body. "Your body is the temple of the Holy Spirit... you are not your own" (1 Cor. 6:19).

5. You must keep your body from **sexual immorality**. "Do you not know that your body is a member of Me? Will you take your body and make it a member of a harlot? Certainly not!... Flee sexual immorality. Every sin that you do to your body is wrong; but sexual immorality is certainly a sin against your body" (1 Cor. 6:15-18).

B. WHAT IS A SANCTUARY?

1. I **live** in a sanctuary; it is the location for My presence. "Make Me a sanctuary that I may dwell with you" (Ex. 25:8).

2. A sanctuary is a location of **worship**. "Praise Me in the sanctuary" (Psa. 150:1). "Lift up your hands in the sanctuary" (Psa. 134:2).

3. A sanctuary has My **attributes**. "Strength and beauty are in My sanctuary" (Psa. 96:6).

    a. What **strength** do you have for Me?

    b. What **beauty** do you have for Me?

C. WHY IS MARRIAGE A GOOD THING?

1. People need **partnerships**. "But for Adam there was not found a helper (helpmeet) compatible for him" (Gen. 2:20).

2. For physical **intimacy**. "They (the two) shall be one (flesh)" (Gen. 2:24).

3. To give children a loving secure **home**. "She is now bone of my bone, and flesh of my flesh" (Gen. 2:23).

4. To give **pleasure** (i.e., The Song of Solomon).

5. Keeps people from **sinning against Me**. "Marriage is honorable among all, and the bed undefiled: because fornication and adulterers, I will judge" (Heb. 13:4).

D. WHAT DOES ADULTERY INCLUDE?

1. **Willful** sexual intercourse with someone other than one's husband or wife.

2. The **source** of lust. "Whosoever looks at a woman to lust after her has already committed adultery with her in his heart" (Matt. 5:28).

3. Adultery also includes the **sexual sins** of rape, homosexuality, incest, and/or sexual abuse of a child.

4. **Single** sexual partners. "The bed is undefiled… but fornicators and adulterers I will judge" (Heb. 13:4). Paul mentions fornication first in list of sins (1 Cor. 5:11; Col. 3:5).

E. WHY IS ADULTERY WRONG?

1. Your relationship with your spouse is based on your relationship to God. "I am the unseen guest at every meal." When you violate your relationship with your spouse, you **violate your relationship to God**.

2. You break your promise to be faithful. This is a **character** issue.

3. You produce children without a **proper home, love, or godly example**.

4. You **destroy** your spiritual life.

5. You expose yourself to **disease**.

6. Tremendous burden on society. How much does sexual unfaithfulness cost you in tax money?

F. SUMMARY/TAKE AWAY

The Seventh Commandment is about consecrating your body as a sanctuary to Me. It is about being faithful to Me, to your mate, yourself, your children, and society.

Lesson 7:

QUESTIONS

THE SEVENTH COMMANDMENT

Seventh Commandment

"You shall not commit adultery" (Exodus 20:14).

I do not have a Commandment about worshipping Me in a temple or sanctuary. I plan to live in your body. I want to be glorified in your body and carry out My ministry through you. "You have heard it said, 'You must not commit adultery. I say don't even have impure intentions, less you commit adultery in your heart'" (Matthew 5:27-28).

A. WHAT I SAY ABOUT YOUR BODY

"What, don't you know your body is the temple of the Holy Ghost? He lives in you. He is a gift to you from the Heavenly Father. Your body does not belong to you. You are bought with the price of My blood, therefore, glorify Me in your physical body, and in your inner spirit" (1 Corinthians 6:19-20).

1. You invite Me _____ at salvation. "But as many as received Me, to that person I gave the right to become the children of the Heavenly Father" (John 1:12). "I in you, the hope of glory" (Col. 1:27).

2. Your body becomes My _____ . "You are My temple, and the Holy Spirit dwells in you" (1 Cor. 3:16).

3. You must keep your body/temple _____ . "If you defile your physical temple the Father will destroy you. For My temple is holy, you are My temple" (1 Cor. 3:17).

4. You do not have the right _____ with your body. "Your body is the temple of the Holy Spirit... you are not your own" (1 Cor. 6:19).

5. You must keep your body from _____. "Do you not know that your body is a member of Me? Will you take your body and make it a member of a harlot? Certainly not!... Flee sexual immorality. Every sin that you do to your body is wrong; but sexual immorality is certainly a sin against your body" (1 Cor. 6:15-18).

B. WHAT IS A SANCTUARY?

1. I _____ in a sanctuary; it is the location for My presence. "Make Me a sanctuary that I may dwell with you" (Ex. 25:8).

2. A sanctuary is a location of _____. "Praise Me in the sanctuary" (Psa. 150:1). "Lift up your hands in the sanctuary" (Psa. 134:2).

3. A sanctuary has My _____. "Strength and beauty are in My sanctuary" (Psa. 96:6).

   a. What _____ do you have for Me?

   b. What _____ do you have for Me?

C. WHY IS MARRIAGE A GOOD THING?

1. People need _____. "But for Adam there was not found a helper (helpmeet) compatible for him" (Gen. 2:20).

2. For physical _____. "They (the two) shall be one (flesh)" (Gen. 2:24).

3. To give children a loving secure _____. "She is now bone of my bone, and flesh of my flesh" (Gen. 2:23).

4. To give _____ (i.e., The Song of Solomon).

5. Keeps people from _____. "Marriage is honorable among all, and the bed undefiled: because fornication and adulterers, I will judge" (Heb. 13:4).

D. WHAT DOES ADULTERY INCLUDE?

1. _____ sexual intercourse with someone other than one's husband or wife.

2. The _____ of lust. "Whosoever looks at a woman to lust after her has already committed adultery with her in his heart" (Matt. 5:28).

3. Adultery also includes the _____ of rape, homosexuality, incest, and/or sexual abuse of a child.

4. _____ sexual partners. "The bed is undefiled... but fornicators and adulterers I will judge" (Heb. 13:4). Paul mentions fornication first in list of sins (1 Cor. 5:11; Col. 3:5).

E. WHY IS ADULTERY WRONG?

1. Your relationship with your spouse is based on your relationship to God. "I am the unseen guest at every meal." When you violate your relationship with your spouse, you _____ .

2. You break your promise to be faithful. This is a _____ issue.

3. You produce children without a _____ .

4. You _____ your spiritual life.

5. You expose yourself to _____ .

6. Tremendous burden on society. How much does sexual unfaithfulness cost you in tax money?

F. SUMMARY/TAKE AWAY

The Seventh Commandment is about consecrating your body as a sanctuary to Me. It is about being faithful to Me, to your mate, yourself, your children, and society.

Lesson 8:

ANSWER KEY

THE EIGHTH COMMANDMENT

Eighth Commandment

"Thou shalt not steal" (Exodus 20:15).

"To the rich young ruler, 'I said... you shall not steal" (Matthew 19:18).

"I wrote through Paul, "You know the commandment, 'You shall not steal'" (Romans 13:9).

A. INTRODUCTION: HOW TO GET STUFF

1. How do I want you to get STUFF... **work**. "Let him that stole steal no longer, but rather let him labor, working with his hands what is good, that he may have something good" (Eph. 4:28).

   a. Work for money and **buy STUFF**.

   b. Work to give you **self-respect and self-esteem**.

2. **Make it**. You can farm, cook, or be a "furniture maker."

3. **Investment**. "I delivered five talents to a servant; look, he has gained five more talents. I said to him, well done, good and faithful servant; you were faithful over a few things, I will make you ruler over many things. Enter into the joy of your lord" (Matt. 25: 20-21, *ELT*).

4. **Inherited**. "That I may cause those that love you to inherit substance; and I will fill your treasures" (Prov. 8:21).

5. **Divine providence**. "Give us this day our daily bread" (Matt. 6:11).

B. HOW CAN A PERSON STEAL?

1. **Thief**. "From old English *to crouch*, one who takes illegally, by secret, or stealthily" (Webster). This is a sneak thief, or burglar.

2. **Robbery or mugging**. To take illegally by force. "A certain man went down from Jerusalem to Jericho, and fell among thieves, which stripped him of his raiment, and wounded him... leaving him half dead" (Luke 10:30).

3. **Seizure**. Using another person's stuff without permission, taking their assets, using and abusing another's possession, etc.

4. **Deceit**. "I hate dishonest scales and dishonest weights" (Prov. 20:23). Mechanics charging for work not done, adding to expenses, false advertising, false claims, exaggerations, selling a person something he/she does not need, or should not have, promises you cannot keep.

5. **Defraud**. "To deprive a person of something by deception; the old English word means *to cheat*." (Webster). To withhold something rightfully due. If you don't pay a debt on time, you defraud and not allow them the use of their money, i.e., stole capital or interest for 120 days. Also, not giving employer eight hours of work for eight hours of pay.

C. WHAT DO THEY STEAL FROM YOU?

1. Your **use** of your possessions.

2. Your **time and talents** to acquire the possession.

3. Your **reputation and respect** that is identified with your possession.

4. Your **love and passion**.

My Attitude About a Thief

He steals your dreams and hopes, your <u>future</u>

He steals your ability to <u>worship and serve</u> God.

He steals your ability to use it to become <u>better and stronger</u>.

D. HOW DO YOU FEEL WHEN SOMETHING IS STOLEN?

1. **Angry**, because you are possessive.

2. **Violated**, because someone took part of your life.

3. **Hurt**, because you need it or miss it.

4. **Confused**, you don't know what to do.

5. You are thankful he didn't take your **ability to make money**.

6. You are thankful he didn't **take your life**.

7. You are thankful you are not **the thief**.

E. DON'T BE LIKE OUR ENEMY

1. "He (the devil) is a murderer from the beginning" (John 8:44). **Don't kill**.

2. "The thief (the devil) cometh not, but for to steal, and to kill, and to destroy" (John 10:10). **He steals**.

3. "He (the devil) is a liar, and the father of it" (John 8:44). **He lies**.

F. WHY STEALING IS A SIN

1. You are made in the image of Me, and if a person would steal from you, he/she would **steal from Me**.

2. "Will a man rob Me"? Yes, but you ask the question where have I robbed the Father? I answer, "You robbed Me in tithes and offerings" (Malachi 3:8-9, *Author's Translation*). **Not paying tithe**.

3. We are to worship and serve God. When things, time or ability are stolen from you, you cannot do **service for Me**.

4. Stealing harms a person **internally**, i.e., discouragement, gives up, vengeful, rage, suicide.

Lesson 8:

QUESTIONS

THE EIGHTH COMMANDMENT

Eighth Commandment

"Thou shalt not steal" (Exodus 20:15).

"To the rich young ruler, 'I said... you shall not steal'" (Matthew 19:18).

"I wrote through Paul, "You know the commandment, 'You shall not steal'" (Romans 13:9).

A. INTRODUCTION: HOW TO GET STUFF

1. How do I want you to get STUFF... _____ . "Let him that stole steal no longer, but rather let him labor, working with his hands what is good, that he may have something good" (Eph. 4:28).

    a. Work for money and _____ .

    b. Work to give you _____ .

2. _____ . You can farm, cook, or be a "furniture maker."

3. _____ . "I delivered five talents to a servant; look, he has gained five more talents. I said to him, well done, good and faithful servant; you were faithful over a few things, I will make you ruler over many things. Enter into the joy of your lord" (Matt. 25: 20-21, ELT).

4. _____ . "That I may cause those that love you to inherit substance; and I will fill your treasures" (Prov. 8:21).

5. _____ . "Give us this day our daily bread" (Matt. 6:11).

B. HOW CAN A PERSON STEAL?

1. _____. "From old English *to crouch*, one who takes illegally, by secret, or stealthily" (Webster). This is a sneak thief, or burglar.

2. _____. To take illegally by force. "A certain man went down from Jerusalem to Jericho, and fell among thieves, which stripped him of his raiment, and wounded him... leaving him half dead" (Luke 10:30).

3. _____. Using another person's stuff without permission, taking their assets, using and abusing another's possession, etc.

4. _____. "I hate dishonest scales and dishonest weights" (Prov. 20:23). Mechanics charging for work not done, adding to expenses, false advertising, false claims, exaggerations, selling a person something he/she does not need, or should not have, promises you cannot keep.

5. _____. "To deprive a person of something by deception; the old English word means *to cheat*." (Webster). To withhold something rightfully due. If you don't pay a debt on time, you defraud and not allow them the use of their money, i.e., stole capital or interest for 120 days. Also, not giving employer eight hours of work for eight hours of pay.

C. WHAT DO THEY STEAL FROM YOU?

1. Your _____ of your possessions.

2. Your _____ to acquire the possession.

3. Your _____ that is identified with your possession.

4. Your _____.

My Attitude About a Thief

He steals your dreams and hopes, your <u>future</u>

He steals your ability to <u>worship and serve</u> God.

He steals your ability to use it to become <u>better and stronger</u>.

D. HOW DO YOU FEEL WHEN SOMETHING IS STOLEN?

1. _____ , because you are possessive.

2. _____ , because someone took part of your life.

3. _____ , because you need it or miss it.

4. _____ , you don't know what to do.

5. You are thankful he didn't take your _____ .

6. You are thankful he didn't _____ .

7. You are thankful you are not _____ .

E. DON'T BE LIKE OUR ENEMY

1. "He (the devil) is a murderer from the beginning" (John 8:44). _____ .

2. "The thief (the devil) cometh not, but for to steal, and to kill, and to destroy" (John 10:10). _____ .

3. "He (the devil) is a liar, and the father of it" (John 8:44). _____ .

F. WHY STEALING IS A SIN

1. You are made in the image of Me, and if a person would steal from you, he/she would _____ .

2. "Will a man rob Me"? Yes, but you ask the question where have I robbed the Father? I answer, "You robbed Me in tithes and offerings" (Malachi 3:8-9, *Author's Translation*). _____ .

3. We are to worship and serve God. When things, time or ability are stolen from you, you cannot do _____ .

4. Stealing harms a person _____ , i.e., discouragement, gives up, vengeful, rage, suicide.

Lesson 9:

ANSWER KEY

THE NINTH COMMANDMENT

Ninth Commandment

"You shall not lie to your neighbor" (Exodus 20:16, ELT).

"I speak what My Father tells Me to say, but you speak what you father tells you... your father is the devil... a murderer from the beginning and does not have the truth in him. I tell you the truth" (John 8:38, 44).

A. INTRODUCTION

1. **Relationship with Me**. Why did I say, you shalt not lie? Because you know when you lie, you cannot lie to yourself. You try to live a lie before Me, but I know the truth.

2. **Destroys self-respect**. If you cannot lie to yourself, how can you harm yourself?

3. **Harms others in many ways**. What does lying do to others?

4. **Satan**. Where does lying come from? "Satan is the father of lies" (John 8:44).

5. **Eve lied first**. Can we blame our lying on someone else? Satan asked, "Did God say you must not eat from any tree in the Garden" (Gen. 3:1, ELT)? Eve exaggerated, "We must not eat ... nor touch" (Gen. 3:3, ELT).

6. **Distorts My Word**. How does Satan lie to you today? Did God really say "no?"

B. ARE THESE LIES?

1. Does lying include **exaggeration**?
   - "Tell them I am not here."
   - "You never do any of the work."
   - "That's the prettiest baby I have ever seen."
   - "My you look younger (or slimmer)."

2. Does lying include **silence**?
   - "Who did this?"
   - Taking **credit** for something you did not do.

C. SEVENTEEN KINDS OF LIES

1. **White lies**: Perceived as good for both teller and the victim of the lie.

2. **Political lies or flattery**: a compliment when you know the thing complimented is not good, but you say what the listener wants to hear

3. **Gossip**: telling what should not be told, i.e., revealing a secret.

4. **Sinister lies**: giving an untruth for your evil purpose.

5. **Jovial lies**: lying in an obvious way without malice, so both teller and listener know it is not true.

6. **Half lies**: telling the truth, but not the whole truth.

7. **Excuse**: misrepresenting the truth about a failure on our part.

8. **Hypocrisy**: your attempt to deceive another about something you are not (the New Testament word referred to an actor using a mask to play the role of another).

9. **Justifying lies**: to convince others they would have taken the similar action.

10. **Face-saving lies**: misrepresentation to avoid embarrassment. (Sarah told Me, she did not laugh).

11. **Evangelistically speaking**: the exaggeration of religious results. (Ananias and Sapphira).

12. **Propaganda**: used in military times to hide one's position.

13. **Advertisement**: sometimes used to exaggerate the merits of a product.

14. **Cheating**: using material that is not yours with a view of misrepresentation (exams and income taxes).

15. **Demonic lies**: evil spirits are the source of mis-representing the nature of righteousness and evil (Rom. 1:25; 2 Thess. 2:11).

16. **Spin**: interpreting obvious fact to your favor (politics).

17. **Plausibility of denial**: people conspire to conceal their involvement by claiming they didn't know.

D. WHY LYING IS WRONG

1. Misrepresents or hides the **truth**.
   - You hurt the other person who does not **know** the truth.
   - The more serious a lie, the more **danger** to the other person.

2. A lie makes a deceiver out of the liar.
   - To **cover up**, or hide something.
   - To **seduce** someone to the liar's advantage.
   - To **get something** (illegally) for the liar.

3. Builds **wrong** relationship with another.
   - The relationship is not built on **honesty**.
   - Lying destroys love and respect.
   - Keeps you separated from others and **from Me**.

4. A lie feeds your **distorted self**. You lie to make yourself look good, or to keep from looking bad.

E. HOW TO OVERCOME LYING

1. Look to Me the **standard**. "I am the way, the truth..." (John 14:6).

2. Recognize the **source** of lies. "You are of your father the Devil... he is a liar, and the father of it" (John 8:44).

3. Admit your human nature is **deceitful**. "Out of the heart proceeds evil thoughts... deceit" (Mark 7:21-22).

4. Recognize the ultimate consequence of lying. "All liars shall have their part in the lake which burns with fire" (Rev. 21:8).

5. Adapt a **conviction** to tell the truth. "Put away all lying, each one speaking truth" (Eph. 4:25).

6. Determine to be a radical disciple (Luke 9:23).

7. Learn to walk in **forgiveness** rather than guilt (Psa. 78:38).

8. Ask for **continued** strength to overcome lying (Phil. 4:13).

9. Decision to always tell the truth.

10. Resolve to be a person of character.

    Character is **habitually** doing the right thing, in the right way.

Lesson 9:

QUESTIONS

THE NINTH COMMANDMENT

Ninth Commandment

"You shall not lie to your neighbor" (Exodus 20:16, ELT).

"I speak what My Father tells Me to say, but you speak what you father tells you... your father is the devil... a murderer from the beginning and does not have the truth in him. I tell you the truth" (John 8:38, 44).

A. INTRODUCTION

1. _____ . Why did I say, you shalt not lie? Because you know when you lie, you cannot lie to yourself. You try to live a lie before Me, but I know the truth.

2. _____ . If you cannot lie to yourself, how can you harm yourself?

3. _____ . What does lying do to others?

4. _____ . Where does lying come from? "Satan is the father of lies" (John 8:44).

5. _____ . Can we blame our lying on someone else? Satan asked, "Did God say you must not eat from any tree in the Garden" (Gen. 3:1, ELT)? Eve exaggerated, "We must not eat ... nor touch" (Gen. 3:3, ELT).

6. _____ . How does Satan lie to you today? Did God really say "no?"

B. ARE THESE LIES?

1. Does lying include _____ ?

    - "Tell them I am not here."
    - "You never do any of the work."
    - "That's the prettiest baby I have ever seen."
    - "My you look younger (or slimmer)."

2. Does lying include _____ ?

    - "Who did this?"
    - Taking _____ for something you did not do.

C. SEVENTEEN KINDS OF LIES

1. _____ : Perceived as good for both teller and the victim of the lie.

2. _____ : a compliment when you know the thing complimented is not good, but you say what the listener wants to hear

3. _____ : telling what should not be told, i.e., revealing a secret.

4. _____ : giving an untruth for your evil purpose.

5. _____ : lying in an obvious way without malice, so both teller and listener know it is not true.

6. _____ : telling the truth, but not the whole truth.

7. _____ : misrepresenting the truth about a failure on our part.

8. _____ : your attempt to deceive another about something you are not (the New Testament word referred to an actor using a mask to play the role of another).

9. _____ : to convince others they would have taken the similar action.

10. _____ : misrepresentation to avoid embarrassment. (Sarah told Me, she did not laugh).

11. _____: the exaggeration of religious results. (Ananias and Sapphira).

12. _____: used in military times to hide one's position.

13. _____: sometimes used to exaggerate the merits of a product.

14. _____: using material that is not yours with a view of misrepresentation (exams and income taxes).

15. _____: evil spirits are the source of mis-representing the nature of righteousness and evil (Rom. 1:25; 2 Thess. 2:11).

16. _____: interpreting obvious fact to your favor (politics).

17. _____: people conspire to conceal their involvement by claiming they didn't know.

D. WHY LYING IS WRONG

1. Misrepresents or hides the _____.
    - You hurt the other person who does not _____ the truth.
    - The more serious a lie, the more _____ to the other person.

2. A lie makes a deceiver out of the liar.
    - To _____, or hide something.
    - To _____ someone to the liar's advantage.
    - To _____ (illegally) for the liar.

3. Builds _____ relationship with another.
    - The relationship is not built on _____.
    - Lying destroys love and respect.
    - Keeps you separated from others and _____.

4. A lie feeds your _____. You lie to make yourself look good, or to keep from looking bad.

E. HOW TO OVERCOME LYING

1. Look to Me the _____. "I am the way, the truth..." (John 14:6).

2. Recognize the _____ of lies. "You are of your father the Devil... he is a liar, and the father of it" (John 8:44).

3. Admit your human nature is _____. "Out of the heart proceeds evil thoughts... deceit" (Mark 7:21-22).

4. Recognize the ultimate consequence of lying. "All liars shall have their part in the lake which burns with fire" (Rev. 21:8).

5. Adapt a _____ to tell the truth. "Put away all lying, each one speaking truth" (Eph. 4:25).

6. Determine to be a radical disciple (Luke 9:23).

7. Learn to walk in _____ rather than guilt (Psa. 78:38).

8. Ask for _____ strength to overcome lying (Phil. 4:13).

9. Decision to always tell the truth.

10. Resolve to be a person of character.

    Character is _____ doing the right thing, in the right way.

Lesson 10:

ANSWER KEY

THE TENTH COMMANDMENT

Tenth Commandment

"You shall not covet your neighbor's house; you shall not covet your neighbor's wife, nor his male servant, nor his female servant, nor his ox, nor his donkey, nor anything that is your neighbor's." (Exodus 20:17).

"I say to you, don't look on your neighbor's wife with impure intentions, lest you commit adultery in your heart" (Matthew 5:28).

"Don't lust after stuff... but seek first My rule in your life, and do the right thing, and your stuff will make you happy" (Matthew 6:30, 33, ELT).

A. INTRODUCTION

1. **Consumerism**. You follow a new "religion." You are constantly preached at to buy newer... faster... bigger... and largest.

2. "Seek first the kingdom of '**stuff**' and you will find happiness."

3. Today René Descartes would say, "I **shop**, therefore I am."

4. The modern Latin conqueror proclaims, "I came... I saw... I **shopped**."

5. The religion of consumerism has theologians as **marketers**, priests as **ad men**, temples as **shopping malls** and worshippers as **shoppers**.

6. What fuels the needs of the new religion? **Greed**.

7. The Roman Catholics combine One and Two Commandments about idols, and separate coveting thy neighbor's wife from coveting thy neighbor's **stuff**.

8. The word covet is to desire, wish for, or crave. The problem is **stuff isn't bad**.

318 THE TEN COMMANDMENTS ACCORDING TO JESUS

B. WHAT COVETING DOES TO US

1. Coveting is seeing what you don't have, and wanting what your neighbor has; therefore, coveting puts us in **competition** with your neighbor. You don't see your neighbor as **I see him/her**.

2. Coveting keeps you from seeing **Me fully**. "I will not withhold any good thing from you" (Psa. 84:11).

3. Coveting keeps you from enjoying **My provision**. "I am able to make all grace abound to you so that you will be satisfied in all ways with all things" (2 Cor. 9:8, ELT).

4. Covetousness is **selfishness**.

C. WHAT IS COVETING?

1. The first Hebrew word *covet* is "sparked by **outward** things seen with the eyes," i.e., your neighbors' house. The second word, *covet* is "driven by deep **inward** desire, i.e., lust after a neighbor's wife.

2. These two words cover the whole spectrum of coveting, i.e., outward **attraction** and inward **lust**.

3. The Tenth Commandment is a major change from the previous Ninth Commandment:
   - The first nine: **behavior**.
   - The tenth: inward **lust and greed**.

4. You break the first nine because of the tenth.
   - The tenth deals with **motives**, i.e., violating the law before breaking it.
   - The tenth reveals the dark regions of **your heart**.

D. WE ALL BREAK THE TENTH

1. Babies wanting other's toys.

2. Teens wanting the physical attractiveness of another.

3. At the gym wanting the physique of another.

4. Men wanting the SUV of another.

5. Women wanting the outfit or slim body of another.

6. Workers discontented with their computer because another has more gadgets.

7. Parents wanting their kids to be like others.

E. WHY COVETING IS WRONG?

1. Most think it is all right to **think**, as long as you don't **act on it**.

2. It's all right to look, **just don't touch**.

3. It's natural to fantasize about **stuff**.

4. All men **look**.

5. What comes out of your heart **makes you unclean**. "What comes out of a person makes them dirty, for out of your heart comes evil fantasizing, urges to take, desires to do away with others, sexual lust, greed, hatred, desire to sneak, sexual liberties… all these evil appetites come from within to make a person dirty" (Mark 7:20-23, *ELT*).

6. People don't become evil by their friends, their environment, circumstance, or lack of money; people **hatch evil in their heart**.

7. People break the Tenth Commandment because of what they **hatch in their hearts**.

8. People eventually **act out** what is in their mind and heart.
   - Coveting is like a **pressure cooker**.
   - Coveting destroys **inward peace**.

F. THE BIG THREE LIES

1. Lie One: Everyone wants stuff, so it must be **all right to want**.

2. Lie Two: When you get what you want, it **quenches your craving**.

3. Lie Three: Wanting stuff is just my **competitive urge** to get ahead of my neighbor.

G. CONTROLLING COVETING

1. I can **control** my heart. "Above all else, guard your heart for it is the source of your life" (Prov. 4:23, ELT).

2. I can **help** control your heart. "I will give you a new heart, and give you a new spirit; I will take away your evil heart and give you a tender heart" (Ez. 36:26, ELT).

3. Make Me **your Lord**. "Set Me as Lord of your heart" (1 Peter 3:15, ELT).

4. First obedience will **lead to more** obedience. "Now you have purified your heart by obeying the truth, so you will have a sincere love for others" (1 Peter 1:22, ELT).

Lesson 10:

QUESTIONS

THE TENTH COMMANDMENT

Tenth Commandment

"You shall not covet your neighbor's house; you shall not covet your neighbor's wife, nor his male servant, nor his female servant, nor his ox, nor his donkey, nor anything that is your neighbor's." (Exodus 20:17).

"I say to you, don't look on your neighbor's wife with impure intentions, lest you commit adultery in your heart" (Matthew 5:28).

"Don't lust after stuff... but seek first My rule in your life, and do the right thing, and your stuff will make you happy" (Matthew 6:30, 33, ELT).

A. INTRODUCTION

1. _____ . You follow a new "religion." You are constantly preached at to buy newer... faster... bigger... and largest.

2. "Seek first the kingdom of '_____' and you will find happiness."

3. Today René Descartes would say, "_____ , therefore I am."

4. The modern Latin conqueror proclaims, "I came... I saw... I _____."

5. The religion of consumerism has theologians as _____ , priests as _____ , temples as _____ and worshippers as _____ .

6. What fuels the needs of the new religion? _____ .

7. The Roman Catholics combine One and Two Commandments about idols, and separate coveting thy neighbor's wife from coveting thy neighbor's _____ .

8. The word covet is to desire, wish for, or crave. The problem is _____ .

B. WHAT COVETING DOES TO US

1. Coveting is seeing what you don't have, and wanting what your neighbor has; therefore, coveting puts us in _____ with your neighbor. You don't see your neighbor as _____ .

2. Coveting keeps you from seeing _____ . "I will not withhold any good thing from you" (Psa. 84:11).

3. Coveting keeps you from enjoying _____ . "I am able to make all grace abound to you so that you will be satisfied in all ways with all things" (2 Cor. 9:8, ELT).

4. Covetousness is _____ .

C. WHAT IS COVETING?

1. The first Hebrew word *covet* is "sparked by _____ things seen with the eyes," i.e., your neighbors' house. The second word, *covet* is "driven by deep _____ desire, i.e., lust after a neighbor's wife.

2. These two words cover the whole spectrum of coveting, i.e., outward _____ and inward _____ .

3. The Tenth Commandment is a major change from the previous Ninth Commandment:

    - The first nine: _____ .
    - The tenth: inward _____ .

4. You break the first nine because of the tenth.

    - The tenth deals with _____ , i.e., violating the law before breaking it.
    - The tenth reveals the dark regions of _____ .

D. WE ALL BREAK THE TENTH

1. Babies wanting other's toys.

2. Teens wanting the physical attractiveness of another.

3. At the gym wanting the physique of another.

4. Men wanting the SUV of another.

5. Women wanting the outfit or slim body of another.

6. Workers discontented with their computer because another has more gadgets.

7. Parents wanting their kids to be like others.

E. WHY COVETING IS WRONG?

1. Most think it is all right to _____ , as long as you don't _____ .

2. It's all right to look, _____ .

3. It's natural to fantasize about _____ .

4. All men _____ .

5. What comes out of your heart _____ . "What comes out of a person makes them dirty, for out of your heart comes evil fantasizing, urges to take, desires to do away with others, sexual lust, greed, hatred, desire to sneak, sexual liberties... all these evil appetites come from within to make a person dirty" (Mark 7:20-23, ELT).

6. People don't become evil by their friends, their environment, circumstance, or lack of money; people _____ .

7. People break the Tenth Commandment because of what they _____ .

8. People eventually _____ what is in their mind and heart.

    - Coveting is like a _____ .

    - Coveting destroys _____ .

F. THE BIG THREE LIES

1. Lie One: Everyone wants stuff, so it must be _____.

2. Lie Two: When you get what you want, it _____.

3. Lie Three: Wanting stuff is just my _____ to get ahead of my neighbor.

G. CONTROLLING COVETING

1. I can _____ my heart. "Above all else, guard your heart for it is the source of your life" (Prov. 4:23, ELT).

2. I can _____ control your heart. "I will give you a new heart, and give you a new spirit; I will take away your evil heart and give you a tender heart" (Ez. 36:26, ELT).

3. Make Me _____. "Set Me as Lord of your heart" (1 Peter 3:15, ELT).

4. First obedience will _____ obedience. "Now you have purified your heart by obeying the truth, so you will have a sincere love for others" (1 Peter 1:22, ELT).

PART FOUR

THE TEN COMMANDMENTS ACCORDING TO JESUS

ADDITIONAL RESOURCES

POWERPOINT SLIDES:

To purchase and download the Powerpoint Slides go to
https://www.norimediagroup.com/pages/elmer-towns

VIDEO:

Video presentations of the PBC are available online at trbc.org/pbc
Television Airing Times for the PBC
Go to hopenow.tv for the current program schedule.

To purchase available video by Dr Towns go to
https://www.norimediagroup.com/pages/elmer-towns

ADD-ON CONTENT

To purchase additional products in this series go to
https://www.norimediagroup.com/pages/elmer-towns

RELATED BOOKS

Available at https://www.norimediagroup.com/pages/elmer-towns

www.ingramcontent.com/pod-product-compliance
Lightning Source LLC
Chambersburg PA
CBHW081914170426
43200CB00014B/2724